BUSINESS AND PROFESSIONAL INCOME
UNDER THE PERSONAL INCOME TAX

NATIONAL BUREAU OF ECONOMIC RESEARCH

Fiscal Studies

Business
and Professional Income
Under the
Personal Income Tax

C. HARRY KAHN

A STUDY BY THE
NATIONAL BUREAU OF ECONOMIC RESEARCH, NEW YORK

PUBLISHED BY
PRINCETON UNIVERSITY PRESS
1964

Printed in the United States of America

To My Parents

RELATION OF THE DIRECTORS TO THE WORK AND PUBLICATIONS OF THE NATIONAL BUREAU OF ECONOMIC RESEARCH

1. The object of the National Bureau of Economic Research is to ascertain and to present to the public important economic facts and their interpretation in a scientific and impartial manner. The Board of Directors is charged with the responsibility of ensuring that the work of the National Bureau is carried on in strict conformity with this object.

2. To this end the Board of Directors shall appoint one or more Directors of Research.

3. The Director or Directors of Research shall submit to the members of the Board, or to its Executive Committee, for their formal adoption, all specific proposals concerning researches to be instituted.

4. No report shall be published until the Director or Directors of Research shall have submitted to the Board a summary drawing attention to the character of the data and their utilization in the report, the nature and treatment of the problems involved, the main conclusions, and such other information as in their opinion would serve to determine the suitability of the report for publication in accordance with the principles of the National Bureau.

5. A copy of any manuscript proposed for publication shall also be submitted to each member of the Board. For each manuscript to be so submitted a special committee shall be appointed by the President, or at his designation by the Executive Director, consisting of three Directors selected as nearly as may be one from each general division of the Board. The names of the special manuscript committee shall be stated to each Director when the summary and report described in paragraph (4) are sent to him. It shall be the duty of each member of the committee to read the manuscript. If each member of the special committee signifies his approval within thirty days, the manuscript may be published. If each member of the special committee has not signified his approval within thirty days of the transmittal of the report and manuscript, the Director of Research shall then notify each member of the Board, requesting approval or disapproval of publication, and thirty additional days shall be granted for this purpose. The manuscript shall then not be published unless at least a majority of the entire Board and a two-thirds majority of those members of the Board who shall have voted on the proposal within the time fixed for the receipt of votes on the publication proposed shall have approved.

6. No manuscript may be published, though approved by each member of the special committee, until forty-five days have elapsed from the transmittal of the summary and report. The interval is allowed for the receipt of any memorandum of dissent or reservation, together with a brief statement of his reasons, that any member may wish to express; and such memorandum of dissent or reservation shall be published with the manuscript if he so desires. Publication does not, however, imply that each member of the Board has read the manuscript, or that either members of the Board in general, or of the special committee, have passed upon its validity in every detail.

7. A copy of this resolution shall, unless otherwise determined by the Board, be printed in each copy of every National Bureau book.

(Resolution adopted October 25, 1926, as revised February 6, 1933 and February 24, 1941)

CONTENTS

CONTENTS

TABLES

TABLES

CHARTS

ACKNOWLEDGMENTS

AMONG the numerous persons who helped me in the course of this study, I am especially indebted to Lawrence H. Seltzer, Daniel M. Holland, and Ralph Nelson of the National Bureau research staff. Their advice and critical comments after reading the entire manuscript resulted in many improvements over the original text. Special thanks are due to Robert E. Lipsey and Joseph A. Pechman. Lipsey gave freely of his time in helping me adopt appropriate statistical procedures. Pechman generously advised me on many occasions on problems involving sources and concepts in connection with Chapter 2. At various stages of its development the manuscript was reviewed critically by Percival F. Brundage, Harold M. Groves, Hal B. Lary, Geoffrey H. Moore, Norman B. Ture, and Joseph H. Willits.

No study of this type would be possible without frequent assistance from government agencies and their personnel. Although in the present case I relied primarily on published data compiled from tax returns by the Statistics Division of the Internal Revenue Service, additional detail and explanation were frequently supplied by Ernest J. Engquist, the Division's director, and Helen F. Demond. Much help was also obtained from persons in the Commerce Department's National Income Division, especially Jeanette Fitzwilliams and the late Selma F. Goldsmith.

Behind the tables in this study are many hours of computations ingeniously performed by Mary H. Faden, Kathryn S. Marin, Irving Miller, and Joan Tron. H. Irving Forman skillfully drew the charts. Joan Tron not only had a part in the statistical work but also served as the manuscript's able editor.

The responsibility for such errors as still remain is as always the author's.

Foreword

TAXATION is an important subject. It is also a complicated subject. Objective description and analysis of the complex features of the tax system should therefore be helpful to all persons concerned with the economic effects of taxation, whatever their views on public policy. It is for this reason that the National Bureau of Economic Research has engaged in studies of the economics of taxation. As with all National Bureau studies, the findings of the tax studies are issued in the form of scientific reports, entirely divorced from recommendations on policy.

This volume by C. Harry Kahn, the latest in the series of tax studies by the National Bureau, is such an objective analysis. It falls into two of the National Bureau's current programs of research in this field. One program, under the direction of Lawrence H. Seltzer, is concerned with various features of the federal individual income tax. The studies already published include: *Interest as a Source of Personal Income and Tax Revenue,* by Seltzer (1955); *Personal Deductions in the Federal Income Tax,* by Kahn (1960); and *Dividends under the Income Tax,* by Holland (1962). The studies now close to publication include: "Personal Exemptions in the Federal Income Tax," by Seltzer; and "The Treatment of Income from Employment Under the Individual Income Tax," by Kahn.

The second research program of the National Bureau in the taxation field is concerned with tax policies in relation to economic growth. This program, which is under the direction of Norman B. Ture, focuses on the effects of the federal individual and corporate income tax structure on business and personal saving and investment, on the amount and character of personal effort, on innovation, and on resource mobility.

The present volume is the first of a two-part study by Kahn concerned with the impact of the individual income tax on unincorporated business enterprises and professional practitioners. Its chief purpose is to provide a detailed examination of the general characteristics of unincorporated business income and its individual income tax treatment. The enterprises considered here represent nine-tenths of the total business population and account for more than a fifth of total business receipts.

The capacity and incentives of unincorporated business and professional practice for survival, assumption of risk, and growth have an important bearing on the growth of the entire economy. In turn, in a number of important respects, various features of the federal income tax on individuals are significant in relation to such capacity and incentives. For this reason, the present report affords background for the second phase of Kahn's study, which is being directed to the problem of economic growth. In particular, it is concerned with the adequacy of the income-averaging provisions in the federal income tax as applied to income from unincorporated business and professional practice.

In the planning and conduct of its studies of the individual income tax the National Bureau has benefited from the advice and guidance of its Committee on Fiscal Research. Similar assistance, in the studies of tax policies for economic growth, is being provided by the National Bureau's Advisory Committee on Tax Policies for Economic Growth. This help is gratefully acknowledged.

SOLOMON FABRICANT
Director of Research

BUSINESS AND PROFESSIONAL INCOME
UNDER THE PERSONAL INCOME TAX

Introduction and Summary

Purpose of the Study

THIS study is intended to summarize and interpret some of the extensive information on income and tax liabilities attributable to the proprietors of unincorporated businesses and professions. Such information has been published for many years in the Treasury Department's annual *Statistics of Income*. The adjustments of business and professional proprietors to a world complicated by a number of income taxes, and indeed their economic behavior in general, have long constituted an uncharted area of empirical knowledge. Proprietors at all times stand at the crossroads of the three taxes which compose our income tax system: the personal income tax, the corporate income tax, and the capital gains tax.

As long as an enterprise is unincorporated, all the proprietor's income from it, whether formally distributed or not, is taxed under the individual income tax as part of his total income. If the enterprise is incorporated, any salary which a proprietor may be paid for his services, and any interest on funds which he may lend to the enterprise, continue to be taxable under the individual income tax. But the remainder of the enterprise's income, which consists of a return on equity capital supplied by the owners and a pure profit residual, is defined as corporate profit by the tax law and subject to corporation income tax. Moreover, distributions to the owners (stockholders) out of these corporate profits are also subject to the individual income tax.[1] Whether the tax position of an enterprise is more favorable when operating as a corporation than under a sole proprietor or partnership depends on the size of total income of the enterprise, the amount of income distributed to the owners, and the size of total income of the owners themselves.

Enterprise income may, under some circumstances, be taxed as a capital gain at long-term capital gains rates. In recent years, these have been one-half of ordinary individual rates or 25 per cent, whichever is lower. The capital gains rates are not intended to apply to entrepreneurial income. Yet the difference between them and ordinary individual rates constitutes an obvious inducement to find ways of converting

---

[1] The first $100 of corporate dividends ($200 when husband and wife own stock jointly and file joint returns) is at present exempt from individual income tax. For a detailed treatment of this subject, and the impact on stockholders of corporate and individual tax combined, see Daniel M. Holland, *The Income-Tax Burden on Stockholders*, Princeton University Press for National Bureau of Economic Research, 1960.

3

ordinary income into long-term gains, though how much influence this possibility actually exerts is difficult to determine.

In what follows, we shall deal only with the part of business and professional income subject to individual income tax rates. Three broad questions concern us.

First, to what extent is sole proprietor and partnership income covered on tax returns? The answer to this question has a bearing on the discussion of the effective rate of tax on this income, which is dealt with later in Chapter 5. To obtain a correct picture of the tax rate imposed on business and professional income, the extent to which the amounts reported on tax returns are representative of actual income must be taken into account. Chapter 2 is largely devoted to this problem.

Secondly, the size and pattern of income reported on the returns with sole proprietor and partnership income is the subject of analysis. We seek to know the quantitative importance of other income types, such as wages and salaries, dividends, etc., on the returns of sole proprietors and partners. The presence of other income permits loss offsets in the current year. Differences in the distribution by income groups of reported net losses and reported net profits are examined, in some detail, in Chapter 3. The specific problem of business loss offsets under the individual income tax is subjected to scrutiny in Chapter 4.

Thirdly, the final broad topic dealt with is the measurement of tax liability attributable to business and professional income. Here, annual effective and marginal rates are presented, enabling us to compare tax rates on unincorporated enterprise with the previously well-known tax rates on corporate enterprise and capital gains.

Profit and Loss Concept in Tax Statistics

Income from unincorporated business and profession appears in the tax return statistics as "profit or loss of sole proprietors from business or profession" (including farming), or as "profit or loss from partnership." It does not necessarily constitute income of persons who are primarily, or even significantly, self-employed proprietors. Both the occasional counseling fees of a college professor and the income of an unincorporated manufacturing establishment whose owner has no other occupation are likely to appear in the same schedule of the tax return. The terms profit and loss as used in these statistics are more inclusive than either the economic or the popular meaning usually attached to them.

Since unincorporated enterprises are usually owner-managed, the sole proprietor and partnership profit and loss data, as tabulated from tax

4

returns, include what may be considered payments to the proprietors for their labor services, as well as interest and a risk premium for capital supplied by them.[2] Therefore it would be more precise to say that only what remains after these implicit income items have been deducted constitutes pure profit (or loss).[3]

With the available statistics, it was not feasible to isolate the profit component from the rest of unincorporated enterprise income. Yet if one were to compare the average effective tax rate on profit under the personal income tax to that under the corporation income tax, the profit concept now used in the personal tax would have to be narrowed. All payments for services and contractual interest on capital supplied by equity owners are excluded in the computation of corporate profits. However, the return on equity capital is included in the corporate profit concept, which gives the latter an intermediate position between the all-inclusive breadth of unincorporated business profits for income tax purposes and the pure profits of economic theory.[4]

The lack of a statistical division of income from unincorporated enterprises into its several components—wages, return on capital, allowance for risk, and profit—has, however, no influence on individual tax liabilities. Even if the separation were always effected, and some of what appears under current practice as net profit were converted into net loss, an individual's tax liability would not thereby be altered. What would be altered is the relative frequency and amount of net profit and net loss reported for a given income group: present practice leads to overstatement of the former and understatement of the latter.

The United States national income accounts also do not divide income from unincorporated business and professions into its capital and labor services components, but break it down by very broad industrial groups:

[2] Since 1954, partnership net profit or loss is reported on partnership information returns (1065) after deducting payments to partners for services, or for the use of capital, to the extent that such payments are contractual, that is, determined without regard to the income of the partnership. Thus, a net loss may be reported on the partnership return although a salary was paid to one or more partners. But *Statistics of Income* for individual returns continues to include such payments in an individual's distributive share of partnership net profit or loss.

[3] When thus defined, profits (losses) are the results of unforeseen events, disequilibria, and monopoly power. To the extent that profits are a residual amount of income resulting from lack of foresight into an uncertain future, they are as likely to be positive as negative. For an extended discussion of the economic meaning of profit, see Frank H. Knight, "Profit" in *Readings in the Theory of Income Distribution,* William Fellner and Bernard F. Haley, eds., Philadelphia, 1946, pp. 533–546.

[4] Annual dividend payments of corporations might be excluded as a rough approximation of return on owners' investment, bringing us a step closer to an accounting concept of pure profits.

business, independent professional practice, and farming. The unincorporated business category is heavily weighted with retail and wholesale trade, construction, and services such as hotels and laundries. The independent professional group includes mainly physicians, dentists, lawyers, accountants, and engineers. The farm group comprises the income of unincorporated farm operators.

Thus, because the income reported comprises more than profit or loss in the economic sense, and because the primary occupation of individuals included on tax returns as proprietors is not always entrepreneurial, the single common denominator of what is reported in the sole proprietor and partnership schedules is income resulting from unincorporated business and professions. Some other terms, widely used elsewhere, might have served nearly as well. Most of this income might also be termed self-employment income; but this does not apply well to the income of partners who are not active in the enterprise. In that case, most of the income is property income, and the term, income from unincorporated proprietorship suggests itself. But here again the occasional independent consulting work of professional persons, where labor is more important than proprietorship, would be poorly defined.

Nature and Limitations of the Data

Data on unincorporated business and professional income have been tabulated by the Internal Revenue Service in two major forms: (1) annually for sole proprietor and partnership profit and loss by size of adjusted gross income (AGI), and (2) for selected years by type of industry. Since the two tabulations are not based on identical sources, their totals are not the same. However, the differences are less than 5 per cent in most years.[5]

The income-size tabulations are available for 1918–60; however, two significant changes in method of tabulation disrupt the continuity of the series. (1) For the years 1918–29 only net profits were tabulated. The net losses reported on some returns were not offset by the net profits reported on others. This means that for this period the figures are only for returns which on balance show a net profit from sole proprietorship or partnership, although losses reported within these schedules, and exceeded by gains, are included. If losses exceeded gains, the net loss was tabulated with miscellaneous deductions. (2) Until 1943, all income-size distributions are by size of statutory net income; thereafter they are by size of

[5] See Appendix A for a comparison of the totals (Table A-1) from the two sources and a discussion of the difference.

AGI. The difference between the two concepts is personal deductions: AGI is net income before personal deductions; the old statutory net income was after personal deductions.

The industrial breakdowns have been tabulated since 1939, at two-year intervals, for sole proprietors. For partnerships, industrial breakdowns are also available beginning with 1939, but at irregular intervals, and tabulated from partnership information returns rather than individual tax returns. Whereas an individual's reported share in partnership income is tabulated in the income-size distribution, in the industrial distribution, partnership net income is tabulated because the partnership is the reporting unit. It is therefore possible that amounts reported on partnership information returns were not reported on individual returns whenever a partner's income was too low to require his filing a return.

Summary of Findings

INCOME FROM BUSINESS AND PROFESSIONS REPORTED ON TAX RETURNS

Income from unincorporated business and professions has, for recent years, constituted one-tenth of total income reported on tax returns. For 1960, sole proprietors reported net income of $21 billion and partners $9 billion. Together they accounted for $30 billion of the total adjusted gross income of $316 billion reported. Nearly three-fourths of their reported net income (profits minus losses) was from three industry groups: agriculture, trade, and services. The rest is largely accounted for by the construction industry and by the finance, insurance, and real estate groups.

Comparison with Total Income from Business and Professions

The $30 billion income reported is, however, not the total amount actually earned from this source. According to the best available estimates for the years 1956–60 (Tables 6 and 8) the reported total was approximately 70 per cent of the actual income from unincorporated enterprise.[6] Part of the discrepancy between the reported and estimated totals is owing to the receipt of unincorporated enterprise income by persons not required to file tax returns. Most of the discrepancy, however, does not seem to be explained by such persons (Table 12). The greater part must be explained by taxpayers' errors in reporting income, and possibly

---

[6] The estimates of total income from unincorporated enterprise were obtained by adjusting Department of Agriculture and Department of Commerce figures to make them compatible with tax return tabulations.

7

insufficient reconciliation between the tax return data, on the one hand, and the Commerce and Agriculture Department estimates, on the other.

Comparison with Total Income Reported by Sole Proprietors and Partners

As explained above, income from unincorporated enterprise includes that of persons for whom it is a secondary, or minor, source. This is strikingly reflected in the comparison of income from unincorporated enterprise and estimated total income reported on the returns of proprietors. The $21.4 billion net income from sole proprietorship reported for 1960 constituted less than half the estimated total income reported on returns with income from that source. For returns with partnership net income the results were even more extreme. Between 1947 and 1960, income from sole proprietorship declined from 67 per cent to 46 per cent of the total income reported by such proprietors; income from partnership declined from 64 per cent of the total income of partners to only 42 per cent.

A small part of the decline over time in the ratio of unincorporated enterprise income to total income of proprietors may be explained by the cross-sectional decline in the ratio when moving up the income scale; but most of it is not. For 1960, the ratio by income-size groups for sole proprietors was as follows:

Total Income (AGI) in Thousands of Dollars	Sole Proprietorship Net Income as Percentage of AGI
Negative income	117
0–2	57
2–3	53
3–5	47
5–10	40
10–25	54
25–50	59
50–100	40
100–500	3
500 and over	−4
Total	46

The decline is very sharp from negative income to the first positive income class; but in the 0-to-$50,000 range, in which the bulk of sole

8

proprietors' income is located (see Table 20), we find no decline. Apparently the declining share of unincorporated enterprise in proprietors' total income is mainly the result of a trend toward more income from other than entrepreneurial sources at any given level of income. A consequence of the declining proportion of income from unincorporated enterprise has been more government sharing in the losses as well as the profits of proprietors, for with increased income diversification, proprietors increasingly have had other income against which to offset losses. This is reflected in the increasing proportion of net losses reported on returns with positive total income:

	Net Losses Reported for Sole Proprietorships On Returns with:			Net Losses Reported for Partnerships On Returns with:		
	Negative Total Income (1)	Positive Total Income (2)	(2) ÷ (1) (3)	Negative Total Income (4)	Positive Total Income (5)	(5) ÷ (4) (6)
1947	520	519	1.0	143	152	1.1
1960	1,059	1,828	1.7	262	529	2.0

The sharp relative decline in income from independent enterprise near the top of the income pyramid, observed in the income-size breakdown shown above, reflects in part a rise of reported net losses relative to net profits at income levels above $50,000. In this one respect, returns in the highest income group resemble those in the very lowest. It is apparent that we are witnessing the results of taxpayers' adjustments to income taxation. A taxpayer subject to high-bracket rates may find it to his advantage to operate an enterprise as an unincorporated business as long as the latter results in net losses, as is frequently the case with young but promising ventures and in particular areas such as oil and gas exploration (Table 31). But for the same reason that losses may make operation in unincorporated form attractive, profits may make it unattractive. The individual now becomes subject to a tax motive either to convert his enterprise into corporate form, where lower tax rates may apply, or to sell his enterprise, thereby capitalizing anticipated profits so as to be taxed at the lower long-term capital gains rates.

In recent years, provisions in the tax law have permitted small businesses, to choose to a limited extent between being taxed as corporations or unincorporated enterprises without being required to change their legal form of organization.

9

With the "Technical Amendments Acts of 1958," corporations with not more than ten shareholders, and subject to certain other limitations, were given the option to elect taxation at the shareholder level like partnerships, provided all shareholders consented. For the fiscal year 1960–61, some 90,000 corporations (or 8 per cent of the total), many of which were in retail and wholesale trade, elected to be taxed like partnerships. Sole proprietors and partnerships were given the option of being taxed as corporations in 1954, but only an insignificant number have elected to do so (Table 28). This striking difference is probably a reflection of the different income tax treatment accorded to pension plan contributions on behalf of employees and self-employed persons. Until 1963, the pension plan contributions of the latter were not deductible from business income whereas those of the former were, as long as they met certain requirements. Thus, provided other things remained equal, the corporate form of organization was advantageous.

Another, equally important reason for the sharp decline of unincorporated enterprise income in relation to total income of proprietors when ascending the income scale, is the occurrence of so-called hobby-losses. The gentleman's farm is the outstanding case in point. We find that for farm sole proprietors with total income (AGI) over $50,000 in 1960, farm net income is negative: reported losses exceed profits. Only the mining group showed equally extreme results in that respect (Table 32).

THE AMOUNT OF NET OPERATING LOSSES DEPENDENT ON CARRYOVERS

As we saw above, the greater part of net losses reported for 1960 was on returns with positive total income ($2.36 billion). Only $1.32 billion was reported on returns with negative income. These net losses may be offset against positive taxable income for other years to the extent that they can qualify as "net operating loss." The estimated total net operating loss for 1960 was $0.75 billion.

At present a net operating loss may be carried back against income of three preceding years and forward against income of five succeeding years. No data on the carryback portion are available. Loss carryforward figures have been published intermittently; most recently for 1960 and 1961. These figures suggest that currently no more than 10 to 20 per cent of net operating losses (largely losses reported on returns with negative total income) are carried forward to other years.

In the neighborhood of $0.64 billion of 1960 net operating losses must have depended on carryback or remained without offset. While this involves less than one-fifth of total net losses reported for 1960, it may nevertheless be that this low aggregate figure is not very representative. Taxpayers who are completely committed to their enterprises with respect to time and capital, and who may therefore have little income from other sources, may find it hard to obtain offsets for their losses.

Data on the frequency of selected income sources for business and professional proprietors reveal that those with negative income for a given year are below average in reporting wages and salaries, dividends, interest, and rental income, but above average in reporting income from both sole proprietorship and partnership (Table 34). For this group of entrepreneurs whose income appears less diversified than that of others, generous loss carryover provisions are of importance.

THE FRACTION OF NET PROFITS AND LOSSES SHARED BY THE INCOME TAX

While the theory underlying the income tax requires that persons be taxed by size of income, regardless of its functional composition, in practice tax liability may vary considerably with variations in income composition. The individual has for this reason some control over the amount of tax he pays on an income of given size. Many, for example, have a choice between operating their enterprise as an unincorporated business or as a corporation. A few have the opportunity of converting ordinary business income into a long-term capital gain, which is taxed at a lower rate.

By prorating each individual's tax liability among his various functional income components (making necessary adjustments for differences in treatment where they exist, e.g., capital gains and dividends), we obtain weighted average effective rates of tax for each. For all business and professional net income reported on taxable returns, the mean effective rate of tax liability for 1960 was nearly 17 per cent. When we include the amount of income reported on nontaxable returns, the mean effective rate drops to 16 per cent, and if we expand the denominator further to include business and professional income not reported on tax returns (but conceptually part of adjusted gross income), the mean rate drops to 11 per cent. Mean effective rates on all individual income other than unincorporated business and professional for 1960 were 13, 12, and 11 per cent respectively.

The averages hide, of course, wide variations by size of income. For 1960, we observe these differences in effective rates on business and professional income by quintiles of tax returns ranked by size of total income (from Table 40):

	Unincorporated Enterprise		Effective
	Net Income	Tax Liability	Tax Rate
	(million dollars)		(2) ÷ (1)
Quintile Group	(1)	(2)	(3)
Lowest	−487	−13	2.7%
Second	2,473	117	4.7
Third	4,005	317	7.9
Fourth	5,523	576	10.4
Highest	18,524	3,783	20.4
Total	30,038	4,780	15.9

The effective rate on reported amounts varied from 3 per cent for the lowest quintile of returns to 20 per cent for the highest. The latter group, however, accounted for over 60 per cent of unincorporated enterprise net income reported for 1960.

The mean effective rate of 15.9 per cent for that year is a composite rate covering returns with net profit and returns with net loss and combining sole proprietors and partners. For the nine years 1952–60, separate means were computed for each (Table 42):

| | Sole Proprietorship | | Partnership | |
| | Net Profits | Net Losses | Net Profits | Net Losses |
	(per cent)		(per cent)	
Taxable returns	15.5	17.9	20.5	23.6
All returns	13.5	8.4	19.7	12.4

The percentages shown express the mean rate at which net profits and net losses were "shared" by the Treasury. Partnership net profits and losses were shared at a higher rate than those for sole proprietors, reflecting the fact that the former were reported by persons with higher income, on average, than were the latter. The same explains why net losses on taxable returns are, on average, shared through the income tax at a higher rate than net profits. In this group, net losses are more concentrated in high-income groups than net profits, a finding which partly reflects our earlier observation that individuals have some discretion over the form in which they obtain their income, and therefore also over the amount of tax they pay on a given amount of business income.

When the averages are computed for net profits and losses reported on taxable and nontaxable returns, inclusion of the latter significantly lowers the effective rate at which net losses are shared. For sole proprietors the mean rate for total net profits is 13.5 per cent; that for net losses, only 8.4 per cent.

One of the difficulties encountered in this study has been lack of data enabling us to break up the distributions between farm and nonfarm proprietors, and between full-time and part-time self-employed persons. However, some limited estimates were possible. For two years, sole proprietors reporting net profits were classified according to the fraction of their total income obtained from business and profession (Table 46). Only a minor difference in effective rates between returns for which net profits were a large fraction of AGI and those for which they were a small fraction was found. For 1960 the mean effective tax rate for returns whose net profit constituted more than one-half of total income was 13.5 per cent, compared to 13.6 per cent for all returns. Estimates of effective rates by farm, business, and profession for all sole proprietors differed more widely. For farm sole proprietors the mean rate was 8.8; for the business group 13.3; and for independent professionals 19.9 per cent (Table 47). The business group, it should be noted, accounted for $12.8 billion of $21.1 billion net income reported by sole proprietors for 1960.

The mean effective rates tell us approximately what fraction of net profit and loss is absorbed by the federal government. They do not tell us the rate at which government shares at the margin, that is, what rate of tax is levied on additional profit or loss. To that end, mean marginal rates for 1952–60, analogous to the mean effective rates, were computed (Table 48):

	Sole Proprietorship		Partnership	
	Net Profits	Net Losses	Net Profits	Net Losses
	(per cent)		(per cent)	
Taxable returns	30.5	34.8	40.1	44.5
All returns	26.5	16.3	37.9	23.7

As before, the mean rate for net losses is higher than that for net profits on taxable returns, but not when mean marginal rates are computed for all returns. The weight assigned to the marginal tax rate of a given return is determined by the amount of net profit (or net loss) reported on it. Therefore, the mean marginal rates shown above are in effect those one would obtain if all net profits and net losses were to change by 1 per cent. If we wanted to know the mean marginal rate per one dollar of change of net profit (or net loss), the weight assigned to each return would have to be the same. The results for all returns for 1960 would be as follows:

	Sole Proprietorship	*Partnership*
Net profits	15.5	23.4
Net losses	14.9	21.8

CHAPTER 2

Sources and Coverage of Business and Professional Income on Tax Returns

Sources of Sole Proprietor and Partnership Income

OF $316 BILLION of adjusted gross income reported by individuals on tax returns for 1960, $30 billion, or close to one-tenth, was from independent business or profession (Table 1). Adjusted gross income from business or profession is obtained by reducing aggregate reported net profits by aggregate reported net losses. Of the $30 billion reported, 70 per cent came from sole proprietors, the rest from partnerships. Next to wages and salaries, which accounted for over four-fifths of AGI reported, they were the second and third largest components.

TABLE 1

ADJUSTED GROSS INCOME AND ITS COMPONENTS AS REPORTED ON TAX RETURNS, 1960

	Amounts (billion dollars)	Per Cent of Total
1. Wages and salaries	258.6	81.7
2. Proprietors' net income	30.0	9.5
Sole proprietorship	21.1	
Partnership	9.0	
3. Property income	25.8	8.2
Dividends	9.9	
Interest	5.1	
Net statutory capital gains	5.3	
Rents and royalties (net)	3.3	
Estates and trusts	0.6	
Pensions and annuities	1.6	
Sales of property other than capital assets	-0.1	
4. Other	2.1	0.7
5. Adjusted gross income	316.5	100.0

Source: Treasury Department, Statistics of Income, 1960.

15

TABLE 2

INDUSTRIAL DISTRIBUTION OF AGI FROM UNINCORPORATED BUSINESS AND
PROFESSIONS REPORTED ON TAX RETURNS, 1960
(dollars in millions)

Industrial Group	Sole Proprietorship		Partnership		Sole Proprietorship and Partnership	
	Net Profit Less Net Loss (1)	Per Cent of Total (2)	Net Profit Less Net Loss[a] (3)	Per Cent of Total (4)	Net Profit Less Net Loss (5)	Per Cent of Total (6)
Agriculture, forestry, and fisheries	2,998	14.2	592	6.3	3,590	11.8
Farms	2,737	13.0	512	5.5	3,590	10.7
Mining and quarrying	-103	-.5	-25	-.3	-128	-.4
Construction	1,898	9.0	730	7.8	2,629	8.6
Manufacturing	645	3.1	708	7.5	1,354	4.4
Transportation, communication, and public utilities[b]	540	2.6	148	1.6	688	2.3
Trade[b]	5,455	25.9	2,686	28.6	8,141	26.7
Wholesale	1,306	6.2	677	7.2	1,983	6.5
Retail	3,869	18.4	1,903	20.3	5,772	19.0
Finance, insurance, and real estate	1,517	7.2	1,209	12.9	2,727	9.0
Professional and personal services	8,060	38.3	3,290	35.1	11,350	37.3
Professional services only[c]	5,544	26.3	2,545	27.1	8,089	26.6
Not allocable	57	.3	47	.5	104	.3
Total[d]	21,067	100.0	9,386	100.0	30,453	100.0

Source: Treasury Department, Selected Financial Data, Statistics of Income, 1960-1961; Table 1 for sole proprietorship, Table 2 for partnership.

a"Ordinary income" less "ordinary loss" plus "payments to partners" as reported on partnership information returns.
bWholesale and retail amounts shown do not add to total because some businesses were not allocable to either of the two.
cProfessional includes medical, legal, educational, engineering and architectural, and accounting, auditing, and booking services.
dDifferences in totals shown here and in Table 1 are explained by differences in sources used (see Appendix A).

Most of the AGI from unincorporated enterprise can be seen to originate from three service sectors: trade; finance, insurance and real estate;
and professional and personal services. In addition, agriculture and
construction accounted for significant amounts (Table 2). In contrast,
manufacturing and the utilities (transport, communication, and power)
accounted for 66 per cent of 1960 corporate net income, but less than
7 per cent of unincorporated enterprise income.

AGI is of course not the sole, or even best, index of industrial composition. Gross receipts, or number of businesses, may for some purposes be
preferred. If gross receipts had been used, over one-half, in contrast to
28 per cent on the basis of AGI, would have been found to originate in
trade; if number of businesses had been used, agriculture would have
accounted for over one-third, in contrast to 11 per cent on the basis of
AGI.[1]

Relation to Total Income

In Table 1 we observed that unincorporated business and professions
contributed slightly less than one-tenth to adjusted gross income reported
on tax returns for 1960. Table 3 shows how this fraction has varied over
time, both on tax returns and for the country as a whole. Business and
professional income and total personal income are shown, first as presented in Commerce Department estimates, which include items not part
of income for tax purposes; secondly, adjusted so as to make the Commerce Department estimates comparable to figures reported on tax
returns—i.e., excluding items not part of income for tax purposes (AGI);
and thirdly, as actually reported on tax returns.

In all three series, the tendency for unincorporated enterprise income
to decline as a fraction of total income is apparent. On individual tax
returns it was 18 per cent of total income reported in 1929, but only one-
tenth for the most recent years. For the other two series the decline was
less. When adjusted for differences in concept, the Commerce Department estimates show a decline from 17 per cent to 12 per cent.

In part, the decline in the relative share of business and professional
income reported on tax returns is the result of the sharp rise in reported
wages and salaries. A breakdown of income reported on tax returns by
employment, property, or unincorporated enterprise is shown in Table 4
and Chart 1 for four decades. The striking changes which have taken
place in the personal income tax over that period are highlighted by the

[1] See *Statistics of Income, U.S. Business Tax Returns, Preliminary, 1960–61*, Tables 1 and 4.

TABLE 3

UNINCORPORATED BUSINESS AND PROFESSIONAL INCOME AS A COMPONENT OF TOTAL PERSONAL INCOME AND ADJUSTED
GROSS INCOME, 1929-60
(dollars in billions)

	Business and Professional Income (Commerce Department estimates) (1)	Total Personal Income (2)	Col. 1 ÷ Col. 2 (per cent) (3)	Business and Professional Income[a] (adjusted estimates) (4)	Adjusted Gross Income[a] (5)	Col. 4 ÷ Col. 5 (per cent) (6)	Business and Professional Income[a] (tax-return figures) (7)	Adjusted Gross Income[a] (tax-return figures) (8)	Col. 7 ÷ Col. 8 (per cent) (9)
1929	14.8	85.8	17.2	13.0	75.8	17.2	4.9	27.2	17.9
1930	11.5	78.9	15.0	9.5	62.4	15.3	3.1	19.6	15.8
1931	8.7	65.7	13.3	6.6	49.1	13.5	2.0	14.1	14.3
1932	5.3	50.1	10.6	4.1	37.1	11.2	1.2	12.3	10.0
1933	5.6	47.2	11.9	5.6	36.5	15.2	1.7	11.7	14.9
1934	7.0	53.6	13.1	7.6	44.2	17.2	2.1	14.1	15.1
1935	10.4	60.2	17.3	8.6	48.5	17.8	2.4	16.3	14.6
1936	10.5	68.5	15.3	10.3	58.0	17.8	3.2	21.0	15.3
1937	12.7	73.9	17.2	10.8	61.9	17.4	3.4	23.2	14.6
1938	11.1	68.6	16.2	9.6	55.8	17.1	3.1	20.7	15.2
1939	11.6	72.9	15.9	10.6	64.9	16.3	3.7	25.2	14.6
1940	13.0	78.7	16.5	11.7	70.4	16.6	5.4	39.6	13.7
1941	17.4	96.3	18.1	16.2	85.6	19.0	8.5	62.7	13.5
1942	23.9	123.5	19.4	21.2	107.6	19.7	12.5	85.1	14.6
1943	28.2	151.4	18.6	26.4	129.5	20.4	15.8	105.9	14.9
1944	29.6	165.7	17.8	27.8	137.8	20.2	17.3	116.9	14.8
1945	30.8	171.2	18.0	28.9	140.5	20.6	19.1	120.6	15.8
1946	36.6	179.3	20.4	34.8	157.1	22.1	23.4	134.8	17.4
1947	35.5	191.6	18.5	35.0	172.2	20.3	23.4	150.3	15.6
1948	40.2	210.4	19.1	35.2	186.1	18.9	24.6	164.1	15.0

(continued)

TABLE 3 (concluded)

	Business and Professional Income (Commerce Department estimates) (1)	Total Personal Income (2)	Col. 1 ÷ Col. 2 (per cent) (3)	Business and Professional Income[a] (adjusted estimates) (4)	Adjusted Gross Income[a] (5)	Col. 4 ÷ Col. 5 (per cent) (6)	Business and Professional Income[a] (tax-return figures) (7)	Adjusted Gross Income[a] (8)	Col. 7 ÷ Col. 8 (per cent) (9)
1949	35.6	208.3	17.1	32.9	186.0	17.7	21.8	161.1	13.5
1950	37.5	228.5	16.4	34.6	203.2	17.0	23.5	179.9	13.1
1951	42.3	256.7	16.5	38.0	228.7	16.6	25.0	203.0	12.3
1952	42.2	273.1	15.5	38.0	242.9	15.6	24.8	216.0	11.5
1953	40.7	288.3	14.1	38.6	256.5	15.1	25.0	228.7	10.9
1954	40.4	289.8	14.0	37.3	255.6	14.6	25.5	229.2	11.1
1955	42.1	310.2	13.6	39.2	275.6	14.2	27.5	248.5	11.0
1956	43.7	332.9	13.1	41.8	296.9	14.1	30.1	267.7	11.3
1957	44.5	351.4	12.7	41.4	309.2	13.4	29.7	280.3	10.6
1958	46.1	360.3	12.8	42.6	313.0	13.6	29.9	281.2	10.6
1959	46.5	383.9	12.1	44.2	337.5	13.1	31.0	305.1	10.2
1960	46.2	400.8	11.5	43.7	350.1	12.5	30.0	315.5	9.5

Source

Cols. 1 and 2: Income and Output, Table II-1, and Survey of Current Business.
Col. 4: Commerce Department and Agriculture Department estimates adjusted for differences in concept (see Table B-3).
Col. 5: Commerce Department estimates adjusted for differences in concept (see Appendix C).
Cols. 7 and 8: Statistics of Income. From 1929 to 1943 only net income was available in this source. For derivation of AGI, see Appendix C.

[a]Excludes fiduciaries 1953–60; adjusted gross income 1954–60 after sick pay and dividend exclusions.

fact that property income exceeded wages and salaries reported on tax returns in 1929, but for 1960 the latter was nearly ten times the amount of the former. Most of this radical change in composition of income reported on tax returns was the result of the lowering of exemptions

TABLE 4

UNINCORPORATED BUSINESS AND PROFESSIONS, WAGES AND SALARIES, AND PROPERTY AS SOURCES OF INCOME REPORTED ON ALL RETURNS, 1918–60
(million dollars)

	Adjusted Gross Income from		
	Wages and Salaries[a]	Business and Professions[b]	Property[c]
1918	8,267	4,268	4,546
1919	10,756	5,608	5,078
1920	15,270	4,791	5,510
1921	13,813	3,560	4,309
1922	13,694	4,128	5,755
1923	14,230	6,223	7,091
1924	13,618	6,411	8,439
1925	9,742	5,383	9,231
1926	9,994	5,168	9,444
1927	10,218	4,889	10,261
1928	10,945	4,858	12,171
1929	11,399	4,869	10,932
1930	10,206	3,102	6,268
1931	8,631	2,015	3,485
1932	8,356	1,229	2,764
1933	7,565	1,746	2,411
1934	8,681	2,125	3,305
1935	9,972	2,387	3,943
1936	11,718	3,210	6,026
1937	14,206	3,376	5,587
1938	13,307	3,132	4,233
1939	16,491	3,689	5,054
1940	27,707	5,427	6,475
1941	47,140	8,495	7,105
1942	65,617	12,455	7,040
1943	82,755	15,805	7,362
1944	91,125	17,340	8,412
1945	91,700	19,102	9,750
1946	99,174	23,384	12,196
1947	114,804	23,400	12,122
1948	125,881	24,598	13,647
1949	124,883	21,777	14,456
1950	139,073	23,514	17,273
1951	160,482	24,961	17,585
1952	174,339	24,844	16,847
1953	187,734	24,951	16,023
1954	186,305	25,452	18,038
1955	201,156	27,454	20,613
1956	216,162	30,137	22,256
1957	228,651	29,698	22,854
1958	228,173	29,905	24,016
1959	248,048	30,995	27,080
1960	258,593	30,038	27,894

which has occurred gradually since the early 1930's.[2] As a consequence, unincorporated business and professional income rose in relation to property income, but fell sharply in relation to wages and salaries on tax returns. The net result has been a decline from about one-fourth to one-tenth of AGI since 1918.

The relative decline of total unincorporated business and professional income is, however, not matched by a decline in the relative frequency of returns with such income. As Table 5 shows, the frequency with which individuals have reported either sole proprietor or partnership income has, if anything, increased since the mid-1940's. Over the same period, the relative share of business and professional income in the total reported has fallen from 15 to 10 per cent. The reason for this divergence will become evident when we examine the composition of income reported on returns with profit or loss from unincorporated business and profession in Chapter 3.

The percentages in Table 3 revealed that business and professional income has been a smaller fraction of AGI on tax returns than of estimated total AGI. For example:

	On Tax Returns	Derived from Personal Income Estimates
1939	.15	.16
1960	.10	.12

[2] Exemptions have declined not merely in absolute dollar amount since the 1930's but also relative to the level of money incomes. Even if there had been no decline in the nominal exemption allowance, the number of family units whose income is below the exemption level would have declined sharply because of the rise, real and inflationary, in the general level of incomes.

NOTES TO TABLE 4

Source: Treasury Department, Statistics of Income.

[a]Wages and salaries include sick pay.

[b]Net profit less net loss of sole proprietors and partners.

[c]Derived residually by subtracting wages and salaries and business and professional income from reported AGI (Appendix C); hence a small amount of the residual may not be property income in a strict economic sense. Included are: dividends (before exclusions), interest, rents and royalties, sale of capital and other assets, income from estates and trusts, pensions and annuities, alimony, gambling profits, and share in current year taxable income of small business corporations electing not to be taxed as corporations.

Note: For 1918-27, amounts shown are only for returns with net income; thereafter, returns with no net income are included. From 1953 on, returns of fiduciaries are excluded.

It follows from these figures that one or more other income components must display an opposite relationship from that found for business and professional income. This is the case for income from employment for recent years:[3]

	On Tax Returns	Derived from Personal Income Estimates
1939	.65	.70
1960	.82	.76

From 1941 on, wages and salaries comprised a greater relative share of income on tax returns than of estimated total income (Chart 2). For business and professional income, the share on tax returns has been smaller than in total income throughout the period 1932-60. The explanation for this could be twofold. First, it is possible that the greater relative dispersion of adjusted gross income on returns with income from unincorporated business or profession than on returns without such income causes its coverage to change over time relative to that for other income components. The less equal distribution of income on returns with business and professional profit or loss than on returns with wages and salaries may affect the extent to which these two income types are covered on tax returns.[4] Though the average AGI of persons with business and professional income has been higher than the average AGI of those with wages and salaries, the relative dispersion of the former was also greater than that for the latter. As long as the average amount of personal exemptions for persons with wage or salary income was above their average taxable incomes, the proportion covered was likely to be lower than for entrepreneurial income. But once personal exemptions were lowered to a level below the average income of those with wages and salaries, the relationship may have been reversed. It is conceivable that the group with a more equal distribution of income, though it has a lower mean income, has a higher coverage ratio than the group with the higher mean income and the less equal distribution.[5]

---

[3] The ratios were computed from the following tables: income from employment, Tables 4 and 6; AGI, Table 3.

[4] See note 14 below for a discussion of the evidence on relative size distribution of income among wage earners and self-employed proprietors.

[5] A simple example will serve to illustrate this point. Assume a universe with two wage earners and two proprietors, whose incomes are as follows:

	Wage Earners	Proprietors
a	$1,200	$ 800
b	1,300	2,000
Average income	1,250	1,400

CHART 1
Business and Professional Income, Wages and Salaries, and Property Income Reported on All Tax Returns, 1918–60

SOURCE: Table 4.

If the exemption for each is $1,500, the proprietors will have a coverage ratio of 71 per cent (assuming exact income reporting) whereas wage earners will have zero coverage. But if the exemption now were lowered to $1,000, wage earners' income will be 100 per cent reported while proprietors' income will continue at 71 per cent coverage.

23

TABLE 5

TOTAL NUMBER OF TAX RETURNS RELATED TO NUMBER WITH
SOLE PROPRIETOR AND PARTNERSHIP INCOME, 1937–60
(in thousands)

	Total No. of Returns (1)	Returns with Sole Proprietorship Income		Returns with Partnership Income		Returns with Sole Proprietorship and/or Partnership Income [a]	
		Number (2)	Col. 2 ÷ Col. 1 (per cent) (3)	Number (4)	Col. 4 ÷ Col. 1 (per cent) (5)	Number (6)	Col. 6 ÷ Col. 1 (per cent) (7)
1937	6,350	850	13.4	263	4.1		
1944	47,204	6,143	13.0	1,187	2.5		
1945	50,046	5,856	11.7	1,539	3.1		
1946	52,938	6,954	13.1	1,709	3.2		
1947	55,209	7,051	12.8	2,095	3.8		
1948	52,173	7,216	13.8	1,818	3.5		
1949	51,914	6,721	12.9	2,257	4.3		
1950	53,175	6,873	12.9	2,132	4.0		
1951	55,563	7,183	12.9	1,919	3.5		
1952	56,662	6,880	12.1	1,843	3.3		
1952	56,529	6,873	12.2	1,833	3.2		
1953	57,838	7,403	12.8	1,891	3.3		
1954	56,747	7,786	13.7	1,817	3.2		
1955	58,250	8,245	14.2	1,955	3.4	9,824	16.9
1956	59,197	8,973	15.2	1,796	3.0		
1957	59,825	8,250	13.8	1,872	3.1		
1958	59,085	8,381	14.2	1,878	3.2		
1959	60,271	8,610	14.3	1,948	3.2	10,173	16.9
1960	61,028	8,599	14.1	1,919	3.1		

The second reason why unincorporated enterprise may be less significant as a source of income as reported on tax returns than of total income as estimated, could be that persons receiving such income report it with less accuracy than is common for some other income types. Reporting practices for business and professional income need not even have changed over time to explain its sharp decline relative to wages and salaries on tax returns. The decline of exemptions, both absolutely and relative to income, may have brought to the fore differences in coverage which had previously been veiled by the greater effect of exemptions on income coverage. We shall devote the following section to a closer examination of the importance of these factors in influencing the coverage of unincorporated enterprise income on tax returns.

Coverage on Tax Returns

In Table 6, entrepreneurial income reported on tax returns and the estimated total are shown for the years 1929–60. The estimated total consists of amounts potentially available for inclusion in the tax base. In accordance with income tax law and practice, which has in general excluded nonmoney income from taxation, it is in effect a money income figure and excludes such items as food and fuel produced and consumed on farms, and imputed income of nonfarm proprietors. We referred to it as a "potentially available" total because it includes earnings of persons whose income is too low to require reporting on tax returns and also income that, though it is reported, is not taxable.

The direction of movement in the two series, relative to one another, is as expected: the amounts reported on tax returns in the decade preceding the 1940's is merely one-third of the estimated total. With the lowering of exemptions and the rise in incomes in the 1940's, coverage had jumped to two-thirds by 1945 and remained at that level through 1953. Thereafter, another small rise occurred. For the three most recent years, 1958–60, coverage has been near 70 per cent.

In comparison, over nine-tenths of wages and salaries have been accounted for on personal tax returns since 1944, and nearly 97 per cent

NOTES TO TABLE 5

Source: Treasury Department, Statistics of Income. Fiduciary returns excluded after 1952.

[a]The number of returns with income from either sole proprietorship or partnership, or both, could only be calculated for 1955 and 1959. For source, see Table 33.

CHART 2
Business and Professional Income and Wages and Salaries as Percentage of Adjusted Gross Income, 1929–60

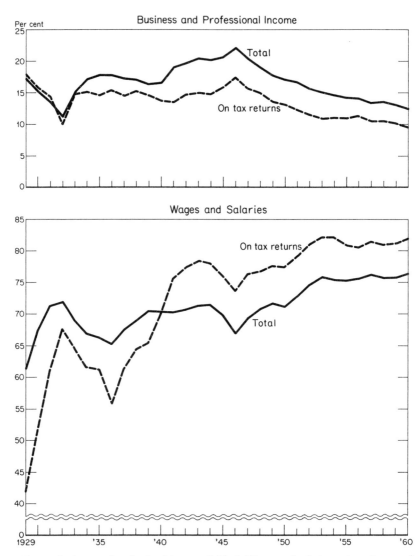

SOURCE: Business and professional income—Table 3. Wages and salaries on tax returns—col. 1, Table 4 divided by col. 8, Table 3. Total wages and salaries—derived as shown in Appendix C.

TABLE 6

BUSINESS AND PROFESSIONAL INCOME REPORTED ON TAX RETURNS RELATED
TO ESTIMATED TOTAL, 1929-60
(million dollars)

	Amount Reported (1)	Estimated Total (2)	Col. 1 ÷ Col. 2 (per cent) (3)
1929	4,869	13,031[a]	37.4
1930	3,102	9,533	32.5
1931	2,015	6,645	30.3
1932	1,229	4,146	29.6
1933	1,746	5,550	31.5
1934	2,125	7,585	28.0
1935	2,387	8,633	27.6
1936	3,210	10,295	31.2
1937	3,376	10,781	31.3
1938	3,312	9,556	32.8
1939	3,689	10,611	34.8
1940	5,427	11,674	46.5
1941	8,495	16,235	52.3
1942	12,455	21,228	58.7
1943	15,805	26,449	59.8
1944	17,340	27,833	62.3
1945	19,102	28,902	66.1
1946	23,384	34,785	67.2
1947	23,400	35,020	66.8
1948	24,598	35,235	69.8
1949	21,777	32,891	66.2
1950	23,514	34,637	67.9
1951	24,961	37,978	65.7
1952	24,844	37,967	65.4
1953	24,951	38,646	64.6
1954	25,452	37,343	68.2
1955	27,454	39,154	70.1
1956	30,137	41,845	72.0
1957	29,698	41,426	71.7
1958	29,905	42,555	70.3
1959	30,995	44,230	70.1
1960	30,038	43,658	68.8

Source

Col. 1: Statistics of Income, Individual Income Tax Returns, including
fiduciary returns through 1952.

Col. 2: Estimated by methods outlined in Table B-3. For an explanation of
the discrepancy between this column and line 12, Table B-3, see
note to lines 9 and 10, Table B-2.

[a]Omits capital gains adjustment for farm proprietors.

27

after 1950. Close to 90 per cent of dividends are reported for 1936–53, and between 80 and 90 per cent for the years thereafter. In contrast, only somewhat over 60 per cent of personal interest receipts were covered on tax returns during 1956–59 (Table 7).

COVERAGE ON TAX RETURNS BY FARM AND NONFARM ENTERPRISE

Additional information on the coverage of unincorporated enterprise income may be obtained by breaking the totals into their farm and nonfarm components. A finer breakdown is not possible with the data at our disposal.

Farm and nonfarm entrepreneurial income accounted for on tax returns is compared with estimated total farm and nonfarm income in Table 8 for selected years, 1939–60. The amounts shown on line 1 differ somewhat from the totals shown under the same heading in Table 6. The difference arises because the data in Table 6 are based on the Internal Revenue Service's annual income-size tabulations whereas those in Table 8 are based on its industrial tabulations, published at irregular intervals. These differences, and the adjustments required to make the tax return figures conceptually consistent with corresponding total income estimates, are fully discussed in Appendix B. However, some weaknesses in the comparison of amounts reported on tax returns and estimated totals should be noted at the outset.

The estimates for total income of nonfarm business and professional proprietors are substantially those of the National Income Division of the Commerce Department. Those for farm proprietors are derived from estimates developed by the Agriculture Department. The Commerce Department estimates of nonfarm *business* income, however, rely heavily on tax return information. Thus circularity enters the comparison of tax return coverage with total income. This is considerably lessened by a number of adjustments made to correct for both underreporting of income and underenumeration of proprietors on tax returns. But to the extent that these corrections (described in more detail in Appendix B) fail to remove some of the peculiarities of tax return data, some circularity remains. The importance of this qualification of the data is reinforced when we recall (as shown in Table 2) that of $30 billion of unincorporated enterprise income reported for 1960, about $19 billion, or nearly two-thirds, originated in the so-called nonfarm business sector. For unincorporated farm enterprise income, two variants are presented in Table 8.[6] Variant I is obtained by treating the depreciation, taxes,

---

[6] For this reason two variants are also shown for total estimated business and professional income, even though only a single variant was calculated for nonfarm business and professional income.

TABLE 7

TOTAL WAGES AND SALARIES, DIVIDENDS, AND INTEREST RECEIPTS REPORTED ON TAX RETURNS COMPARED WITH ESTIMATED TOTAL, 1936-60
(billion dollars)

	Wages and Salaries			Dividends[a]			Interest		
	Reported on Tax Returns (1)	Estimated Total (2)	Col. 1 ÷ Col. 2 (per cent) (3)	Reported on Tax Returns (4)	Estimated Total (5)	Col. 4 ÷ Col. 5 (per cent) (6)	Reported on Tax Returns (7)	Estimated Total (8)	Col. 7 ÷ Col. 8 (per cent) (9)
1936	11.7	37.8	31.0	4.0	4.3	93.7			
1939	16.5	45.7	36.1	3.3	3.5	93.1			
1941	47.1	60.0	78.5	4.2	4.1	102.6			
1943	82.8	92.2	89.8	3.7	4.1	91.1			
1945	91.7	98.1	93.5	3.9	4.3	91.2			
1947	114.8	119.4	96.2	5.5	5.9	93.3			
1949	124.9	133.2	93.7	6.6	6.8	97.6			
1953	187.7	194.5	96.5	7.6	8.3	90.7			
1954	186.0	192.7	96.5	7.6	8.6	89.1			
1955	200.7	207.6	96.7	8.5	9.8	86.5			
1956	215.6	224.5	96.1	9.3	10.4	88.9			
1957	228.1	235.5	96.9	9.8	10.7	91.5	3.5	5.5	62.5
1958	227.6	236.6	96.2	9.1	10.1	89.8	4.0	6.5	61.2
1959	247.4	255.6	96.8	9.7	10.8	90.2	4.4	7.0	62.7
1960	257.9	267.1	96.6				5.4	8.2	65.4

Source

Cols. 1 and 2: See Appendix Table C-1.

Cols. 4 and 5: Daniel M. Holland, Dividends Under the Income Tax, Princeton for NBER, 1962, Table 26, Variant 2, lines 4 and 14. For 1958 and 1959, President's Tax Message along with Principal Statement, Detailed Explanation, and Supporting Exhibits and Documents, 1961, p. 143.

Cols. 7 and 8: President's Tax Message, p. 145.

[a] Includes fiduciaries 1936-57. Other differences between the two sources are minor.

TABLE 8

INCOME FROM UNINCORPORATED ENTERPRISE REPORTED ON TAX RETURNS AS PERCENTAGE OF ESTIMATED TOTAL, BY FARM AND NONFARM, 1939-60
(dollars in millions)

	1939	1941	1943	1945	1947	1949	1953	1955	1956	1957	1958	1959	1960
1. Total reported on tax returns	4,042	8,456	15,761	18,837	22,784	21,933	25,401	26,612	29,836– 30,740	29,981	30,337	31,386	30,453
2. Nonfarm business and professional	3,881	6,597	11,812	15,052	16,923	17,106	21,592	23,627– 23,442	25,809	26,120	25,974	28,191	27,204
3. Farm operators	161	1,859	3,949	3,785	5,859	4,827	3,810	2,985– 3,170	4,027– 4,931	3,861	4,363	3,195	3,249
4. Estimated total													
Variant 1	10,593	16,199	26,373	28,841	34,939	32,834	38,733	39,262	41,943	41,537	42,671	44,350	43,772
Variant 2	10,054	15,625	25,727	28,128	33,821	31,800	37,446	37,986	40,613	40,169	41,277	42,893	42,304
5. Nonfarm business and professional	7,498	11,526	16,955	19,111	21,359	22,141	27,645	30,537	32,517	32,994	32,456	35,320	34,069
6. Farm operators													
Variant 1	3,095	4,673	9,418	9,730	13,580	10,693	11,088	8,725	9,426	8,543	10,215	9,030	9,703
Variant 2	2,556	4,099	8,772	9,017	12,462	9,659	9,801	7,449	8,096	7,175	8,821	7,573	8,235
7. Reported amounts by estimated total													
Variant 1	.38	.52	.60	.65	.65	.67	.66	.68	.71–	.72	.71	.71	.70
Variant 2	.40	.54	.61	.67	.67	.69	.68	.70	.73– .76	.75	.73	.73	.72
8. Nonfarm business and professional	.52	.57	.70	.79	.79	.77	.78	.77	.79	.79	.80	.80	.80
9. Farm operators													
Variant 1	.05	.40	.42	.39	.43	.45	.34	.34– .36	.43– .52	.45	.43	.35	.33
Variant 2	.06	.45	.45	.42	.47	.50	.39	.40– .43	.50– .61	.54	.49	.42	.39

and interest connected with farm dwellings as a personal nondeductible expense, as required by tax law. This is the variant used for the analysis below, except as otherwise noted. Variant II is obtained by following a possibly widespread practice of treating all, or most, expenses connected with a farm dwelling as part of the farm business expense. The separation between personal and business expense on a farm is in any case difficult and bound to involve arbitrary divisions. Variant-II estimates are therefore presented alongside Variant-I estimates. A significant portion of farm income appears to be derived from livestock sales. If the animals sold were used for breeding, draft, or dairy purposes, many farmers report the net income from such sales as long-term capital gain rather than in the farm business schedule. Estimates of such capital gains were subtracted from the farm income estimates derived from the Department of Agriculture figures.[7]

Of an estimated $34 billion adjusted gross income obtained by proprietors from nonfarm business and profession, $27 billion, or 80 per cent, is accounted for by tax return tabulations. For farm operators, only $3.2 billion of an estimated total of $9.7 billion, or between 33 and 40 per cent, was accounted for. Both of these coverage ratios had reached this level during the first half of the 1940's. For 1939, the single prewar year for which we have an industrial breakdown, only 5 per cent of

[7] The reported figure for net long-term capital gains from the sale of livestock for 1959 was $701 million (see Treasury Department, *Sales of Capital Assets Reported on Individual Income Tax Returns for 1959, Statistics of Income,* Supplemental Report, Table 2). This figure served as a benchmark for the estimates for other years (see Appendix Table B-3).

NOTES TO TABLE 8

Source: Lines 1 through 3: Table B-1, except for lines 1 and 3 in 1956 which were obtained as the difference between the nonfarm figure from the industry tabulation ($25,809) and total unincorporated enterprise income from the annual income-size tabulation for individuals (shown in Table A-1, col. 6). Since the income figures from the two sets of estimates are hardly ever precisely the same, the "industry" figure having in recent years varied from 99 to 102 per cent of the "income-size" figure (see Table A-1), these two percentages were used to estimate a likely range for the farm net income estimate:

lower limit	upper limit
30,137 x .99 = 29,836	30,137 x 1.02 = 30,740
−25,809	−25,809
4,027	4,931

Lines 4 through 6: Table B-3.

Note: Variant 1 refers to farm operators' net income before deduction of depreciation, taxes, and mortgage interest on farm dwellings. Variant 2 is farm net income after deduction of these items.

31

farm operators' income, but over one-half of unincorporated business and professional income, was accounted for on tax returns. By 1941, after the drastic cut in personal exemptions and the rise in incomes that accompanied the outbreak of the war, 40 per cent of farm and 57 per cent of nonfarm enterprise income were covered. Thus, most of the increase in coverage between 1939 and 1941 is explained by the sharp rise from 5 to 40 per cent in the coverage of the farm component.[8]

In the years following, both farm and nonfarm proprietors' income rose steeply. But the coverage of farm income on tax returns did not increase substantially. By 1947, total farm income had reached a peak of $13.7 billion, triple the amount of 1941, and filing requirements had been further reduced by one-third below 1941. At the same time, the number of farms had declined from 6.3 to 5.9 million—a factor one might expect to operate in the same direction as income and exemptions in increasing the coverage of farm income. Yet the coverage of farm operators' income rose only from 40 to 43 per cent between 1941 and 1947. By 1953, total farm operators' net income had declined to $11.2 billion from its 1947 peak; but the number of farms had now fallen to 5 million and filing requirements were still below the 1941 level. In the face of this moderate decline, 1953 coverage fell sharply to one-third of farm enterprise income. Since 1953, both the estimated total of farm income and the amount reported on tax returns have continued the irregular decline begun in the 1940's (lines 3 and 6, Table 8). However, the decline in total farm net income has not been accompanied by a further decline in coverage on tax returns but remained at roughly one-third as late as 1960 (line 9, Table 8), and somewhat over 40 per cent in the period 1956–58.[9] The decline in coverage after 1958 is difficult to explain.

---

[8] Assume, for instance, that the coverage of farm income had been the same in 1939 as in 1941, so that only the coverage of the nonfarm component would have risen. In that case, 48 per cent of the total would have been reported in 1939, and the rise would have been only 4 percentage points between 1939 and 1941.

[9] Starting in 1955, self-employed farmers were included in Old Age and Survivors Insurance (Social Security). In connection with this, they were also subject for the first time to the payment of a self-employment tax. The data presented in Tables 8 through 10 do not unambiguously suggest that their liability to self-employment tax (which is paid in conjunction with income tax) has had a pronounced or identifiable influence on farmer income coverage. A rise in coverage from one-third to over 40 per cent occurred in 1956 and remained at that level until 1958. The probable effect of the self-employment tax is most clearly observed in the change in number of farm sole proprietors filing returns (Table 10). The latter rose from 3.1 to 3.4 million from 1953 to 1955 and then remained at that level. In contrast to this evidence, it must be noted (Table 8) that after 1958 farm income coverage returned to its 1953–55 level of one-third.

Total farm net income declined only from $10.4 to $9.8 billion, whereas the reported amount showed a sharp drop from $4.4 to $3.2 billion. Tables 9 and 10 give further evidence of the striking discrepancy between total farm net income as estimated and as reported on tax returns. For 1939 and 1941 the average amounts accounted for on returns are much higher than the averages for the country as a whole. This is what one would expect, considering that only about one in forty farms for 1939 and one in five for 1941 were represented on tax returns. Those who are reporting may be presumed to have larger incomes, on

TABLE 9

AVERAGE FARM INCOME FROM FARM ENTERPRISE AS REPORTED
ON TAX RETURNS AND AS ESTIMATED, 1939-60

	Average Farm Net Income Reported		Estimated Average Farm Net Income[a]		Col. 3 ÷ Col. 2	Col. 4 ÷ Col. 2
	Sole Proprietors (1)	Sole Proprietors and Partnerships (2)	Variant 1 (3)	Variant 2 (4)	(5)	(6)
1939	771	1,019	479	396	.47	.39
1941	1,417	1,545	741	650	.48	.42
1943	1,365	1,507	1,543	1,437	1.02	.95
1945	1,256	1,373	1,626	1,507	1.18	1.10
1947	1,780	1,941	2,307	2,117	1.19	1.09
1949	1,430	1,551	1,864	1,684	1.20	1.09
1953	1,079	1,168	2,221	1,963	1.90	1.68
1955	773	n.a.	1,871	1,597	n.a.	n.a.
1957	967	1,109	1,952	1,639	1.76	1.48
1958	1,115	1,243	2,413	2,084	1.94	1.68
1959	782	908	2,206	1,850	2.43	2.04
1960	815	932	2,455	2,084	2.63	2.24

Source: Col. 1: Line 8, Table B-1 divided by column 1, Table 10.
Col. 2: Line 3, Table 8 divided by column 3, Table 10.
Col. 3: Line 13 minus line 9, Table B-2 divided by column 4, Table 10.
Col. 4: Line 14 minus line 10, Table B-2, divided by column 4, Table 10.

[a]See Table 8 for explanation of variants.

33

TABLE 10

NUMBER OF FARM BUSINESSES ACCOUNTED FOR ON INDIVIDUAL TAX RETURNS,
1939-60
(in thousands)

| | | | Number of Noncorporate Farms | | |
	Sole Proprietors (1)	Partnerships (2)	On Tax Returns (Col. 1 + Col. 2) (3)	Total (4)	Col. 3 ÷ Col. 4 (per cent) (5)
1939	140	18	158	6,433	2.5
1941	1,161	42[a]	1,203	6,285	19.1
1943	2,560	60[a]	2,620	6,082	43.1
1945	2,659	97	2,756	5,961	46.2
1947	2,904	114	3,018	5,864	51.5
1949	2,987	125[a]	3,112	5,714	54.5
1951	3,139			5,420	
1953	3,126	135	3,261	4,975	65.5
1955	3,417			4,645	
1957	3,343	137	3,480	4,361	79.8
1958	3,374	135	3,509	4,220	83.2
1959	3,387	132	3,518	4,083	86.2
1960	3,359	126	3,485	3,933	88.6

Source: Cols. 1-3: _Statistics of Income._
Col. 4: U. S. Department of Agriculture, _Farm Situation_, July
1962, p. 46, number of farms minus number of farm corporations as given in _Statistics of Income._

[a]Total number of partnership returns are available by year in _Statistics of Income_, 1949, p. 71. These figures were multiplied by the ratio of farm returns to total returns of partnerships for the years this ratio was available.

average, than those who are not reporting.[10] The share of the reporting group in the income total is thus also larger than its share on a population basis: the 20 per cent of farms represented on returns in 1941 accounted for 40 per cent of farm net income. But this expected rela-

[10] Among those not reporting were undoubtedly many farm operators with extremely small incomes. According to estimates by Nathan M. Koffsky and Jeanne E. Lear for 1946, about 2.7 million farm operators out of a total of 5.9 million had gross cash farm incomes of less than $1,000. See their "Size Distribution of Farm Operators' Income in 1946," _Studies in Income and Wealth_, 13, New York, NBER, 1951, p. 228.

tion had changed by 1943. Beginning with that year, the proportion of farms reported on exceeded by increasing amounts the proportion of income accounted for. In the latest year, 1960, the number of tax returns with farm income equalled 89 per cent of the estimated number of unincorporated operating farms. Yet the net income reported accounted for only 33 to 39 per cent of the total, as we have seen. The relation is the opposite of what one would expect to find.

For business and professional income, coverage rose from 57 per cent in 1941 to a level of 79 per cent in 1945. It has remained within 2 percentage points of that level since then. The small rise in the over-all coverage ratio since the war does not appear to be explained by a rise in coverage within either the farm or business and professional groups, but mainly by the increasing relative share of the nonfarm sector (see lines 5 and 6 of Table 8). As the weight of nonfarm income, with its "higher" coverage ratio, increases, the over-all coverage ratio for unincorporated enterprise income rises.[11]

No attempt is made to show the relative number of nonfarm proprietors represented on tax returns, as was done for farmers in Table 10. What constitutes an unincorporated business or a self-employed person is subject to various definitions. On the tax return, anyone with self-employment income may use the business schedule of the return to list such income. This naturally makes the number of self-employed proprietors larger on tax returns than that estimated with more restrictive definitions by the Commerce Department's National Income Division. The latter counts as self-employed only those active proprietors of enterprises who devote the major portion of their time to the business. In the statistics on business firms, only those firms are included which have at least one paid employee or an established place of business. Consequently we find the following frequencies for nonfarm unincorporated businesses (in thousands):

	NID[a] (1)	Tax Returns[b] (2)	(2) ÷ (1) (3)
1945	2,664	3,171	1.19
1947	3,239	3,994	1.23
1953	3,640	4,826	1.33

[a] Betty C. Churchill, "Business Population by Legal Form of Organization," *Survey of Current Business,* April 1955, p. 15.
[b] IRS, *Statistics of Income.*

[11] The qualifications of the nonfarm unincorporated business estimates on pp. 28 and 31 should be noted and borne in mind.

35

The above figures do not include professional practitioners such as doctors, lawyers, and accountants. For this group, the NID estimates of the number of active proprietors may be more nearly comparable with the tax return figures, since most professional practitioners probably devote the major portion of their working time to their profession. But even here the IRS figure includes some professionals who are, for the most part, employees, and we may double count some who are both partners and sole proprietors, or who are partners in more than one partnership.[12]

From the figures presented it is apparent that the difference in coverage between unincorporated enterprise income and wages and salaries is not solely attributable to the low coverage of farm income. Nonfarm enterprise income has also had a lower coverage than that of employees since 1941 (Table 11). It is frequently thought that withholding of tax at the source accounts for the difference in coverage between wages and salaries and other income types not subject to withholding. Yet the coverage ratio for wages and salaries exceeded that for nonfarm enterprise income as early as 1941, two years before withholding at the source was instituted. This would suggest that the reporting of wages and salaries was more accurate than that of enterprise income even before World War II. If the income of employees were found to have risen more than that of nonfarm proprietors over the years in question, a relative

[12] The respective frequencies (in thousands) are as follows:

	NID Active Proprietors[a] (1)	IRS Sole Proprietors and Partners[b] (2)	(2) ÷ (1) (3)
1939	519	220	.42
1945	433	354	.82
1947	513	457	.89
1953	586	555	.95
1956	625	669	1.07
1957	638	694	1.09
1958	641	704	1.10
1959	648	782	1.21
1960	651	756	1.16

[a] Department of Commerce, *U.S. Income and Output,* and *Survey of Current Business,* Table VI-13 and VI-16, lines 75–78.

[b] Internal Revenue Service, *Statistics of Income.* The number of partnerships for 1939 and 1945 were multiplied by 2.62, the ratio of partners per professional partnership for 1947. For 1953 and 1959 the ratios were 2.63 and 2.79, respectively. Simple straight-line interpolation was used to estimate the ratios for 1956–58. For 1960, the 1959 ratio was used.

TABLE 11

INCOME FROM WAGES AND SALARIES AND NONFARM BUSINESS AND PROFESSIONS: AVERAGE
AMOUNT PER RECIPIENT AND PERCENTAGE REPORTED ON TAX RETURNS, 1939-60

	Nonfarm Entrepreneurial Income		Wages and Salaries	
	Percentage Reported (1)	Average Per Proprietor (dollars) (2)	Percentage Reported (3)	Average Per Employee (4)
1939	52	1,514	36	1,253
1941	57	2,292	78	1,392
1943	70	3,751	90	1,692
1945	79	4,167	94	1,816
1947	79	3,746	96	2,503
1949	77	3,809	94	2,815
1953	78	4,436	96	3,509
1955	77	4,757	97	3,770
1956	79	4,965	96	3,963
1957	79	4,996	97	4,132
1958	80	4,938	96	4,269
1959	80	5,211	97	4,483
1960	80	5,045	97	4,634

Source

Col. 1: Table 8.
Col. 2: Line 9 minus line 2, Table B-3, divided by number of active pro-
prietors (Commerce Department, Income and Output and Survey of
Current Business, July, 1962, Tables VI-13 and VI-16).
Col. 3: Column 3, Table 7 (figures rounded).
Col. 4: Wages and salaries as derived in Appendix Table C-1 divided by
number of full-time equivalent employees (Commerce Department.
Income and Output and Survey of Current Business, July, 1962,
Table VI-13).

rise in coverage of wages and salaries could be explained by the increased
amount of taxable income from that source rather than more accurate
reporting practices. But it is unlikely that the incomes of employees rose
more than those of nonfarm proprietors. As shown in Table 11, average
business and professional income rose from $1,514 to $4,167 between

37

1939 and 1945, whereas average wages and salaries rose only from $1,253 to $1,816.[13]

It is also possible, as explained earlier in this chapter, that the relative size distributions of two income types differ so radically that the one with the lower average per recipient has nevertheless a higher ratio of reported to total income. Applied to the case under study, if employee income were equally distributed and exceeded the exemption level, it might be nearly 100 per cent reported despite a low average income per employee. On the other hand, if entrepreneurial income were unequally distributed, so that some proprietors had extremely high and others very low incomes, this group could conceivably have a lower reporting ratio than employees and yet a higher average income per proprietor. While entrepreneurial income is indeed less equally distributed than wages and salaries,[14] the difference does not appear large enough to explain the lower reporting ratio for proprietors. This judgment is based on the data presented in the next section, where the unincorporated enterprise income of persons with income too low to require reporting is discussed.

Effect on Coverage of Income Below Filing Requirement

As we have seen, the difference between estimated and reported business and professional income is large. Barring estimating or conceptual errors

[13] Both proprietors and employees usually have, of course, some income from other sources, and many are employees in some capacities and self-employed in others. But if this were taken into account, it would tend to raise the income figures of proprietors more than that of employees. As we shall see below (Table 18), income from unincorporated enterprises accounted for 50.2 per cent of estimated adjusted gross income of sole proprietors and partners for 1959. In contrast, wages and salaries constituted 93 per cent of estimated adjusted gross income on returns of employees.

[14] We have no direct evidence for all years regarding the equality of the distribution of income among wage earners and persons with self-employment income. The usual Lorenz distributions are by size of the specified receipt rather than total income of recipients. For the mid-thirties, data on variability of total income for wage earners and proprietors show greater variability for the latter than the former. But, strictly speaking, these data are not as inclusive as required for our purpose. They cover the total income of units whose largest source of income is wages and salaries or entrepreneurial income, and therefore do not include the income of those whose wages and salaries or entrepreneurial profit and loss are a secondary source of income. See Frank A. Hanna, Joseph A. Pechman, and Sidney M. Lerner, *Analysis of Wisconsin Income*, Studies in Income and Wealth, 9, New York, NBER, 1948, pp. 91–92; and Milton Friedman and Simon Kuznets, *Income from Independent Professional Practice*, New York, NBER, 1945, pp. 71–73. Our statistics, of course, deal with all unincorporated enterprise income and, in a strict sense, require an estimate of the total income of all persons with such income, regardless of whether the latter is the major or only a minor source of the income of which it is a component. For 1955, we were able to estimate total AGI for returns showing wage and salary income and for returns with entrepreneurial income by size of AGI. The coefficient of inequality for wage and salary recipients is .40, whereas that for persons reporting entrepreneurial income is .57.

of that magnitude, the difference must be explained by (1) taxpayers' errors in reporting their income, and/or (2) the amounts received by persons with incomes too low to be required to file a tax return.

An estimate of the amount of business and professional income legally not required to be reported should ideally take into account two filing requirements. First, that any person with gross income over $600 ($1,200 if a person is over 65) must file a tax return. Second, that any person with net income from business or profession of $400, or more, is subject to self-employment tax and must for this reason file a tax return. The only exceptions to the latter requirement are income from the performance of services as a doctor of medicine, or when an individual had wages of $4,800 or more which were subject to social security tax. To obtain a precise estimate of unincorporated business and professional income received by persons not required to file a return, it would be necessary to construct a distribution of taxpayer units by size of business and professional income and by size of AGI. This would allow the identification of those with income below the general filing requirement as well as less than $400 from self-employment. Such a distribution should of course be independent of the tax return tabulations of the Treasury Department. But the necessary data are not readily available.

For our present purpose it appears sufficient to obtain a rough and approximate notion of how important income below the filing requirement might be in explaining the gap between reported and total entrepreneurial income. Accordingly, we used the Census Bureau's frequency distributions for families and unrelated individuals by size of specific source as a basis for judgment. The Census frequency of families and unrelated individuals reporting income of less than $500 from self-employment is compared to the number of tax returns on which less than $500 from sole proprietorship and/or partnership is reported (Table 12).[15] Evidently the Census and tax return frequencies are so close as to give no basis for supposing that income below the filing requirement could account for any substantial omission of entrepreneurial income from tax returns. For each of the three groupings shown in Table 12, the frequencies from the two sources correspond closely, and it is as close for the total as for the two lower size groups shown. The latter would argue against the possibility that underreporting on tax returns moved a spuriously large number into the lowest size groups.

[15] The lowest size group in the Census tabulations is $500 and less. It was thus the nearest grouping to the $400 filing limit for persons with self-employment income. The institution of the $400 filing requirement for the self-employed in 1955 probably explains the relative increase in tax return frequencies between 1954 and 1956 (Table 12).

TABLE 12

NUMBER OF PERSONS WITH BUSINESS AND PROFESSIONAL INCOME LESS THAN
$500, LESS THAN $1,000, AND TOTAL: TAX-RETURN AND CENSUS DATA,
1954, 1956, AND 1960
(in thousands)

| | Number on Tax Returns (1) | Census Frequency of Families and Individuals with | | | Col. 1 ÷ Col. 4 (5) |
		Farm Self-Employment Income (2)	Nonfarm Self-Employment Income (3)	Total (4)	
		UNDER $500			
1954	2,657	1,720	1,062	2,782	.96
1956	2,955	1,747	1,198	2,945	1.00
1960	3,287	1,369	1,669	3,038	1.08
		UNDER $1,000			
1954	3,737	2,330	1,517	3,847	.97
1956	4,159	2,308	1,602	3,910	1.06
1960	4,393	2,176	1,798	3,974	1.11
		TOTAL			
1954	9,249	5,284	4,018	9,302	.99
1956	10,372	5,469	4,131	9,590	1.08
1960	10,135	6,495	3,431	9,926	1.02

Source

Col. 1: Statistics of Income. Total frequencies for 1954 and 1956
were reduced by the 1955 (1960 by the 1959) percentage of returns with
sole proprietorship or partnership income which showed income from both
these sources (column 8, Table 33). For the number of returns with less
than $500 and less than $1,000, it was assumed that the same duplication
ratio applied but that the combined income from both sole proprietorship
and partnership on returns with duplication was sufficient to raise the
total self-employment income above $500 and $1,000 respectively; hence,
all returns with duplication were eliminated by reducing the frequency
of sole proprietors and partners by twice the duplication ratio.
Cols. 2 and 3: Commerce Department, Current Population Reports,
Consumer Income; #20, p. 20; #27, p. 31; and #37, p. 37.

Even if one were to assume that all of the Census frequencies with
income less than $500 did not file and had self-employment income of
$200 each, the total amount thereby accounted for would only be $.63
billion for 1956 and $.61 billion for 1960.[16] Recalling that the unexplained

[16] This figure is still much above any other estimates dealing with the same topic. For
instance, see Ulric Weil, "A Note on the Derivation of Income Estimates by Source of
Income of Persons Making Less than $500 per Annum, 1944–1948," *Journal of the American
Statistical Association,* Vol. 45, p. 440. Weil's estimate of the entrepreneurial component, in the

gap shown in Table 8 was near $12 billion and $13 billion, respectively, it must be concluded that the filing requirement level explains little of the discrepancy and that strenuous attempts at greater precision with respect to this item would seem uncalled for.

Comparisons With Other Studies

How do the findings presented above compare with those of other studies? The first thoroughgoing, and by now classic, appraisal of the extent of income coverage on tax returns was that by Selma F. Goldsmith for the years 1944, 1945, and 1946, and later extended to 1951 and 1952.[17] Since the method used in this study follows closely that employed by Mrs. Goldsmith in her two studies, it is not surprising that the results closely agree. Mrs. Goldsmith found that of total unincorporated enterprise income estimated by the NID, the amount covered on tax returns varied between 66 and 72 per cent for the five years mentioned above. For 1951, tax returns accounted for 85 per cent of nonfarm business and professional income and 41 per cent of farm income, according to her estimates.

The most direct evidence that has yet become available regarding income coverage on federal tax returns are the reports on the Internal Revenue Service's Audit Control Program (ACP) for 1948–50. Only results for 1948 and 1949 have been publicly reported, mainly in several papers by Marius Farioletti.[18] The absolute amount of error uncovered was not nearly as large as the discrepancies noted in either Mrs. Goldsmith's or the present study. For 1949, ACP estimates indicate that audit

income group with $500 and less, varied from $230 to $320 million for 1944–48, i.e., an average of 9 per cent of money income for that group. Elsewhere, we have estimated the total income below the filing-requirement level for 1955 at roughly $3.41 billion (C. Harry Kahn, *Personal Deductions in the Federal Income Tax*, Princeton for NBER, 1960, Table A-2). Assuming the Weil figure for the relation of entrepreneurial to total income, we would get about $.31 billion, that is, $3.41 billion multiplied by .09. In one important respect our estimate as shown in Table 12 differs from Weil's: the farm component of income below the filing level is over twice as large as the nonfarm, whereas in the Weil estimates the nonfarm exceeds the farm component.

[17] Selma F. Goldsmith, "Appraisal of Basic Data Available for Constructing Income Size Distributions," in *Studies in Income and Wealth*, 13, New York, NBER, 1951, p. 302 and "The Relation of Census Income Distribution Statistics to Other Income Data," in *An Appraisal of the 1950 Census Income Data*, Studies in Income and Wealth, 23, Princeton for NBER, 1958, pp. 79–80. See also Daniel M. Holland and C. Harry Kahn, "Comparison of Personal and Taxable Income," *Federal Tax Policy for Economic Growth and Stability*, Joint Committee on the Economic Report, 1955, pp. 337–338.

[18] Marius Farioletti, "Some Results from the First Year's Audit Control Program of the Bureau of Internal Revenue," *National Tax Journal*, March 1952; and "Some Income Adjustment Results from the 1949 Audit Control Program," in *1950 Census Income Data*.

TABLE 13

ESTIMATED INCREASE IN GROSS RECEIPTS AND IN NET PROFIT LESS LOSS
AFTER AUDIT OF 1949 TAX RETURNS FOR SOLE PROPRIETORS, BY FARM AND NONFARM INCOME
(dollars in millions)

	Gross Receipts			Net Profit Less Net Loss		
	Total Disclosable by Audit (1)	Increase over Reported Amount (2)	Col. 2 ÷ Col. 1 (per cent) (3)	Total Disclosable by Audit (4)	Increase over Reported Amount (5)	Col. 5 ÷ Col. 4 (per cent) (6)
Total income	107,417	1,916	1.8	16,293	2,715	16.7
Farm	18,192	541	3.0	5,010	939	18.7
Nonfarm	89,225	1,375	1.5	11,283	1,776	15.7

Source: Marius Farioletti, "Some Income Adjustment Results from the 1949 Audit Control Program," in An Appraisal of the 1950 Census Income Data, Studies in Income and Wealth 23, Princeton for NBER, 1958, Table 5.

of all sole proprietorship returns for that year would have produced an increase in net profit (less net loss) of $2.7 billion (Table 13).[19] Even with generous allowance for amounts not reported because the recipients, though legally required to file, were nontaxable after exemptions and nonbusiness taxes, the estimated change disclosed by audit was well below the discrepancy shown in Table 8. But, as Farioletti has repeatedly noted, the ACP estimates were not intended to disclose all errors, "but only the errors that experienced Internal Revenue examining officers would find if all of the returns of the taxpayers were audited with about the same experience and time factors." It was decided beforehand that "it would not be practicable to establish standards of audit needed to estimate all errors that taxpayers make."[20] Even in the absence of such a decision it would be difficult to find all taxpayer errors by audit methods.

It is, however, of interest to note some of the relative magnitudes brought out in the ACP. Thus, although returns with profit or loss from

[19] No comparable estimate is given for partnership income. The only evidence for partnership income is for returns reporting less than $10,000 adjusted gross income on Forms 1040 for which a change in tax liability is indicated, with the largest portion attributable to error in AGI. The AGI change on returns on which partnership income was the major income item in error was $329 million. (See Farioletti in 1950 Census Income Data, p. 255.) Thus, total estimated audit change for partnership income may be in the neighborhood of $400 million, which would bring the audit change for all unincorporated enterprise income to $3.1 billion.

[20] Ibid., pp. 242–243.

42

sole proprietorship have accounted for less than one-tenth of total adjusted gross income reported, they accounted for 54 per cent of the total adjusted gross income change for returns examined in the 1949 ACP. In the 1948 ACP, underreporting errors were found on more than one out of every three returns with income or loss from sole proprietorship. The significance of this ratio is best stated in Farioletti's words: "Based on results of the Bureau's Audit Control Program, it is estimated that the 7 million 1948 income tax returns filed by individuals with business and professional incomes are more frequently in error, have larger amounts of tax change, and produce more dollars of tax change per man-year of examination effort expended than is the case regarding the 45 million returns without business incomes."[21]

The most significant 1949 ACP findings for sole proprietors are assembled in Table 13. The relative size of the increase in net profit (less net loss) after audit was somewhat greater for farm than for non-farm proprietors, 18.7 as compared to 15.7 per cent, but the difference was much less than might be expected from the relative gap between estimated totals and amounts reported, as shown in Table 8 above. This suggests the possibility that the NID estimates of net income from non-farm business, which are largely based on IRS data,[22] may not have been adjusted upward sufficiently. If so, much of the difference in the proportion of farm and nonfarm business and professional income accounted for on tax returns may be apparent rather than real.[23]

The only other study which approached the problem of income coverage on tax returns through the "audit" method is that recently reported on by Harold M. Groves.[24] While of great interest in many respects, its relevance to the subject of this inquiry is limited by the fact that it deals with the coverage of farm and rental income under the Wisconsin state income tax. Wisconsin probably cannot be considered representative of the nation since its tax returns have long been open to public inspection, a circumstance which made the Groves study possible and which undoubtedly has considerable effect on income tax administration. The Groves group found that a reasonable estimate of farm net

[21] Farioletti, in *National Tax Journal,* March 1952, p. 77.

[22] See footnote 5, above.

[23] It will be recalled that the estimates of farm operators' income, with which the tax return figures are compared, were derived independently, whereas the nonfarm business estimates lean on IRS and audit data which cannot be presumed to disclose all of the underreporting likely to occur.

[24] Harold M. Groves, "Empirical Studies of Income Tax Compliance," *National Tax Journal,* December 1958, especially pp. 297–301.

income coverage on Wisconsin tax returns is in the range of 60 to 75 per cent, which exceeds even our variant 2 estimate of 52 per cent for 1957. Another recent study, which deals only with farm operators' income, is that by Stocker and Ellickson[25] of the U.S. Department of Agriculture. Stocker and Ellickson restricted themselves almost entirely to a thorough-going analysis of the coverage of gross farm receipts on federal tax returns. As the authors note in their concluding remarks, it is of course the coverage of net income rather than gross income that matters in the analysis of problems relating to the income tax. Equity requires that the measure used as the tax base is adequately reported. Stocker and Ellickson find that, for 1955, all but $4.2 billion of gross receipts, or 86 per cent of the total, can be accounted for after some skillful adjustments. They draw from this the sanguine conclusion "that one of the last large economic groups to remain essentially untouched by federal income taxation has apparently been brought under the tax."[26] While acknowl-edging the possibility that the overstatement of expenses as well as the understatement of gross receipts can cause errors in reported net income, they suggest (in line with a finding by Groves)[27] that farmers may well understate rather than overstate their expenses. From this they suggest that farm net income may be as fully reported as farm gross income.

Actually, the gap for gross farm receipts reported by Stocker and Ellickson is not irreconcilable with our own seemingly much larger gap (shown in Table 8 above). The divergence in the two findings is only superficial. For 1955 we estimated farm operators' net income at $8.9 billion. Stocker and Ellickson report $4.2 billion of gross farm income as unaccounted for. To be consistent with our estimates (see Appendix Table B-3) their figure was reduced to $3.3 billion.[28] But even $3.3 billion of missing gross receipts, when compared with $8.9 billion net income, can mean an understatement of 37 per cent in the latter. Unless accompanied by understatement of expenses, a relatively small omission of gross receipts has an important effect on net income. According to the ACP findings (summarized in Table 13), underreporting of gross receipts was not offset by underreporting of business expense. On the contrary, it was reinforced by overreporting errors, as suggested by the fact that

[25] Frederick D. Stocker and John C. Ellickson, "How Fully Do Farmers Report Their Incomes?" *National Tax Journal,* June 1959.

[26] *Ibid.,* p. 124.

[27] *National Tax Journal,* December 1958, p. 300.

[28] Stocker and Ellickson obtain their gap of $4.2 billion by inclusion of intrastate livestock sales of $0.9 billion in gross receipts (in *National Tax Journal,* June 1959, p. 122). For lack of data our estimates did not include this item.

44

the audit increase in net income was 1.7 times as large as that for gross receipts.[29] If we apply this ratio to the missing gross receipts for 1955, the unexplained amount would be raised from $3.3 billion to $5.7, as follows:

1. Farm entrepreneurial net income estimate   8.9
2. Minus: gross receipts not accounted for   3.3
3. Minus: overstatement of business expenses (line 2 x .74)   2.4
4. Equals: 3.2
5. Our estimate of farm net income accounted for (Table 8)   3.0–3.1

Needless to say, the above calculations are hypothetical. They are intended to show that the seeming disparity between either Mrs. Goldsmith's or our estimates on the one hand, and those presented by Stocker and Ellickson on the other, can be reconciled without much difficulty.

In conclusion, it should be stressed once more that while the amount of farm operators' income not accounted for is large, the evidence that a relatively smaller amount of business and professional income is unaccounted for rests on shaky ground. Certainly the ACP data presented in Table 13 furnished scant support for such a conclusion.

Coverage by Size of Income Reported

Data on tax changes resulting from tax return audits have been tabulated by size and type of income reported on returns with error. This was done as part of the Audit Control Program for 1948.[30] Although the income groups chosen are extremely broad and the source of tax error is not entirely clear,[31] certain patterns are nevertheless revealed.

Table 14 suggests that audit would disclose nearly one-half of the returns with business income to be in error. This compares with 23 per

---

[29] Expense overreporting may be an important factor. Many farmers may fail to prorate property taxes and mortgage interest between personal and business expense (a possibility taken into account in our variant 2 estimates). Others may deduct as an expense the value of work performed by the farmer's wife or dependent children although no explicit money wage payments may take place.

[30] The figures presented in this section are based on U.S. Treasury Department, *The Audit Control Program, A Summary of Preliminary Results,* 1951, and some detailed breakdowns supplied by the Internal Revenue Service.

[31] The 1948 ACP classified its data by collectors' and agents' returns. Collectors' returns are forms 1040 A and forms 1040 with AGI under $7,000. Agents' returns are forms 1040 with AGI over $7,000 or gross receipts from business or professional over $25,000. They are classified into groups with under $25,000, $25,000 to $100,000, and over $100,000 AGI. Because a sizable number of returns had gross receipts over $25,000 but AGI less than $7,000, no clean break between the under $7,000 and $7,000 to $25,000 AGI groups was possible.

It should also be noted that the tax changes shown in the tables, though occurring on returns with unincorporated enterprise income, are not necessarily always errors in entrepreneurial income. The latter may be responsible for only part of the tax change on a return.

SOURCES AND COVERAGE

TABLE 14

NUMBER OF SOLE PROPRIETOR RETURNS WITH TAX ERROR, BY INCOME GROUPS, 1948
(in thousands)

AGI (thousand dollars)	Total Number Filed (1)	Number with Error		Percentage of Total with Error		Number with Error in Business Income (6)
		Under-stating Tax (2)	Over-stating Tax (3)	Under-stating Tax (2)÷(1) (4)	Over-stating Tax (3)÷(1) (5)	
Under 7	5,970	2,358	207	39.5	3.5	2,147
7 - 25ᵃ	1,207	804	84	66.6	7.0	777
25 - 100	78	55	7	70.5	9.0	48
100 and over	4.4	3.2	0.5	72.7	11.4	2.2
Total	7,260	3,222	298	44.4	4.1	2,974

Source: See Appendix D.

ᵃRoughly 45 per cent of returns in this group have AGI of less than $7,000 but gross receipts greater than $25,000.

cent for returns without business income.[32] But not all the errors were due to underreporting. Of the estimated 3.5 million returns of sole proprietors, which audit would disclose to be in error, 0.3 million, or 8.5 per cent, had errors resulting in a decrease in tax liability. For the other 91.5 per cent, disclosure of error would have resulted in an increase in tax liability. Most of these errors may be presumed to consist of under-reporting of income, inasmuch as 3 million of the 3.5 million returns of sole proprietors had errors in their business income schedule (Table 14, column 6).

The relative frequency of both types of error tends to rise as income rises. Returns of sole proprietors for which audit resulted in a tax increase were 40 per cent of those with less than $7,000 reported income and 73 per cent of those with over $100,000. Returns for which audit led to a tax decrease, though much less frequent, rose even more steeply—from 3.5 to 11.4 per cent over the same income range.

Of the tax change disclosable by audit of sole proprietors' returns, $688 million constituted tax increase and $30 million tax decrease (Table 15). These tax changes are attributable to returns reporting tax

[32] Treasury Department, *Audit Control Program,* p. 22.

46

TABLE 15

TAX CHANGE DISCLOSABLE BY AUDIT ON RETURNS OF SOLE PROPRIETORS,
BY INCOME GROUPS, 1948
(dollars in millions)

| AGI (thousand dollars) | Tax Liability Reported on | | Change Resulting in | | Tax Change as Percentage of Column 2 | | Tax Change [a] on Returns with Error in Business Income |
	All Returns of Sole Proprietors (1)	Returns of Sole Proprietors with Error (2)	Tax Increase (3)	Tax Decrease (4)	Col. 3 ÷ Col. 2 (5)	Col. 4 ÷ Col. 2 (6)	(7)
Under 7	742	431	308	10	71.5	8.3	285
7 - 25 [b]	1,170	921	288	12	31.3	1.3	279
25 - 100	870	700	75	6	10.7	.9	66
100 and over	590	530	17	2	3.2	.4	15
Total	3,372	2,582	688	30	26.6	1.2	644

Source: See Appendix D.

[a] Sum of tax increase and tax decrease without regard to sign.

[b] Roughly 45 per cent of returns in this group have AGI of less than $7,000 but gross receipts greater than $25,000.

47

TABLE 16

ESTIMATED INCREASE IN DISPOSABLE AGI DUE TO UNDERREPORTING ON RETURNS OF
SOLE PROPRIETORS WITH TAX ERROR, BY INCOME GROUPS, 1948

AGI (thousand dollars)	Tax Liability Reported on Returns of Sole Proprietors with Error (1)	Net Tax Increase Disclosable by Audit[a] (2)	Estimated AGI for Returns with Error				
			Amount Reported (3)	Additional AGI Disclosed by Audit (4)	Total (Col. 3 + Col. 4) (5)	Disposable AGI (Col. 5 Minus Cols. 1 and 2) (6)	Col. 2 ÷ Col. 6 (per cent) (7)
Under 7	431	298	5,130	1,795	6,925	6,196	4.8
7 - 25[b]	921	276	7,997	1,358	9,356	8,159	3.4
25 - 100	700	69	2,435	152	2,587	1,818	3.8
100 and over	530	15	800	20	821	276	5.4
Total	2,582	658	16,363	3,325	19,689	16,449	4.0

Source: See Appendix D.

a Tax increases minus tax decreases disclosable by audit; col. 3 minus col. 4, Table 15.

b Roughly 45 per cent of returns in this group have AGI of less than $7,000 but gross receipts greater than $25,000.

48

liability of $2,582 million. Thus, the tax increase disclosable by audit constitutes 27 per cent of the voluntarily reported amount, the tax decrease 1 per cent. But this average again hardly describes the relationship of tax increase to amount reported for different income groups. It was found that tax liability is raised by 72 per cent through audit of returns with reported AGI under $7,000; by 11 per cent for returns reporting $25,000 to $100,000; and by 3 per cent for returns with $100,000 and over. The size of tax decreases, when viewed relative to reported amount of tax, also declined over this income range—from 2.3 to 0.4 per cent. Thus, though the frequency of tax error rises sharply over the income range, as we observed in Table 14, the relative amount of tax error declines. Understatement of tax is large in relation to tax liability at the lower end of the income scale and comparatively small at the top.

Reductions in tax liability, whether brought about by reductions in rates or by the unilateral action of some taxpayers, need not be viewed solely against the background of tax liabilities themselves. An alternative, frequently chosen,[33] is to view the change against disposable income. In Table 16 the net tax increase disclosable by audit (i.e., the amount of net understatement of tax liability) is viewed as an increase in disposable income. To stay within the statistical framework laid down by the income tax the net tax understatement of each income group was compared with its disposable AGI. The latter was estimated by subtracting from the total AGI of each group its reported tax liability plus the net understatement of tax liability. Total AGI is reported AGI plus estimated net understatement of AGI.[34]

When the net tax understatement disclosed by audit is compared with estimated disposable AGI, average disposable income is enhanced by 4.0 per cent, and the variation in this percentage among the four income groups is not systematic by size of income. The group with less than $7,000 increased its disposable income by 4.8 per cent; taxpayers reporting $25,000 to $100,000 raised theirs by 3.8 per cent; and those reporting $100,000 and over added 5.4 per cent.

Evidently, sole proprietors' net understatement of tax liability does not vary greatly in relation to disposable income, although it declines sharply

---

[33] See, for instance, R. A. Musgrave and Tun Thin, "Income Tax Progression, 1929–48," *Journal of Political Economy*, 1948, pp. 498–514.

[34] Net understatement of AGI was estimated by dividing the net understatement of tax of each group by its average marginal rate of tax, thus obtaining an income equivalent for the Treasury Department's tax change figure. The reported amount of AGI is given for all returns with sole proprietor income in *Statistics of Income* for 1948. The amount for returns with error was obtained by prorating.

in relation to tax liability itself. This, of course, is in the nature of the complementary relationship between tax liability and disposable income: under a progressive tax, tax liability rises as a percentage of disposable income as income rises. Hence any variable which maintains a stable relation to disposable income must decline in relation to tax liability as income rises.

Size and Pattern of Income on Returns
with Profit or Loss from Business and Professions

As a prelude to the discussion of the tax rates that have been applied to unincorporated enterprise income, it is necessary to have a detailed picture of the size distribution and pattern of net profits and losses reported under the headings of sole proprietorship and partnership. Business and professional profits and losses reported on personal tax returns exhibit peculiarities not found in other distributions of proprietors' income. The latter usually cover the total income of "proprietors," which includes only persons whose main occupation, or source of income, is proprietorship. In contrast, the present study covers all unincorporated enterprise income reported, regardless of its size in relation to the recipient's total income or occupational status. The result of this broad coverage is strikingly reflected in Table 17.

TABLE 17

CUMULATIVE PERCENTAGE DISTRIBUTION OF NET PROFITS AND NET LOSSES REPORTED
BY SOLE PROPRIETORS AND PARTNERS, BY SIZE OF NET PROFIT AND LOSS, 1960

Size of Net Profit or Loss	RETURNS OF SOLE PROPRIETORS				RETURNS OF PARTNERS			
	With Net Profit		With Net Loss		With Net Profit		With Net Loss	
	Number	Amount[a]	Number	Amount[a]	Number	Amount[a]	Number	Amount[a]
Under 100	3.3	b	10.8	.3	4.3	b	16.7	.3
Under 500	17.5	1.3	41.5	5.7	15.7	.6	46.0	3.6
Under 1,000	32.7	4.5	63.0	15.5	25.7	1.8	63.6	9.2
Under 5,000	81.1	39.4	94.7	55.9	65.1	19.4	90.6	34.1
Under 10,000	93.0	62.6	98.1	69.9	83.4	40.0	95.6	48.2
Under 25,000	98.7	86.0	99.5	83.0	95.8	69.8	98.9	68.8
Under 50,000	99.8	96.1	99.9	90.7	99.2	87.9	99.6	78.1
Total	100.0	100.0	100.0	100.0	100.0	100.0	100.0	100.0
Total[c]	6,831	23,959	1,768	2,887	1,589	9,757	330	791

Source: The frequency distribution is based on Statistics of Income, 1960. The dollar distribution was estimated from this frequency distribution, using methods discussed in Appendix F. Absolute totals are from Statistics of Income, 1960.

[a]These percentages are of absolute totals given. To the extent that these totals differ from the sum of profits estimated, the difference was placed, as a residual, in the highest income class.

[b]Less than .05 per cent.

[c]Dollars in millions; frequencies in thousands.

Distribution by Size of Profit or Loss

A large number of returns show only "very small" [1] amounts of income from unincorporated enterprises. For 1960, one-third of the returns with net profit from sole proprietorship and one-fourth of those with net profit from partnership reported less than $1,000 net profit. Of course, very small amounts of net income from business for any given year do not necessarily mean very small business. Even the owner of a sizable enterprise may at times experience a small net profit or loss. Among returns with net loss, small amounts also predominate. On close to two-thirds of these returns, for both sole proprietors and partners, net losses were less than $1,000 (Table 17).

Not unexpectedly, the major industrial source of the large number of returns with net profit or loss below $1,000 is the farm sector.[2] It is possible that many of the returns, with net profit below $1,000, both farm and nonfarm, are filed by persons whose enterprise is merely a secondary source of income to them. A comparison of estimated mean ratios of net profit to total income (AGI) by returns with net profit under $1,000 and returns with net profit of $1,000 and over for 1960 appears to corroborate this:[3]

	Net Profit	
	Under $1,000	Over $1,000
Sole Proprietors	.15	.74
Partners	.06	.66

By this test, unincorporated enterprise appears more likely to be a secondary source of income for returns with less than $1,000 net profit than for returns with net profit exceeding $1,000. The wider relative spread in the means for partners than for sole proprietors conforms to

[1] Use of the term "very small" is deliberate since the term "small business," as commonly employed, is by no means limited to persons who derive incomes as small as $1,000, or even $10,000, from independent enterprise.

[2] See *Statistics of Income, U.S. Business Tax Returns, 1960–61* (Preliminary), Table 3, where a breakdown by industry and size of net profit is presented. For 1960, of the sole proprietorships with net profit under $1,000, 45 per cent were in agriculture, forestry, and fisheries. Of those with net loss, 55 per cent were in that industrial category. The frequencies cited are for number of businesses rather than number of returns filed as in Table 17. Distributions by number of businesses and number of returns are roughly comparable but not identical because an individual's return showing income from sole proprietorship may cover more than one business. In distributions having the individual as their focus, such a return is counted once; in distributions focusing on the business establishment, it counts as more than one frequency.

[3] The ratios were estimated from a cross tabulation of frequencies by size of net profit and size of adjusted gross income presented in *Statistics of Income, Individual Income Tax Returns, 1960,* Table 8. For each group of frequencies (some 200 in number) total net profit and AGI were estimated, and the ratio of net profit to AGI was computed from these estimates.

one's expectation that the above test applies to partners even more than to sole proprietors.

An alternative explanation might be found in year-to-year variability of income. The tax return with a low net profit for the year may be that of a full-time entrepreneur whose business income fluctuates widely, but whose stable secondary source of income (e.g., interest) will cause him to have a low ratio of net profit to total income for the year. Variability of business income would cause the reverse to hold true for returns with large net profits. Of course, only to the extent that unincorporated enterprise income fluctuates more widely than other income sources, can year-to-year variability be a cause of lower ratios of net profit to total income on returns with low net profits. It is doubtful that income variability alone can explain the wide difference observed in the ratios of net profit to total income.

In conclusion, it should be observed that while returns with net profits below $1,000 account for a very large proportion of the number of unincorporated enterprise returns, they account for only a small fraction of net profits reported on them: 5 per cent of the total for sole proprietors and 2 per cent for partners.

Relation of Income from Business or Profession to Total Income of Proprietors

In Table 18 unincorporated enterprise income is grouped by size of proprietors' total income (AGI) rather than by its own size as in the preceding section. We find that throughout the income scale, income from unincorporated enterprise tends to be substantially supplemented by income from other sources. On returns of proprietors, reported adjusted gross income for 1960 amounted to nearly $63 billion, which was almost evenly divided between net income from their enterprises and other sources. For none of the groups shown in the table, except that with negative income, did the business and professional component approach as much as two-thirds of income reported.[4] The extent to which unincor-

---

[4] In addition to our estimates of AGI of proprietors, the Internal Revenue Service has tabulated for some years (and published in *Statistics of Income*) the AGI reported on returns with self-employment tax (dollars in billions):

	On Returns with Self-Employment Tax (reported)	On Returns with Business or Professional Income over $400 (estimated)
1956	37.3	43.9
1958	37.6	43.9

A large part of the discrepancy in the figures is explained by (a) the exemption of physicians from self-employment tax, and (b) the fact that self-employment tax was only incurred when wages and salaries subject to the tax and reported on the same return were less than $4,200. Working in the opposite direction, however, is the optional inclusion of ministers, members of religious orders, and Christian Science practitioners, in self-employment tax.

53

SIZE AND PATTERN OF INCOME ON RETURNS WITH

TABLE 18

DISTRIBUTION OF BUSINESS AND PROFESSIONAL INCOME AND AGI
OF PROPRIETORS, BY INCOME GROUPS, 1960
(dollars in millions)

Adjusted Gross Income (thousand dollars)	Business and Professional				
	Net Profits (1)	Net Losses (2)	Net Income (Col. 1 minus Col. 2) (3)	Estimated AGI (4)	Col. 3 ÷ Col. 4 (5)
Negative AGI	84	1,321	-1,237	-958	129.1
0 - 2	1,805	355	1,450	2,495	58.1
2 - 3	1,849	265	1,584	3,010	52.6
3 - 5	4,507	411	4,096	8,342	49.1
5 - 10	8,306	540	7,766	18,339	42.3
10 - 25[a]	9,734	324	9,410	16,834	55.9
25 - 50	4,934	150	4,785	8,047	59.5
50 - 100	1,894	122	1,773	3,931	45.1
100 - 500	571	159	412	2,136	19.3
500 and over	33	34	b	632	-.1
Total	33,716	3,679	30,038	62,810	47.8

Source: Statistics of Income, 1960. AGI estimates were obtained by multiplying average AGI for all returns in each AGI class by the number of returns reporting business and professional income. The frequencies used were corrected for double counting of returns reporting both sole proprietorship and partnership income by re- ducing them by the 1959 fraction of returns in each income group showing both income sources (shown in column 8 of Table 33).

[a]Includes all nontaxable returns with AGI of $10,000 or more.

[b]Less than $500,000.

porated enterprise income is supplemented (or even exceeded) by other sources increases with the size of income reported by sole proprietors and partners. Business and professional income was nearly three-fifths of the total reported in the 0–$2,000 AGI group, but less than one-fifth of the total on returns with AGI exceeding $100,000.

In addition to the cross-sectional decline of business and professional income relative to total income of proprietors, we also find that a decline has occurred over time. In Table 19, estimates of total adjusted gross income reported on returns of sole proprietors and partners are shown for selected years, 1939–60. There has been a pronounced downward trend in the proportion of proprietors' income derived from independent enterprise. For sole proprietors the business and professional component declined from two-thirds to less than one-half between 1945 and 1960. For partners the decline was even greater.

54

PROFIT OR LOSS FROM BUSINESS AND PROFESSION

TABLE 19

BUSINESS AND PROFESSIONAL NET INCOME AND AGI REPORTED ON RETURNS WITH BUSINESS AND
PROFESSIONAL INCOME OR LOSS, 1939-60
(dollars in millions)

	Sole Proprietors			Partners		
	Estimated AGI (1)	Net Income (2)	Col. 2 ÷ Col. 1 (per cent) (3)	Estimated AGI (4)	Net Income (5)	Col. 5 ÷ Col. 4 (per cent) (6)
1939	3,868	2,480	64.1		n.a.	
1941	9,651	6,226	64.5		n.a.	
1945	17,845	11,943	66.9	10,537	7,060	67.0
1947	22,978	15,341	66.8	12,528	7,953	63.5
1949	22,599	14,231	63.0	13,557	7,474	55.1
1951	29,559	16,466	55.7	15,406	8,412	54.6
1953	30,213	16,664	55.2	13,167	8,287	54.6
1954	33,014	16,926	51.3	16,099	8,526	53.0
1955	36,325	18,430	50.7	18,168	9,024	49.7
1956	42,425	21,285	50.2	18,327	8,852	48.3
1957	40,173	20,339	50.6	19,253	9,359	48.6
1958	41,301	20,674	50.1	19,459	9,232	47.4
1959	45,389	21,431	47.2	21,688	9,563	44.1
1960	46,156	21,072	45.7	21,514	8,966	41.7

Source: *Statistics of Income*. AGI was estimated by assuming average AGI
for returns with entrepreneurial income to be the same as AGI for all returns
in a given income group.
Note: AGI figures shown in this table for 1960 add to a greater total than
that shown in Table 18 because some returns show income from both sole proprietor
and partnership. Fiduciary returns are excluded from this table for all years.

There are a number of possible reasons for this trend. The cross-
sectional decline of unincorporated enterprise relative to other sources,
when moving upwards along the income scale (Table 18), could be
responsible for the decline over time. This appears to be only a partial
explanation of the downward trend when we examine the cross-sectional
pattern for five selected years (Tables 20 and 21). It is true that for both
sole proprietors (Table 20) and partners (Table 21), independent enterprise declines in relative importance as a source with rising total income
in every one of the five years shown. But in the range in which the bulk
of the income reported by proprietors has been concentrated, the relative decline of unincorporated enterprise income has not been so large
as to explain the sharp decline from 1945 to 1960, which we noted above.
For 1945, when the bulk of sole proprietors' adjusted gross income was
reported in the 0-$25,000 income range, the part which originated in
sole proprietorship varied from 65 to 75 per cent of the total (Table 20).

TABLE 20

SOLE PROPRIETORSHIP NET INCOME[a] AND ESTIMATE OF AGI REPORTED
ON RETURNS OF SOLE PROPRIETORS, BY INCOME GROUPS,
SELECTED YEARS, 1939-60

Adjusted Gross Income Class (thousand dollars)	Adjusted Gross Income (million dollars) (1)	Net Income	
		Amount (million dollars) (2)	Percentage of AGI (3)
1939[b]			
Negative AGI	-65	-108	166.0
0 - 2			
2 - 3	2,019	1,572	77.9
3 - 5			
5 - 10	871	576	66.1
10 - 25	578	322	55.7
25 - 50	218	85	38.9
50 - 100	117	29	24.8
100 - 500	86	6	7.2
500 and over	45	-2	-3.6
Total	3,868	2,480	64.1
1945			
Negative AGI	-248	-279	112.4
0 - 2	3,186	2,386	74.9
2 - 3	2,772	1,809	65.2
3 - 5	3,627	2,387	65.8
5 - 10	3,278	2,419	73.8
10 - 25	2,993	2,112	70.6
25 - 50	1,159	705	60.9
50 - 100	578	279	48.2
100 - 500	384	117	30.4
500 and over	116	8	7.0
Total	17,845	11,943	66.9
1953			
Negative AGI	-923	-910	98.6
0 - 2	2,690	1,728	64.2
2 - 3	3,094	1,976	63.9
3 - 5	6,838	3,687	53.9
5 - 10	8,126	4,287	52.8
10 - 25[c]	4,928	3,224	65.4
25 - 50[c]	3,583	2,164	60.4
50 - 100	1,032	420	40.7
100 - 500	633	89	14.1
500 and over	211	-2	-1.2
Total	30,213	16,664	55.2

(continued)

56

TABLE 20 (concluded)

Adjusted Gross Income Class (thousand dollars)	Adjusted Gross Income (million dollars) (1)	Net Income	
		Amount (million dollars) (2)	Percentage of AGI (3)

1955

Negative AGI	-757	-839	110.8
0 - 2	2,903	1,896	65.3
2 - 3	3,183	1,911	60.0
3 - 5	7,174	3,542	49.0
5 - 10	10,043	4,573	45.5
10 - 25	7,801	4,886	62.6
25 - 50	3,358	1,877	55.9
50 - 100	1,394	535	38.4
100 - 500	884	59	6.7
500 and over	342	-10	-2.9
Total	36,326	18,430	50.7

1960

Negative AGI	-862	-1,006	116.7
0 - 2	2,295	1,314	57.3
2 - 3	2,714	1,437	52.9
3 - 5	7,321	3,421	46.7
5 - 10	14,989	5,949	39.7
10 - 25^d	11,654	6,329	54.3
25 - 50	4,786	2,822	59.0
50 - 100	1,964	794	40.4
100 - 500	958	26	2.7
500 and over	337	-14	-4.2
Total	46,156	21,072	45.7

Source: Statistics of Income.

[a]Sole proprietorship net profits minus net losses.

[b]For 1939, returns are classified by size of statutory net income.

[c]For 1953, the class limit is $20,000 instead of $25,000.

[d]Includes all nontaxables with AGI of $10,000 and over.

For 1960, the bulk of sole proprietors' income was reported in the 0–$50,000 range, and in it, sole proprietorship income constituted between 40 and 59 per cent of the total. A similar trend is evident for net income from partnership. Both in 1945 and 1960, reported adjusted gross income of partners was heavily concentrated in the $3,000–$100,000 income range. In that group, the proportion of AGI derived from partnership varied between 63 and 70 per cent for 1945, and between 37

TABLE 21

PARTNERSHIP NET INCOME[a] AND ESTIMATE OF AGI REPORTED ON RETURNS
OF PARTNERS, BY INCOME GROUPS, SELECTED YEARS, 1939-60

Adjusted Gross Income Class (thousand dollars)	Adjusted Gross Income (million dollars) (1)	Net Income	
		Amount (million dollars) (2)	Percentage of AGI (3)
		1939[b]	
Negative AGI	-10	-18	171.6
0 - 2			
2 - 3	n.a.	372	n.a.
3 - 5			
5 - 10	521	309	59.3
10 - 25	548	300	54.6
25 - 50	282	133	47.3
50 - 100	169	70	41.5
100 - 500	106	27	25.9
500 and over	25	1	3.6
Total	n.a.	1,195	n.a.
		1945	
Negative AGI	-31	-50	159.7
0 - 2	481	346	71.9
2 - 3	671	423	63.0
3 - 5	1,230	777	63.2
5 - 10	1,884	1,302	69.1
10 - 25	2,812	1,968	70.0
25 - 50	1,708	1,190	69.7
50 - 100	1,047	711	67.9
100 - 500	641	361	56.4
500 and over	94	32	33.7
Total	10,537	7,060	67.0
		1953	
Negative AGI	-179	-230	128.8
0 - 2	405	293	72.4
2 - 3	543	359	66.0
3 - 5	1,637	989	60.4
5 - 10	3,262	1,873	57.4
10 - 25[c]	3,076	1,867	60.7
25 - 50[c]	3,666	2,056	56.1
50 - 100	1,523	732	48.1
100 - 500	995	343	34.5
500 and over	238	6	2.7
Total	15,167	8,287	54.6

(continued)

58

TABLE 21 (concluded)

Adjusted Gross Income Class (thousand dollars)	Adjusted Gross Income (million dollars) (1)	Net Income	
		Amount (million dollars) (2)	Percentage of AGI (3)

1955

Adjusted Gross Income Class (thousand dollars)	Adjusted Gross Income (million dollars) (1)	Amount (million dollars) (2)	Percentage of AGI (3)
Negative AGI	-117	-177	150.4
0 - 2	329	197	60.0
2 - 3	531	328	61.8
3 - 5	1,578	960	60.8
5 - 10	3,611	1,951	54.0
10 - 25	5,019	2,784	55.5
25 - 50	3,419	1,714	50.1
50 - 100	1,954	838	42.9
100 - 500	1,429	401	28.1
500 and over	416	27	6.6
Total	18,168	9,024	49.7

1960

Adjusted Gross Income Class (thousand dollars)	Adjusted Gross Income (million dollars) (1)	Amount (million dollars) (2)	Percentage of AGI (3)
Negative AGI	-141	-231	163.2
0 - 2	243	136	56.0
2 - 3	348	147	42.4
3 - 5	1,246	675	54.2
5 - 10	4,065	1,817	44.7
10 - 25^d	6,672	3,080	46.2
25 - 50	4,431	1,963	44.3
50 - 100	2,617	978	37.4
100 - 500	1,578	386	24.5
500 and over	456	14	3.0
Total	21,514	8,966	41.7

Source: Statistics of Income.

[a]Partnership net income minus net losses.

[b]For 1939, returns are classified by size of statutory net income.

[c]For 1953, the class limit is $20,000 instead of $25,000.

[d]Includes all nontaxable with AGI of $10,000 and over.

and 54 per cent for 1960. Clearly the declining share of business and professional income in the total income reported by proprietors is not merely the result of their movement over time into higher income groups; that is, not the outcome of a mere movement along a curve but rather of a drop in the curve itself. The fact that the trend is observable for both sole proprietors and partners seems to rule out as the sole cause the relative decline of farm income in the postwar years. For farmers, the decline in the relative share of entrepreneurial income may have been especially pronounced.[5] But since they are, as we have seen, mainly sole proprietors, the relative decline of farm income cannot explain the decline of partnership income as a component of partners' AGI.

For both sole proprietors and partners the decline in entrepreneurial income relative to total income is very sharp at the top of the income pyramid. For sole proprietors in the $100,000–$500,000 AGI group, only 7 per cent of their income in 1955 and 3 per cent in 1960 was from their independent enterprises. The highest ratio on record for this group was 30 per cent for 1945.[6] For those reporting incomes over $500,000, the business and professional component was negative for all years except 1945. A similar, but less extreme pattern is revealed for partners.

We have so far viewed business and professional income as the algebraic sum of the net profits reported by some taxpayers and the net losses reported by others. It is therefore possible that the decline relative to total income of proprietors which has been observed—over time, and to some extent upwards over the income scale—is the result of a rise in net losses relative to net profits. We consider this possibility next.

PROFITS AND LOSSES IN RELATION TO TOTAL INCOME OF PROPRIETORS

In Tables 22 and 23 unincorporated enterprise income and AGI are shown separately for returns with net profit and returns with net loss by size of AGI. Two years, 1945 and 1960, were selected for close examination but data for other years may be found in Appendix G.

For both sole proprietors and partners the tendency for the share of entrepreneurial income to fall with rising income persists when net profit returns alone are viewed. For 1960, net profits fell from 82 to 70 per cent of AGI of sole proprietors over the 0–$50,000 income range. An even sharper drop may be observed for partners: from 86 to 55 per cent.

Net losses, not unexpectedly, trace a similar pattern: they decline sharply relative to the AGI of which they are reported as a negative component. For sole proprietors reporting the very highest incomes, that is, on returns with AGI over $500,000, the net losses reported by some exceed in absolute amount the net profits reported by others for most years. This was reflected in the negative incomes from sole proprietorship in four of the five years shown in Table 20. Thus, while the

[5] See Jacob Schiffman, "Multiple Jobholders in May 1962," *Monthly Labor Review*, May 1963, p. 517, and Bureau of the Census, "Multiple Jobholding: July 1958," *Current Population Reports*, Series P-50, No. 88, Table 1.

[6] This most probably reflects the brief period during World War II when, because of the excess profits tax, some businesses changed from corporate to unincorporated form.

TABLE 22

SOLE PROPRIETORSHIP INCOME AND ESTIMATED AGI, BY RETURNS WITH NET
PROFIT AND NET LOSS AND BY INCOME GROUPS, 1945 AND 1960
(dollars in millions)

AGI Class (thousand dollars)	Returns with Sole Proprietorship Net Profits			Returns with Sole Proprietorship Net Losses		
	AGI (1)	Net Profits (2)	Col. 2 ÷ Col. 1 a (3)	AGI (4)	Net Losses (5)	Col. 5 ÷ Col. 4 a (6)
			1960			
Negative AGI	-41	53	-129.6	-821	1,059	129.0
0 - 2	1,987	1,625	81.8	308	311	-100.9
2 - 3	2,264	1,635	72.2	450	198	-44.1
3 - 5	5,839	3,777	64.7	1,482	356	-24.0
5 - 10	11,983	6,383	53.3	3,006	434	-14.4
10 - 25	10,135	6,550	64.6	1,519	221	-14.5
25 - 50	4,173	2,911	69.8	613	89	-14.5
50 - 100	1,486	876	59.0	478	82	-17.2
100 - 500	418	140	33.6	541	115	-21.2
500 and over	78	8	9.8	259	22	-8.4
Total	38,321	23,959	62.5	7,836	2,887	-36.8
			1945			
Negative AGI	-11	11	-106.3	-237	290	122.4
0 - 2	2,960	2,503	84.6	226	118	-52.0
2 - 3	2,533	1,855	73.2	239	46	-19.3
3 - 5	3,381	2,429	71.8	246	41	-16.7
5 - 10	3,092	2,457	79.4	186	38	-20.6
10 - 25	2,747	2,159	78.6	246	46	-18.9
25 - 50	981	732	74.6	178	26	-14.8
50 - 100	425	296	69.6	153	17	-11.1
100 - 500	216	131	60.9	169	14	-8.6
500 and over	31	11	35.0	84	3	-3.5
Total	16,356	12,583	76.9	1,489	640	-43.0

Source: Statistics of Income.

a Percentages computed from unrounded figures.

decline of business and professional income relative to AGI of proprietors cannot be ascribed to the rising ratio of net loss to net profit over
the income scale, it was nevertheless reinforced by it.

In Tables 24 and 25, total reported net profits and net losses and total
estimated AGI on returns with net profits and net losses, respectively,
are shown for selected years of the period 1939–60. These tables sum

TABLE 23

PARTNERSHIP INCOME AND ESTIMATED AGI, BY RETURNS WITH NET
PROFIT AND NET LOSS AND BY INCOME GROUPS, 1945 AND 1960
(dollars in millions)

AGI Class (thousand dollars)	Returns with Partnership Net Profits			Returns with Partnership Net Losses		
	AGI (1)	Net Profits (2)	Col. 2 ÷ Col. 1[a] (3)	AGI (4)	Net Losses (5)	Col. 5 ÷ Col. 4[a] (6)
			1960			
Negative AGI	-26	31	-120.9	-116	262	226.4
0 - 2	210	180	85.6	33	44	-132.1
2 - 3	301	214	70.9	46	66	-143.5
3 - 5	1,061	730	68.8	185	55	-29.6
5 - 10	3,438	1,923	55.9	627	106	-16.9
10 - 25	5,691	3,184	56.0	981	104	-10.6
25 - 50	3,706	2,024	54.6	726	60	-8.3
50 - 100	2,116	1,018	48.1	501	39	-7.8
100 - 500	1,091	430	39.4	487	44	-9.1
500 and over	199	26	12.9	258	12	-4.6
Total	17,786	9,757	54.9	3,728	791	-21.2
			1945			
Negative AGI	-6	13	-203.9	-25	62	252.3
0 - 2	449	366	75.0	33	20	-62.2
2 - 3	620	431	69.6	52	8	-16.2
3 - 5	1,162	786	67.6	68	9	-13.4
5 - 10	1,798	1,316	73.2	86	14	-16.0
10 - 25	2,681	1,985	74.0	131	17	-12.6
25 - 50	1,626	1,199	73.7	82	9	-11.0
50 - 100	983	716	72.8	63	6	-8.9
100 - 500	571	365	63.8	69	3	-4.9
500 and over	69	32	46.7	25	b	-1.7
Total	9,953	7,209	72.4	584	149	-25.5

Source: Statistics of Income.

[a]Percentages computed from unrounded figures.

[b]Less than $1 million.

up the two conclusions which one may draw from the discussion thus
far in this section:

1. Unincorporated enterprise income has become increasingly reported
together with income from one or more other sources. This is reflected
in the fact that both net profits and net losses have declined over time
relative to the incomes of which they are components. The nature of
this supplementation will be discussed below.

2. The fact that income from business and profession has been increasingly supplemented with other income has given rise to increased loss offsets under the income tax. Net losses which might not have been reported, or indeed not acquired, at one level of income diversification, make their appearance at another level when there is enough income from other sources to offset losses.

One might ask whether a decline in the profitability of independent enterprises could not explain the falling share of business and professional income in the total income of proprietors. But if this were the case, not only would we observe a fall in net profits as a component of proprietors' AGI, but also a rise in the ratio of net losses to AGI on returns with losses. As we have seen in Tables 24 and 25, this has not been the case. Between 1945 and 1960, net losses reported by sole proprietors declined from 43 to 37 per cent of estimated AGI of these proprietors; those reported by partners from 26 to 21 per cent.

Our observations suggest that greater income diversification rather than a decline in the fortunes of unincorporated business lies behind the

TABLE 24

TOTAL REPORTED NET PROFIT AND NET LOSS FROM SOLE PROPRIETORSHIP AS PERCENTAGE OF ESTIMATED AGI ON RETURNS OF SOLE PROPRIETORS, SELECTED YEARS, 1939–60

| | Net Profit (1) | Net Loss (2) | AGI on Returns with | | Col. 1 ÷ Col. 3 (per cent) (5) | Col. 2 ÷ Col. 4 (per cent) (6) |
			Net Profit (3)	Net Loss (4)		
1939	2,712[a]	223[a]	3,332	536	81.4	−41.6
1941	6,475[a]	228[a]	8,862	799	73.1	−28.5
1945	12,583	640	16,356	1,489	76.9	−43.0
1947	16,381	1,039	21,125	1,853	77.5	−56.1
1949	15,630	1,399	20,445	2,154	76.4	−64.9
1951	18,163	1,697	25,943	3,616	70.0	−46.9
1953	18,678	2,014	26,418	3,795	70.7	−53.1
1954	19,235	2,309	28,129	4,885	68.4	−47.3
1955	20,597	2,167	30,950	5,376	66.5	−40.3
1956	23,662	2,377	36,011	6,414	65.7	−37.1
1957	22,526	2,187	34,418	5,756	65.4	−38.0
1958	22,890	2,216	35,199	6,102	65.0	−36.3
1959	24,323	2,892	38,267	7,122	63.6	−40.6
1960	23,959	2,887	38,321	7,836	62.5	−36.8

Source: Statistics of Income.

[a] Includes taxable fiduciary returns with net income.

63

TABLE 25

TOTAL REPORTED NET PROFIT AND NET LOSS FROM PARTNERSHIP
AS PERCENTAGE OF ESTIMATED AGI ON RETURNS OF PARTNERS,
SELECTED YEARS, 1945-60

	Net Profit (1)	Net Loss (2)	AGI on Returns with		Col. 1 ÷ Col. 3 (per cent) (5)	Col. 2 ÷ Col. 4 (per cent) (6)
			Net Profit (3)	Net Loss (4)		
1945	7,209	149	9,953	584	72.4	-25.5
1947	8,249	295	11,727	800	70.3	-36.9
1949	7,912	438	12,244	1,314	64.6	-33.3
1951	8,871	459	13,873	1,533	63.9	-29.9
1953	8,803	516	13,601	1,566	64.7	-33.0
1954	9,004	478	14,320	1,778	62.9	-26.9
1955	9,553	529	15,910	2,259	60.0	-23.4
1956	9,393	541	15,868	2,459	59.2	-22.0
1957	9,964	605	16,664	2,592	59.8	-23.3
1958	9,810	578	16,662	2,796	58.9	-20.7
1959	10,220	657	18,261	3,427	56.0	-19.2
1960	9,757	791	17,786	3,728	54.9	-21.2

Source: Statistics of Income.

[a]Includes taxable fiduciary returns with net income.

trends observed. As a consequence, the likelihood that losses as well as profits are shared by society through the income tax appears to have risen.

Conversion of Unincorporated Enterprise Profits into Other Income

The decline in the ratio of total reported unincorporated enterprise income to AGI of proprietors over time may be explained by increased amounts of income from other sources. In contrast, the sharp cross-sectional decline in this ratio, when moving above $50,000 in the income scale, requires further explanation. It will be recalled that the cross-sectional decline of the ratio of business and professional to total income of sole proprietors was found to be so sharp as to turn negative for the group with AGI over $500,000 in four of the five years selected in Table 20. Not only did net losses for the group exceed net profits in dollar amounts, but the frequency of returns with net loss also exceeded that of returns with net profit for sole proprietors reporting AGI over $100,000 and for

TABLE 26

NUMBER OF RETURNS REPORTING NET PROFIT OR NET LOSS FROM SOLE
PROPRIETORSHIP AND PARTNERSHIP, BY NET PROFIT AND NET
LOSS AND BY INCOME GROUPS, 1955 AND 1960

Adjusted Gross Income (thousand dollars)	1955 Returns with		1960 Returns with	
	Net Profit	Net Loss	Net Profit	Net Loss
SOLE PROPRIETORSHIP				
Negative AGI	12,549	351,226	16,303	327,383
0 - 2	2,299,420	319,644	1,854,380	309,934
2 - 3	1,110,584	169,273	908,161	179,823
3 - 5	1,486,357	346,185	1,477,772	370,660
5 - 10^a	1,240,297	247,617	1,719,163	441,735
10 - 25	481,791	52,547	705,168	109,045
25 - 50	87,167	13,661	125,074	18,381
50 - 100	15,691	5,312	22,593	7,267
100 - 500	2,523	2,954	2,734	3,087
500 and over	56	243	79	229
Total	6,736,435	1,508,662	6,831,427	1,767,544
PARTNERSHIP				
Negative AGI	7,898	48,552	10,247	46,113
0 - 2	255,968	42,245	185,588	33,711
2 - 3	185,285	26,363	120,587	18,697
3 - 5	350,716	47,845	264,504	45,082
5 - 10	461,849	53,390	480,355	87,515
10 - 25^b	302,788	31,746	377,550	66,228
25 - 50	90,979	10,320	111,065	21,752
50 - 100	25,108	4,330	32,167	7,620
100 - 500	6,780	2,121	6,920	2,740
500 and over	199	190	200	224
Total	1,687,570	267,102	1,589,183	329,682

Source: Statistics of Income.
^{a}Includes all nontaxable returns with AGI of $5,000.
^{b}Includes all nontaxable returns with AGI of $10,000 or more.

partners reporting over $500,000 (Table 26).[7]

While it is not improbable for annual losses to exceed annual gains
for some income groups, we do not expect to find it year after year in
the upper reaches of the income distribution. The occurrence of a business loss imparts a downward bias to a person's income: for that year it

[7] For sole proprietors, the number of net loss returns has exceeded net profit returns in the
group reporting income over $500,000 for every year since 1937; in the group reporting in-
comes between $100,000 and $500,000, in every year except one since 1952 and in the period
1937–40. For partners, the ratios of loss to profit frequencies have been less extreme, and only
since 1953 have loss frequencies begun to outnumber profit frequencies in the highest
income groups.

may place him in a lower income group. In the same sense, a business profit imparts an upward bias: the higher the profit, the higher of course a proprietor's total income for that year. For these obvious reasons we expect loss returns to be concentrated at low levels of income and profit returns at higher levels. To find that business and professional net losses outweigh net profits at high income levels is certainly contrary to our expectation.

The net profit and loss pattern which one might expect is found in the distribution of net capital gains and losses. In Table 27 such a distribution is shown for 1960 alongside that for unincorporated enterprise net profit and loss. The differences are striking. Net capital gains in the highest AGI groups were $1,047 million and losses only $4 million. In contrast, unincorporated enterprise net profits were $33 million and losses $34 million.

The question arises as to why the distribution for net capital gains and losses conforms to one's reasonable expectations while that for unincorporated enterprise profit and losses does not. From the mere size of

TABLE 27

BUSINESS AND PROFESSIONAL NET PROFITS AND LOSSES AND REALIZED
NET GAINS AND LOSSES FROM SALE OF CAPITAL ASSETS REPORTED
ON ALL RETURNS, BY INCOME GROUPS, 1960
(million dollars)

Adjusted Gross Income (thousand dollars)	Business and Professional		Capital[a]		AGI on Tax Returns
	Net Profit (1)	Net Losses (2)	Net Gains (3)	Net Losses (4)	(5)
Negative AGI	84	1,321	376	155	-1,091
0 - 2	1,805	355	445	205	14,546
2 - 3	1,849	265	407	160	17,333
3 - 5	4,507	411	757	274	54,915
5 - 10[b]	8,306	540	1,673	556	140,032
10 - 25	9,734	324	2,481	711	63,496
25 - 50	4,934	150	1,482	247	14,710
50 - 100	1,894	122	1,285	90	6,648
100 - 500	571	159	1,794	40	3,808
500 and over	33	34	1,047	4	1,070
Total	33,716	3,679	11,747	2,441	315,466

Source: Statistics of Income.
[a]Excluding gain or loss from sale of other property and after carryover. Both gains and losses are included at 100 per cent before net long-term capital gains deduction and statutory limitations on loss deduction.
[b]Includes all nontaxable returns with $10,000 or more AGI.

capital gains reported at the top of the tax return distribution one might conclude that most of the returns in that group for a given year are swept into it because of their capital gains. Other income types are therefore reported on these returns only incidentally. But this reasoning cannot explain why those who are "swept" into the topmost group have a disproportionately high unincorporated business loss experience.

It is possible that these results reflect a number of tax-law influences on the conduct of business, all of which tend to operate in the same direction. One of the explanations for the rising loss ratios at high income levels may be the conversion of would-be unincorporated business net profits into statutory long-term capital gains. A taxpayer subject to a high marginal tax rate will find it to his advantage to report his losses as ordinary negative personal income, which can be offset against other income in full, but to convert profits whenever possible into long-term capital gains, which are subject to a 25 per cent maximum effective rate limitation.[8] The simultaneous occurrence of long-term gains and unincorporated business losses on high income tax returns seems to support the explanation offered. For instance, on tax returns with AGI over $500,000, we find the following reporting frequencies:[9]

	Total	*With Net Capital Gain*	*With Sole Proprietor and/or Partnership*	
			Net Profit or Loss	Net Loss
1959	982	856	614	387
1960	1,018	882	584	361

These figures show that for 1960, at least 448, or 77 per cent, of the 584 returns with unincorporated enterprise income reported also net capital gain; at least 225, or nearly two-thirds of the 361 with net loss from unincorporated enterprise reported net capital gain. These are only minima based on the conservative, indeed extreme, assumption that the

---

[8] Net long-term capital gains are included in adjusted gross income at only 50 per cent of their value and subject to a maximum effective rate of 50 per cent. Hence, even for taxpayers subject to the lowest marginal rates, the conversion of business profits into net long-term capital gains is advantageous. But once a taxpayer's marginal tax rate exceeds 50 per cent, the relative gap widens between his rate on a long-term capital gain and that on a business profit.

[9] The frequencies for the group total and net capital gains are as tabulated in *Statistics of Income*. Those shown for sole proprietorship and partnership are corrected for estimated overlap, since the tabulated frequencies are given for sole proprietorship and partnership separately. Uncorrected frequencies for 1960 are 732 for sole proprietor and partnership profit or loss; 453 for those with only loss. The figures were reduced by the 1959 per cent of returns reporting both sole proprietor and partnership profit or loss (see column 8, Table 29).

number of returns with business and professional income or capital gain (or both) is equal to the number for the class. If we assume that the incidence of the two types of income within the income group is entirely random (i.e., zero correlation between business net loss and capital gain), then 313 of the 361 returns with unincorporated enterprise loss, or 87 per cent, had also net capital gain.[10]

The fact that entrepreneurial losses and net capital gains are frequently associated on high-income tax returns does not, of course, prove that some of these capital gains are in fact the capitalization of unincorporated enterprise profits. But there are a number of reasons for this hypothesis. High-bracket taxpayers have a strong inducement, in the absence of other factors, to conduct promising, but deficit-incurring, ventures in unincorporated form because a large part of current loss is offset by the consequent reduction in the individual's tax liability. The loss is shared by the Treasury at the individual's highest bracket rate. But the opposite occurs as soon as the venture begins to show the expected profits: for the same reason that losses make operation in unincorporated form attractive, profits make it unattractive. The individual becomes subject to a tax motive to convert either the expected *future* profits into a capital gain, or to convert his business into corporate form. In the one case, the proprietor's capitalized future profits become subject to the lower long-term capital gains rates; in the other, he avoids the personal income tax (but of course not the corporate tax) on earnings retained in the business.

In recent times the tax law has contained explicit recognition of the varying advantages in organizing as a corporation or unincorporated business. Under the 1954 Code, unincorporated businesses were granted the option to be taxed as corporations provided there were no more than 50 partners (in case of a partnership). Since 1958, corporations with no more than ten shareholders, and subject to certain other limitations,[11] have been permitted to elect partnership treatment under the income tax. Provided all shareholders consent, their profits are taxed at the shareholder level without loss of the benefits of incorporation. Whereas a corporation can at any time revoke its election to be taxed as a partnership, it cannot subsequently renew it for a period of five years.

The extent to which businesses have been able, and desirous, of electing optional tax treatment is shown in Table 28. Corporations have

[10] The figure was obtained as follows: $\frac{882}{1,018} \cdot 361 = 313$.

[11] For detail, see Internal Revenue Service, *Tax Guide for Small Business*, Publication No. 334, 1961 ed., pp. 125–129.

TABLE 28

NUMBER OF CORPORATIONS AND UNINCORPORATED ENTERPRISES ELECTING
OPTIONAL TAX TREATMENT AS PERCENTAGE OF TOTAL NUMBER, 1957–60

| | Total Number | | NUMBER ELECTING OPTIONAL TAX | | | |
| | | | Corporations | | Unincorporated Businesses | |
	Corporations (1)	Unincorporated Businesses (2)	Number (3)	Per Cent of Total (4)	Number (5)	Per Cent of Total (6)
1957–58	940,147	9,708,292			200	a
1958–59	990,381	9,753,551	43,945	4.4	560	a
1959–60	1,074,128	10,091,755	71,140	6.6	445	a
1960–61	1,140,575	10,030,545	90,221	7.9	n.a.	n.a.

Source: U.S. Treasury Department, Statistics of Income, U.S. Business Tax Returns.

aLess than 0.1 per cent.

clearly made the greater use of the option: for 1960–61, 8 per cent of corporations compared to less than 0.1 per cent of unincorporated businesses have chosen optional treatment.[12] The data suggest that small businesses use the option largely to carry losses directly to the individual; few in order to have profits taxed at the corporate level. For the corporations electing to be taxed as partnerships, 38 per cent had a net loss for 1960–61 (Table 29).[13]

In addition to these general considerations, a few special situations tend to create a bias among high-income taxpayers in favor of net losses from unincorporated enterprise. Partnerships (or syndicates) are often formed for the purpose of owning and operating depreciable real estate. Because physical assets are by far the most important input for the real estate industry, to the extent that depreciation for tax purposes proceeds at a faster rate than actual depreciation, tax accounting net income may for many years be greatly reduced or nonexistent. Writing of private investment in rental housing, Louis Winnick concludes that "the combi-

[12] Even if only partnerships are included in the denominator for unincorporated businesses, the number electing to be taxed as corporations is less than 0.5 per cent.

[13] However, this relative loss frequency is no greater than for corporations not electing optional treatment, after the data are standardized for asset size. For corporations with a similar asset-size distribution, but filing regular corporation tax returns, the percentage reporting net loss was: 39.2 in 1958–59; 38.7 in 1959–60; and 43.5 in 1960–61. For 1959–61, the relative loss frequency is greater for corporations using the regular return than for those choosing partnership treatment. For a possible explanation of this surprising result, see the hypothesis advanced in footnote 31 below.

TABLE 29

NUMBER AND NET INCOME OF CORPORATIONS ELECTING TO BE TAXED
AS PARTNERSHIPS, BY NET PROFIT AND LOSS, 1958-60

	Number with			Amount (million dollars) of	
	Net Profit (1)	Net Loss (2)	Net Loss as Percentage of Total (3)	Net Profit (4)	Net Loss (5)
1958–59	25,203	18,742	42.6	287.9	199.0
1959–60	46,037	25,103	35.3	605.3	210.1
1960–61	56,123	34,098	37.8	678.5	296.0

Source: U.S. Business Tax Returns.

nation of mortgage interest and depreciation allowance on real estate improvements seems to be sufficient, in most cases, to wipe out the tax liability entirely or else to reduce it to relatively insignificant amounts."[14] In such situations, operating a real estate venture in unincorporated form may be preferable, although the corporate form offers advantages which frequently outweigh any tax considerations.[15] In the early years of a venture the combination of mortgage interest and depreciation is particularly high relative to gross income. As mortgage interest and, possibly, depreciation[16] decline, and as taxable income from the venture rises, the owners become subject to a tax motive to sell the property and to realize a long-term capital gain in consequence. In this case accumulated past taxable income is converted into a capital gain. The bias toward so-called tax losses is confirmed by the relation of net losses to net profits reported for sole proprietors and partnerships classified as real estate operators and lessors (Table 30). This relation differs markedly

[14] *Rental Housing: Opportunities for Private Investment,* New York, 1958, p. 145. Because of its size relative to true net income, and a depreciation rate allowed by the Treasury that is faster than actual, this item has occupied a crucial position for many real estate investors for whom "depreciation is not considered an expense, even if it is so regarded by the Treasury, but a tax-free income." *Ibid.,* p. 151.

[15] *Ibid.,* p. 153. "While depreciation may yield the investor a tax-free cash surplus, the transfer of this cash from the corporation to his own bank account exposes the typical investor to a high personal income tax liability. This would not be the case if the apartment property were held by an individual proprietorship or partnership . . ." For further discussion of the same points, see W. J. Casey, *Tax Shelter in Real Estate,* New York, 1957.

[16] Where the taxpayer elects a form of accelerated depreciation, as permitted under the 1954 Tax Code, depreciation deductions as well as interest deductions for a given real estate improvement decline. However, accelerated depreciation is restricted to original owners, and further, according to Winnick, "many investors in FHA projects with 90 per cent mortgages are quite content to use straight-line depreciation." See Winnick, *Rental Housing,* p. 147.

TABLE 30

NET PROFIT, NET LOSS, AND DEPRECIATION OF REAL ESTATE OPERATORS AND
LESSORS REPORTING AS SOLE PROPRIETORS AND PARTNERSHIPS, 1958-60
(million dollars)

	Net Profit (1)	Net Loss (2)	Net Profit Less Loss (3)	Depreciation on Returns with		
				Net Profit (4)	Net Loss (5)	Total (6)
			1958			
Sole proprietors	113.2	53.7	59.5	46.6	42.4	89.0
			1959			
Sole proprietors	176.6	51.2	125.5	50.7	33.8	84.5
			1960			
Sole proprietors	152.2	47.4	104.9	n.a.	n.a.	78.7
Partnerships[a]	515.0	156.1	358.9	262.3	170.6	433.0

Source: *Statistics of Income: Selected Financial Data,* 1958-59, 1959-60, 1960-61.

[a] Partnership net income and loss are after payments to partners are added back. For payments to partners, see *U.S. Business Tax Returns,* 1960-1961, p. 70.

from that reported for the rest of unincorporated enterprises whose reported losses are much smaller in relation to net profits (Tables 24 and 25).

Another special situation which may give rise to some asymmetry in tax treatment is individual participation in mineral exploration, especially oil exploration. Aspects of this type of enterprise have been widely discussed and need not be gone into in detail here.[17] It may suffice to note that a large proportion of exploration and development costs (referred to in the Tax Code as intangible costs)[18] incurred in the search for oil can be written off currently. These include the cost of surveys, exploratory drilling, labor, power, materials, etc. In addition, salvageable equip-

[17] See, for instance, the papers in Joint Committee on the Economic Report, *Federal Tax Policy for Economic Growth and Stability,* Washington, 1955, pp. 419–493, especially that by Arnold C. Harberger, "Taxation of Mineral Industries;" the Committee on Ways and Means, *Tax Revision Compendium,* Washington, 1959, vol. 2, pp. 933–1060, especially the paper by Peter O. Steiner, "Percentage Depletion and Resource Allocation;" and an exhibit on "Comparative Tax Benefits in Investment in Oil Property and in Depreciable Facilities," by Senator Paul H. Douglas in *Congressional Record,* June 18, 1960, p. 13291.

[18] *Internal Revenue Code of 1954,* Sec. 263 (c).

ment used is depreciated at ordinary rates. Each search is in effect a separate venture, and as long as an individual has other income, the cost of an unsuccessful search is for the most part written off and treated as a loss on the tax return. On the other hand, if a venture is successful, in addition to deducting intangible development costs in the year incurred and depreciation deductions for equipment, it is permissible to make a depletion deduction from taxable income of 27.5 per cent of the gross value of the output of the property, but not to exceed 50 per cent of net income attributable to it. As an alternative to producing oil from his discovery, the individual may sell it after a six-month interval and pay a capital gains tax limited to 25 per cent of the gain.

To the extent that high-income investors engage in oil ventures in unincorporated form,[19] there is thus ample reason for the pattern of net losses and profits displayed in Table 27. Some confirmation that mining ventures have contributed to the pattern observed can be obtained from industry breakdowns of unincorporated enterprise tax returns for six selected years in the period 1953–60 (Table 31). For these years, net losses for unincorporated mining enterprises, most of which were engaged in oil and gas production, were nearly as great as net profits. Indeed, for 1953, 1958, and 1960, net losses exceeded net profits in the mining sector. This situation was very different from the aggregate for unincorporated enterprises whose net profits for 1960 were over nine times as large as net losses (Table 27). For the corporate mining sector (included in Table 31 for comparison), the allowance of depletion also reduced the ratio of net profit to loss, but this ratio was nevertheless much higher for corporations than for unincorporated business. Apparently, we are observing the result of a bias in favor of reporting the less successful ventures in the unincorporated enterprise category and the more successful ones as long-term capital gains.[20]

---

[19] Much of the exploration for oil in the United States has been carried out by individuals in recent times. In a paper by Paul Haber, "Writeoffs, Cost Depletion, and Percentage Depletion—An Appraisal" (inserted into the *Congressional Record,* June 18, 1960, pp. 13292–13293, by Senator Paul H. Douglas), it is asserted that "at least 40,000 wells a year, out of a total of 55,000, are drilled by individual taxpayers and only 15,000 are drilled by major oil companies . . . ."

[20] In contrast to the annual net profit-net loss relation for mining ventures observable in Table 31, the following relation is found in the sale of natural resources which are reported as long-term capital assets (assets held longer than six months) on individual tax returns for 1959:

Gross sales	$382
Long-term capital gains	276
Long-term capital losses	13

The above figures are from the Treasury's special study *Sales of Capital Assets Reported on Individual Income Tax Returns for 1959* (*Statistics of Income, 1959,* Supplemental Report), Table 2. The

In addition to the possible capitalization by individuals of future, and in some cases past, net income through sale of the enterprise to a corporation or other individuals, the observed bias may also be the result of conversion of unincorporated businesses into corporations. When an operation becomes profitable (in the tax-law sense), an individual has a tax motive to convert it into a corporation, for he is then able to avoid the personal income tax on the earnings retained in the business. If the accumulation of retained earnings in the business is desired, and possible,[21] there may be a tax motive against making the takeover by a corporation the occasion for realizing capital gains. The individual will then avoid capital gains tax until the stock in the corporation itself is sold; and if death intervenes, the tax will be avoided forever.[22]

The above analysis may also shed light on a problem raised by Irwin Friend and Irving Kravis.[23] They note that, according to survey data, the unincorporated enterprise sector has a high marginal propensity to save and accounts for a major share of personal saving; and that "unincorporated nonfarm enterprises have played a significant role in capital formation."[24] In other words, a large proportion of proprietors' savings is offset by investment in inventories, plant, and equipment. Yet Friend and Kravis also note that, according to aggregate data, the annual changes in equity of proprietors in unincorporated business enterprises have grown surprisingly little. In the postwar period (1946–54), changes in net physical investment of unincorporated businesses were found to be 24 per cent of personal saving, whereas the net increase in unincorporated business equity was only 3 per cent of personal saving.[25]

The authors pose the question "Can this conflict be reconciled?" and consider the possibility that conceptual differences between the various estimates might account for the apparent paradox. The savings data used in the Friend-Kravis study are for the most part survey estimates of both

---

"natural resources" category used in the capital assets study includes the sale of timber and timber royalties; oil and mineral rights and leases; oil well ventures; coal royalties; and production payments in oil and minerals. The figures for sole proprietorship and partnership income do not include timber or forestry operations and the data are to that extent not entirely comparable.

[21] That is, if there are suitable opportunities to invest retained earnings through the corporation so as not to incur the penalty tax on undistributed earnings provided for in Section 102 of the Code.

[22] The Code provides that if property is exchanged solely for stock of a corporation, which is controlled by the transferor, no gain or loss is to be recognized at the time of the exchange. See *Internal Revenue Code of 1954*, Sec. 351.

[23] "Entrepreneurial Income, Saving, and Investment" *American Economic Review*, June 1957, pp. 269–301.

[24] *Ibid.*, pp. 282–283.

[25] *Ibid.*, p. 281.

TABLE 31
MINING NET PROFIT AND LOSS, DEPRECIATION, AND DEPLETION, REPORTED
FOR SOLE PROPRIETORS, PARTNERSHIPS, AND CORPORATIONS, 1953-60
(million dollars)

	Net Profit (1)	Net Loss (2)	Depreciation (3)	Depletion (4)
		1953		
Sole proprietors	87	96	n.a.	n.a.
Partnerships	353	411	82	77
Corporations	1,101	156	443	743
		1956		
Sole proprietors	209	182	185	190
Partnerships[a]	157	144	94	84
Corporations	1,470	303	593	845
		1957		
Sole proprietors[a]	167	134	85	86
Partnerships	182	89	146	105
Corporations	1,287	338	665	882
		1958		
Sole proprietors[a]	109	105	144	200
Partnerships	140	168	107	81
Corporations	1,190	358	645	797
		1959		
Sole proprietors[a]	105	110	94	71
Partnerships	122	84	91	68
Corporations	1,152	479	678	n.a.
		1960		
Sole proprietors	116	219	134	202
Partnerships	127	152	104	98
Corporations	1,260	521	720	893

Source: The following supplements to _Statistics of Income_ were used: _U.S. Business Tax Returns_; _Corporation Income Tax Returns_; _Partnership Returns_, 1953; _Business Indicators, Sole Proprietorships Partnerships, Corporations_, 1956-57; and _Selected Financial Data_ for the four most recent years in the table.

a
After 1953, "payments to partners" became a deductible item on partnership information returns. Estimates of payments to partners were therefore added back to the ordinary income and loss data as tabulated. Total payments to partners for 1957-60 were tabulated in _Selected Financial Data_; only the total for 1956 was therefore estimated by us. However, no breakdown of this item between net income and net loss returns was available, and the division was therefore made on the assumption that payments to partners are divided between income and loss returns in proportion to gross receipts on such returns.

74

personal and business savings of businessmen; the data for changes in unincorporated business equity are based on Commerce estimates which cover business saving and capital transfers between personal and business accounts. The authors, noting that capital transfers between personal and business assets would have to be negative to help the reconciliation, feel that these differences "can at best account for only part of the difference between the survey and Commerce estimates." Their discussion suggests strongly that the disparity may be accounted for by weaknesses in the annual Commerce estimates of changes in unincorporated business equity.[26]

While an attempt at quantitative reconciliation of the findings from cross-sectional surveys and annual aggregates would be clearly outside the scope of the present study, it is nevertheless noteworthy that the tax-return data suggest that the "conflict" may indeed be largely a matter of capital transfers. Proprietors may at any moment of time invest most of their savings in their own businesses, and yet year-to-year data may show only small increases in unincorporated business equity. Such a development will occur if proprietors sell profitable businesses to corporations, or incorporate them on their own.[27] It will show up on asset account as a transfer from unincorporated business to personal holdings. Our data suggest that this may have taken place over time. To the extent that this explanation is valid, there is no conflict between the Commerce Department "equity" estimates and the survey findings.

---

[26] *Ibid.*, pp. 286–287.

[27] The number of sole proprietorships and partnerships that were converted into corporations during any one year appears to be very small in relation to the total number of unincorporated businesses. IRS tabulations of first-year corporation returns for 1946 and 1954 show the following:

	New Corporation Returns of Previously Unincorporated Enterprises		Number of Unincorporated Enterprises in Preceding Year		Per Cent of Total Converted	
	Total (1)	Nonfarm (2)	Total (3)	Nonfarm (4)	Total (5)	Nonfarm (6)
1946	22,473	22,232	6,316,522	3,520,331	0.36	0.63
1954	16,346	16,108	8,673,103	5,319,895	0.19	0.30

Source: Cols. 1 and 2: *Statistics of Income, Corporation Returns,* 1946 and 1954.
Source: Cols. 3 and 4: *Statistics of Income, Individual Returns,* 1945 and 1953, and *Partnership Returns* (Supplements), 1945 and 1953.

It is, however, difficult to conclude anything from frequencies alone in the present context. Even if small in number relative to the total, the businesses changing into corporations are likely to be among the largest and to control a disproportionate share of assets. Furthermore, even a small outmigration of firms may offset much of the increase in equity of all the remaining firms for the same period, since the former represents the cumulation of past years' increases in equity (a stock) whereas the latter is only the increase over that period (a flow).

Another set of situations, which operates to reduce the reported net-profit-to-loss ratio on tax returns, consists in attributing expenses to unincorporated enterprises which are actually unrelated to them. Individuals may pursue hobbies which are difficult to distinguish from enterprises conducted to produce income. The most frequently cited case in point is the so-called gentleman's farm. In this case the business aspect of the farm may be incidental to the consumption purpose which it has for its owner, and the loss at which it is operated is thus questionable within the usual business terms. Similar instances are the occasional antique or gift shop, which permits its owner to deduct the cost of travel as a business expense, and various resort enterprises, such as the operation of a ski-tow, which permit the mingling of business and pleasure.[28] A clue to the possible quantitative importance of hobby-losses among sole proprietors of farms and recreational enterprises can be obtained from a breakdown of net income for these industries by total income (AGI) of the proprietors. Such a tabulation became available for the first time for 1960. In Table 32 net income from farming, recreational services, mining, and real estate operation is shown by AGI groups. For the latter two, the figures shown are the algebraic sum of the net losses and net profits shown separately in Tables 30 and 31. No separate tabulation of net losses and net profits by size of AGI and industry groups are available. However, even the net income (net profits minus net losses) tabulations in Table 32 show conclusively that, for the four industry groups in question, net losses are highly concentrated at the upper extreme of the income scale. Net income originating in mining and farming turned negative from the $50,000 level on. The reasons why this may be so for mining have already been discussed. For farming it suggests the existence of a significant hobby-loss element at high income levels. Indeed, the hobby-loss farm appears to contribute a large part, though by no means all, of the explanation for the peculiar relation of unincorporated enterprise net income to AGI on tax returns when moving up along the income scale.

Probably more prevalent at low-income levels is the practice of some to ascribe a disproportionate part of professional or business expense to part-time self-employment. For example, an employed scientist may deduct from small or occasional consulting fees most of his professional expenses, such as the cost of journals and depreciation of professional

---

[28] The so-called hobby-loss provision of the Tax Code is intended to curb this practice. It applies to individuals whose expenses relating to an enterprise exceeds gross income therefrom by $50,000 or more in each of five consecutive years. See *Internal Revenue Code* of 1954, Sec. 270.

PROFIT OR LOSS FROM BUSINESS AND PROFESSION

TABLE 32

SOLE PROPRIETORSHIP NET INCOME: TOTAL AND FOUR SELECTED INDUSTRIES,
BY INCOME GROUPS, 1960
(million dollars)

AGI (thousand dollars)	All Industries (1)	Mining (2)	Real Estate Operators and Lessors (3)	Farms (4)	Recreational Services (5)	All Other (6)
Under 1	-714	-50	-12	-241	-8	-403
1 - 2	1,027	2	14	460	1	550
2 - 5	4,840	4	24	1,336	30	3,446
5 - 10	5,943	-17	36	808	32	5,084
10 - 20	5,058	12	23	333	30	4,660
20 - 50	4,113	10	18	96	20	3,970
50 - 150	813	-50	2	-23	4	880
150 - 500	1	-9	a	-22	-4	36
500 and over	-15	-6	a	-10	-2	3
Total	21,067ᵇ	-103	105	2,737	103	18,226

Source: Cols. 1-5: U.S. Treasury Department, U.S. Business Tax Returns, 1960-61, Table 6. Col. 6: col. 1 minus the sum of cols. 2-5.

ᵃLess than 0.5 million (negative for the $500,000 and over group).

ᵇThis total differs by $5 million from that shown in Table 19 whose source is Statistics of Income, Individual Income Tax Returns, 1960.

library. He could not deduct such expenses at the same time as using the standard deduction if he were merely an employee.[29] The practice results in understatement of his independently obtained income, and indeed may result in a small business loss.

Effect on Business Organization of Tax Treatment of Pension Plan Contributions

The data presented earlier in this chapter are influenced by the treatment of employer contributions to pension funds. Subject to certain limitations, such contributions have in recent times been a deductible current expense to employers, the same as cash wage payments, and a form of deferred compensation to employees. The treatment as deferred compensation under the income tax means that beneficiaries are not taxed currently on either the employer contributions made on their behalf nor on the accumulated investment income of the fund, but only

[29] Occupational and professional expenses of employees may be deducted and are part of the so-called personal deductions on the individual return, Form 1040. For persons who itemize, it is therefore immaterial whether they include these expenses among their personal deductions or among their business deductions in the business schedule of the return. But for persons who take the standard deduction, an advantage arises from shifting occupational expenses into the business schedule.

at the time when payments are actually made to them. The effect of this deferral is a considerable lowering of tax liability over time. Owner-managers of corporations, because they are employees, have long been able to obtain substantial tax advantages through qualified pension plans.[30]

Until recently owner-employees of unincorporated enterprises have not had this opportunity. In order to obtain the same tax treatment with respect to retirement contributions as has been available to employees, self-employed persons had to incorporate their business or profession and pay themselves a salary. Many state laws were amended to enable professional persons to do so. This may have been an important consideration, in addition to the possibility of lower corporate tax rates, in causing some proprietors to incorporate. For some, as has been discussed earlier in the chapter, it has been possible to do both; namely to incorporate and, at the same time, to carry any income (loss) directly to the proprietors. This may also explain why few partnerships and sole proprietors, but a substantial number of corporations, choose optional tax treatment (see Table 28).[31]

Beginning with January 1, 1963, self-employment income has received some of the favorable tax treatment available for employment income.[32] One-half of the contributions to approved retirement plans up to 10 per cent of earned self-employment income, or $2,500 annually, whichever is lower, may be deducted. That is, the amount deducted cannot exceed $1,250, must be matched 100 per cent by nondeductible contributions to the plan, and the combined total cannot exceed 10 per cent of income. Any full-time employee with a minimum of three years of service must be included on a nondiscriminatory basis under the plan, and any contributions on his behalf must be vested immediately.

The new provisions concerning self-employment income thus appear, at least initially, less favorable than those for stockholder-employees of corporations. Many proprietors may therefore continue to find incorporation combined with the option to be taxed as a partnership more

---

[30] The term "qualified" in this context means that a plan has met all the requirements of the Internal Revenue Service in order to qualify for the desired tax treatment.

[31] It might also explain why the incidence of losses was found to be no greater among corporations electing optional partnership tax treatment than among corporations not electing (Table 29). It would mean that those electing to be taxed as a partnership incorporated mainly to obtain the more advantageous treatment of retirement contributions but otherwise found it advantageous to be taxed at individual, rather than corporate, tax rates.

[32] See "Self-Employed Individual Tax Retirement Act of 1962" (P.L. 87-792).

favorable. It is, of course, too early for any of the effects of the new provisions to be reflected in the data available at the time of writing.

Pattern of Income on Returns With Profit or Loss From Business or Profession

Table 33 shows the relative frequency of returns with profit or loss from sole proprietorship or partnership, or both, for 1955 and 1959. These are the only recent years for which data are available in sufficient detail to make possible the elimination of double-counting of returns filed by persons who are both sole proprietors and partners. In every income group above the $10,000 level, more than one-third of the returns have profit or loss from unincorporated enterprise. Above the $100,000 level, the frequency is more than one-half. This is in sharp contrast to the relatively small, if any, net profits from that source reported for that income range, and is another indication that some of this entrepreneurship may be so in name only, or may be largely directed toward the accumulation of capital gains through sale of the enterprise.

We also see in Table 33 that the proportion of returns reporting profit or loss from both sole proprietorship and partnership rises continuously from the bottom of the income scale to the top, except for the group with negative income. Nearly one out of ten returns with business or professional income in the $10,000-$25,000 group was filed by a person who was both a sole proprietor and a partner. On returns with adjusted gross income of $100,000 and over, this proportion was greater than two in ten. For the total of returns in the two annual distributions, only four out of one hundred had both sole proprietor and partnership income. However, the relative frequency of multiple business returns is greater than that, since no account is taken of returns with income from more than one sole proprietorship or more than one partnership. The important aspect of this diversification is that it lowers the chance of unaveraged losses. The loss in one enterprise can be offset against the profit in another.

Such loss offsets are of course not dependent on multiple business ownership. As Table 34 shows, at least 57 per cent of returns with business and professional income for 1955 and 1959 also reported income from one or all of these other sources: wages, salaries, dividends, interest, rents, and royalties.[33] One-third of those with negative income and

---

[33] Hereafter referred to, for brevity, as "other sources." Capital gains or losses and the smaller income sources were omitted from the basic tabulation from which Table 34 is derived.

79

TABLE 33

NUMBER OF RETURNS WITH UNINCORPORATED ENTERPRISE PROFIT OR LOSS AS PERCENTAGE OF ALL
RETURNS FILED, 1955 AND 1959
(in thousands)

1955

Income Group (thousand dollars)	All Returns (1)	Number with Profit or Loss from			Percentage of Returns with Profit or Loss from			
		Sole Proprietorship (2)	Partnership (3)	Sole Proprietor and/or Partnership[a] (4)	Sole Proprietorship (2) ÷ (1) (5)	Partnership (3) ÷ (1) (6)	Sole Proprietor and/or Partnership (4) ÷ (1) (7)	Sole Proprietor and Partnership[b] (8)
Negative AGI	432.0	363.8	56.4	399.2	84.2	13.1	92.4	5.3
0 – 2	15,691.1	2,619.1	298.2	2,872.2	16.7	1.9	18.3	1.6
2 – 3	8,428.7	1,279.9	211.6	1,457.0	15.2	2.5	17.3	2.4
3 – 5	16,673.6	1,832.5	398.6	2,158.8	11.0	2.4	12.9	3.3
5 – 10	14,461.5	1,487.9	515.2	1,912.6	10.3	3.6	13.2	4.7
10 – 25	2,153.0	534.3	334.5	791.2	24.8	15.5	36.7	9.8
25 – 50	311.0	100.8	101.3	177.2	32.4	32.6	57.0	14.1
50 – 100	77.6	21.0	29.4	43.6	27.1	38.0	56.3	15.6
100 – 500	20.8	5.5	8.9	11.9	26.3	42.7	57.0	21.0
500 and over	0.9	0.3	0.4	0.5	33.7	43.9	61.6	26.0
Total	58,250.2	8,245.1	1,954.7	9,824.2	14.2	3.4	16.9	3.8

(continued)

80

TABLE 33 (concluded)

1959

Income Group (thousand dollars)	All Returns (1)	Number with Profit or Loss from			Percentage of Returns with Profit or Loss from			
		Sole Proprietorship (2)	Partnership (3)	Sole Proprietor and/or Partnership[a] (4)	Sole Proprietorship (2)÷(1) (5)	Partnership (3)÷(1) (6)	Sole Proprietor and/or Partnership (4)÷(1) (7)	Sole Proprietor and Partnership[b] (8)
Negative AGI	433.1	355.0	51.9	388.6	82.0	12.0	89.7	4.7
0 – 2	14,315.2	2,273.7	232.6 ⎫	3,702.3	15.9	1.6 ⎫	17.3	1.7
2 – 3	7,128.2	1,105.6	153.7 ⎬		15.5	2.2 ⎬	14.9	2.7
3 – 5	14,065.1	1,823.0	331.8	2,098.4	13.0	2.4	13.1	3.9
5 – 10	19,546.4	2,079.0	575.0	2,554.6	10.6	2.9	26.3	8.8
10 – 25	4,217.9	784.6	421.2	1,107.8	8.6	10.0	55.6	14.5
25 – 50	422.7	145.5	123.7	235.0	34.4	29.3	61.0	16.5
50 – 100	114.8	35.9	45.8	70.1	31.3	39.8	57.6	18.7
100 – 500	26.8	6.9	11.4	15.5	25.8	42.6	61.3	25.4
500 and over	1.0	.3	.5	.6	29.8	47.0		
Total	60,271.3	8,609.7	1,947.8	10,172.9	14.3	3.2	16.9	3.8

Source: Statistics of Income, Individual Income Tax Returns, 1955 and 1959, Tables 6 and 8 respectively.

[a] Derived from Tables 6 and 8 in above source.

[b] Col. 2 plus col. 3 divided by col. 4 minus 1.

TABLE 34

RELATIVE FREQUENCY OF RETURNS WITH UNINCORPORATED ENTERPRISE PROFIT OR LOSS
AND INCOME FROM OTHER SOURCES, 1955 AND 1959

PERCENTAGE OF RETURNS WITH ENTERPRISE INCOME AND:

Income Group (thousand dollars)	Wages and Salaries 1955 (1)	Wages and Salaries 1959 (2)	Dividends 1955 (3)	Interest 1955 (4)	Rents and Royalties 1959 (5)	Income from Other Sources[a] 1955 (6)	Income from Other Sources[a] 1959 (7)
Negative AGI	22.0	23.2	6.1	11.3	17.0	32.9	36.0
0 – 2	27.2	31.2	3.7	10.1	14.7	36.8	41.9
2 – 3	42.6	53.9	4.8	13.4	17.2	53.3	63.7
3 – 5	54.3	63.3	6.6	15.1	21.2	64.4	73.2
5 – 10	60.4	50.6	13.8	25.4	28.8	74.9	66.2
10 – 25	44.8	44.4	36.7	46.3	36.0	75.5	64.1
25 – 50	45.4	50.6	62.2	64.0	40.3	85.8	70.2
50 – 100	56.1	60.0	79.3	73.8	46.2	93.4	78.1
100 – 500	67.2	88.1	90.2	83.5	58.0	98.1	88.1
500 and over	71.1		97.4	89.4		99.5	
Total	43.6	46.3	10.7	19.0	19.0	56.9	57.4

Source: See source to Table 33.

[a] For 1955, income from other sources means wages and salaries, dividends, and interest. For 1959 it means wages and salaries and rents and royalties.

nearly all those reporting adjusted gross income over $100,000 for 1955 had income from these sources in addition to that from unincorporated enterprise.[34] As the percentages show, for those reporting incomes below $10,000, the most frequent source of other income was wages and salaries; for those with higher income, dividends and interest were the most frequent other sources.

[34] These relative frequencies may be compared with data from the Survey of Consumer Finances for 1949–52, presented by L. R. Klein and J. Margolis in "Statistical Studies of Unincorporated Business," *Review of Economics and Statistics*, February 1954, p. 40. Klein and Margolis dealt with unincorporated business exclusive of farm operators, professionals, and self-employed artisans who have no employees "and little or no capital plant or equipment." They found that 62 per cent of the entrepreneurial spending units in their sample received money income outside the business; 52 per cent if the units are limited to those in which the owner himself receives outside income. From these figures we could expect a tax return sample to show a range of 52 to 62 per cent for outside income, and our figure for 1955 indeed falls into that range. But for receipt of income from dividends, interest, trust funds, or royalties, Klein and Margolis present us with a range of only 13 to 14 per cent. The large difference between this and our figure of 23 per cent for dividends and interest alone may be primarily the result of differences in concept between the tax return distributions and the Klein-Margolis sample. The latter excludes professional practitioners, a category which is included in the tax return distribution. This group is likely to have a high property income frequency which would explain the difference in the two studies.

CHAPTER 4

The Treatment of Losses

IN EVERYDAY DISCOURSE a business loss is defined as negative net income from business. Such usage is meaningful as long as allowance for all cost elements is made in the definition of income. When allowance is not made, as often occurs in accounting practice[1] and income tax definitions of business income, a true loss may exist long before income from business becomes negative. After explicit allowance for an owner-manager's salary and return on his capital, we might find a loss where the tax return now shows a profit. Business losses as reported on tax returns are therefore understated.

However, in terms of tax treatment this understatement has little practical significance since it is a taxpayer's total income, that is, the sum of negative and positive components, that determines his tax liability. An economically correct definition of business profit would merely lower an individual's business income and raise his other income (salary, interest, etc.) commensurately; his total income would not be affected.[2]

To what extent do losses then present us with a problem that requires separate mention? Are losses not merely an extreme aspect of income variability, which is present whenever a person's income declines?

We are interested in the tax experience of losses, first, because of the widely held belief that the federal Treasury shares in profits but not in losses. This arises naturally from the fact that the income tax does not, with some exceptions, allow averaging of income over time. Therefore, a person whose loss results in negative over-all income may find the Treasury not sharing his loss as it shares his profit. If, on the other hand, a loss is offset against positive other income, it is no longer different from

---

[1] Many self-employed proprietors do, of course, make some imputation for the value of their services in the business. For instance, it is reported from the 1951 Survey of Consumer Finances that "11 of 13 interviews with entrepreneurs who clearly state that they had a business loss show positive total business income—withdrawals exceeding the stated loss" (Klein and Margolis, *Review of Economics and Statistics,* February 1954, p. 44). This finding does not prove, however, that most proprietors consider their services a business cost; it merely suggests that of those reporting losses, many do so after some imputation.

[2] For example, assume an individual proprietor whose business ends a given year with a $1,000 loss, without allowance for implicit costs such as the use of his capital and labor. If his income from other sources was $4,000, his total income for the year was accordingly $3,000. If he paid himself $10,000 for the services of his capital and labor, his business loss would mount to $11,000. But his total income would remain unchanged:

Income from other sources	4,000
Business income	− 11,000
Amount imputed for services and capital supplied by owner	10,000
Total	3,000

84

any other decline in income, though the latter may not have the same label attached to it. The peculiarity of loss treatment is then the peculiarity of the treatment of income fluctuations in general; this, in turn, arises from the absence of averaging and the existence of progressive tax rates. The only way in which tax treatment of losses may thus differ from that of other income declines is in the absence of any offset against positive income. We inquire into the extent of this bias.

The second reason for our interest in the amount and distribution of net losses is to obtain some indirect information on income variability. It would be preferable, of course, to have data for an identical group of taxpayers over an extended period of time. This would show year-to-year income fluctuations for each taxpayer and hence the varying rates at which the Treasury actually participates in increases and decreases in income. In the absence of such a sample, the statistics on annual net profit and net loss furnish us with some insight into income variability (see the discussion of average effective and marginal rates in the next chapter).

The Extent of Loss Offset

In Table 18, both net profits and net losses from unincorporated enterprises were shown separately by income groups. As indicated in that table, most of the aggregate net loss was reported on returns with positive total income. This was evidently because individuals reporting net losses from sole proprietorship or partnership had significant amounts of income from other sources. The figures for 1960 in Table 18 may be summarized as follows:

Net loss reported on returns with positive AGI $2.36 billion
Net loss reported on returns with negative AGI $1.32 billion

Of close to $3.7 billion net losses reported, almost $2.4 billion must be considered offset by other income simply because it was reported on returns which, after taking the net loss from unincorporated enterprise into account, had nevertheless positive total income. An estimated $0.57 billion of even the $1.32 billion net loss reported on returns with negative incomes was offset by positive income from other sources.[3] This

---

[3] In addition to $1,321 million net losses from unincorporated enterprises reported by individuals on returns with negative AGI, $875 million positive income (including net long-term capital gains at 100 per cent) was also reported in this income group. If we prorate this positive income to the sole proprietors and partners in the group, an offset of $569 million against the reported net losses results. The error in estimating the offset through simple prorating is likely to be small, for of the 435,000 returns with negative AGI, some 373,000 had also net loss from sole proprietorship or partnership.

85

TABLE 35

NET OPERATING LOSS CARRYFORWARD DEDUCTIONS AND ESTIMATED
NET OPERATING LOSSES FROM UNINCORPORATED ENTERPRISES ON
RETURNS WITH NEGATIVE AGI, 1943-61
(dollars in millions; frequencies in thousands)

	Net Operating Loss Carryforward		Net Operating Loss on Returns with Negative Income			Carryforward as Percentage of		Number of Carryforward Returns as Percentage of Number with Net Loss and Negative Income for Preceding Year (2) ÷ (5)
	Amount (1)	Number of Returns (2)	Amount (3)	Weighted Average Amount for Years from Which Loss Carried Forward[a] (4)	Frequency of Sole Proprietor or Partnership Net Loss (5)	Preceding Year's Loss (1) ÷ (3) (6)	Average Loss for Years from Which Carried (1) ÷ (4) (7)	(8)
1943[b]			153.5		n.a.			
1944[b]			219.9		150.7			
1945[b]	80.5	n.a.	225.9	197.8	147.3	36.6	40.7	n.a.
1948			665.6		285.9			
1949			812.5		365.1			
1950			742.6		307.0			
1951	105.2[c]	30.6[c]	736.1	751.6	293.7	14.2	14.0	10.0
1952	134.6[c]	30.0[c]	745.6	748.9	334.3	18.3	18.0	10.2
1953	202.3[c]	38.2[c]	993.9	742.4	372.5	27.1	27.2	11.4
1954	145.0[c]	34.8[c]	879.3	876.9	397.7	14.6	16.5	9.3
1955			827.2		399.8			
1956			785.5		365.0			
1957			735.7		358.0			
1958			717.1		316.1			
1959			913.7		382.7			
1960	165.6[c]	13.9[c]	751.2	829.0	373.5	18.1	20.0	3.6
1961	91.9[c]	15.1[c]	n.a.	789.0	358.4	12.2	11.6	4.0

leaves $0.75 billion of net losses not offset against current-year positive income.

Such net losses are, subject to certain restrictions, eligible for so-called loss carryover. A net operating loss (as distinct from a capital loss) may be offset against the positive income of preceding years (referred to as carryback), and after the carryback possibilities have been exhausted, it may be offset against positive income in future years (referred to as carryforward). At present, a three-year carryback and a five-year carryforward are allowed. Statistics have been published only for 1945, 1951–54, and 1960–61, and then only for the carryforward portion. The total loss carryforwards reported for these years, and their relation to preceding years' estimated net operating losses for returns with negative total income, are shown in Table 35. On the basis of a projection of the 1960–61 level of reported loss carryforwards, an estimated $0.11 billion of the $0.75 billion not offset against other income in that year is carried

---

NOTES TO TABLE 35

Note: Number of years allowed for loss carryover.

Income Year	Loss Carryback	Loss Carryforward
1942–47	2 Years	2 Years
1948–49	2 Years	3 Years
1950–53	1 Year	5 Years
1954–57	2 Years	3 Years
1958–63	3 Years	5 Years

Source: Cols. 1, 2, and 5 as tabulated in Statistics of Income. Col. 3 estimated by subtracting from reported net losses of sole proprietors and partners with negative AGI a prorated amount of positive income.

[a]Amounts shown are the weighted average of the figures in col. 3 for the following years (the numbers in parentheses are the weights attached to the net loss of the year shown):

1945: 1943 (.5), 1944   (1).
1951: 1948 (.25), 1949 (.5), 1950   (1).
1952: 1949 (.25), 1950 (.5); 1951 (1).
1953: 1950 (.25), 1951 (.5); 1952 (1).
1954: 1950 (.12), 1951 (.25), 1952 (.5), 1953   (1).
1960: 1955 (.06), 1956 (.12), 1957 (.25), 1958 (.5), 1959 (1).
1961: 1956 (.06), 1957 (.12), 1958 (.25), 1959 (.5), 1960 (1).

[b]Data for 1943–45 are for sole proprietors only.

[c]For 1952–54 and 1960–61 the net operating loss carryforward includes an undetermined amount of carryover of casualty loss on nonbusiness property.
    Positive income reported on returns with negative AGI was prorated on the basis of frequencies with net loss from unincorporated enterprise as a percentage of the total frequency in the group. The prorated share of net long-term capital gain was included at 100 per cent to correspond with the requirement that the net operating loss must be computed before the 50 per cent net long-term capital gains deduction. For detail, see Appendix I.

87

forward against future income. Net losses reported for 1960 may thus be accounted for in this manner:

Total net loss reported	$3.68 billion
Offset on returns with positive total income	2.36
Offset on returns with negative total income	
Against positive components (estimated)	0.57
Loss carryforward (estimated)	0.11
Loss carryback	n.a.
Net loss carried back or not offset	$0.64 billion

At most, one-sixth of reported net losses were not offset against positive income. How much of the $0.64 billion which we failed to account for was carried back against preceding years' income cannot be estimated with the information now at hand. A carryback requires the filing of an amended return and therefore does not appear on regular tax returns from which the *Statistics of Income* information is drawn. Yet a net operating loss must be carried back first, and only the amounts not offset in this manner can be carried forward. Carrybacks may therefore be substantial, depending largely on the degree of income variability experienced by the relevant group of taxpayers.

No mention has yet been made of losses which were offset by gains reported in the same schedule of the tax return. For a given taxpayer, no loss is shown if that from one business he owns is offset by the gain from one or more others. The net losses shown are those of taxpayers whose loss from one business exceeds the gain from others they may own. There is consequently some understatement of loss offsets on this account.

It is evident from the figures presented that all but a small proportion of the total losses from unincorporated enterprises are taken into account in computing taxable income. To the extent that this is so, losses are treated more symmetrically with profits than is frequently assumed,[4] and the adverse effect of the income tax on the disposition to assume risks may not be as great as it first appears. However, since our discussion of loss offsets has so far been confined to the aggregate of reported

[4] Henry C. Simons' view of loss treatment is representative of widely held opinion on this subject. "Our tax laws are crude, niggardly, and patently unfair in their treatment of losses. . . The possibility of deducting losses would largely counterbalance the prospective tax on speculative gains, except for persons and enterprises whose small resources prohibit diversification of investments." (See *Personal Income Taxation,* Chicago, 1938, p. 21.) Simons' impressions of a quarter century ago may be more valid for capital losses for which offsets are largely limited to the amount of capital gains. For operating losses his generalization, as we have seen, appears less valid.

net losses, the finding that a large proportion has been offset in recent years may not apply equally to all taxpayers. For instance, taxpayers who devote full time to their enterprise and have little or no income from other sources may find it much harder to obtain loss offsets under current provisions than taxpayers whose independent enterprise is a part-time activity and who obtain, therefore, a large proportion of their income elsewhere. A business loss will result in over-all negative income for those without other income whereas it may not for those with diverse sources. Therefore, one would expect to find "other income" less frequently on returns with negative total income than on returns higher up in the distribution of annual income.[5]

This expectation is confirmed in Tables 33 and 34, where we observed the patterns of income on returns with unincorporated enterprise profit or loss. The negative income group has a somewhat above-average frequency of returns with more than one business, but is below average with respect to the number reporting wages and salaries, dividends, and interest. The percentage of returns with income from unincorporated enterprise and specified other sources is reproduced below:

	Sole Proprietor and Partnership Profit or Loss		Wages and Salaries		Dividends	Interest	Rents and Royalties
	1955	1959	1955	1959	1955	1955	1959
Negative AGI	5.3	4.7	22.0	23.2	6.1	11.3	17.0
Total	3.8	3.8	43.6	46.3	10.7	19.0	19.0

These frequencies suggest that losses leading to negative income are relatively more likely for persons with few or no income sources besides unincorporated enterprise. The same, however, does not seem to hold for taxpayers with more than one enterprise[6]: negative income occurs with greater frequency among taxpayers who are both partners and sole proprietors than among those who are only one or the other. It is possible, though our data are not sufficient to establish it, that persons

[5] Whereas this expectation seems reasonable and may at first sight appear obvious, it assumes a random distribution of losses. A different pattern is conceivable. If the taxpayers who engaged in risky enterprises were also the ones with other income sources, whereas those without other sources were engaged in relatively riskless businesses, the negative income group could show a higher average frequency of income sources per return than some positive income groups.

[6] As noted in the preceding chapter, the frequencies presented are actually only for the number of returns with both sole proprietorship and partnership profit or loss. Multiple business ownership is thereby understated since only one frequency is recorded when a taxpayer has more than one business in the same category, e.g. sole proprietorship.

strongly inclined to independent enterprise (as we may assume those who are both partners and sole proprietors to be) are also engaged in more risky ventures than single-enterprise persons.

It is evident that the provisions extending loss offsets over a number of years are of greater importance for taxpayers whose major, or sole, source of income is from unincorporated enterprise than for those with other income sources. If the trend (noted in Chapter 3) toward an ever-rising share of income from other sources in the total income of proprietors continues, the need for loss offsets extending over long periods will of course correspondingly decrease. In the meantime, the adequacy of loss carryovers is still an important question.

Provisions for Loss Carryover Deductions

The history of loss carryover provisions is largely one of varying combinations of loss carryback and carryforward periods. Through most of the 1940's the carryback period was two years and the carryforward period at first two and later three years. In 1950 the emphasis was shifted from carryback to carryforward. The former was reduced to one year, the latter increased to five. While the length of the carryforward period has remained the same since then, the carryback has been lengthened twice: in 1954 to two years, and again in 1958 to three years. The principle of operation of the carryover system has remained the same throughout. A net loss not fully offset in the current year must, after appropriate adjustments, first be carried back to the earliest year possible, and then to each successive year until fully offset. A business loss incurred in 1950, for example, had to be offset in the following sequence:

Offset year	2	1	3	4	5	6	7
Calendar year	1949	1950	1951	1952	1953	1954	1955

Under the provisions in force during the four years 1950–53, a business loss thus had a potential offset period of seven years. Over a seven-year period, an occasional operating loss, even if six times as large as a taxpayer's usual positive income (ignoring signs), can in principle be fully offset. In addition, losses over a succession of years can be offset, as long as their numerical value is not far out of line with the taxpayer's usual positive income. Under the law applicable to the 1950–53 period, operating losses for six successive years, if numerically the same as positive income in other years, could in principle be offset over a twelve-year period:

Year	Income		Year	Income
1949	+		1955	−
1950	−		1956	+
1951	−		1957	+
1952	−		1958	+
1953	−		1959	+
1954	−		1960	+

In the above example, an extreme case of course, the taxpayer's 1950 net operating loss could be carried back to 1949; the loss for 1951 five years forward to 1956; that for 1952 forward to 1957, and so forth until 1960.

Beginning with 1954, Congress extended the carryback period to two years (starting with the earlier year), so that the loss for any one year could now be offset over an eight-year span, and a succession of losses could in principle be averaged over a fourteen-year period. Seven poor years could be offset against seven good years, a provision that would have been adequate to Egypt's feast and famine sequence in the days of Joseph. Beginning with 1958, Congress extended the carryback period once more by an additional year, so that at present, any year's net loss can be offset against taxable income over a nine-year period.[7]

To what extent have these provisions resulted in loss offsets? As already indicated, there is only scant information on the adequacy of loss carryovers. For the seven years for which we have data on loss carryforwards (Table 35), the amounts carried forward to any one year have varied from $80 million for 1945 (sole proprietors only) to $202 million for 1953. In the latter figure (as well as those for other years from 1952 on) an undetermined, but probably small,[8] amount of nonbusiness casualty-loss carryforwards are also included. The 1945 deduction is the result of losses carried forward from two preceding years; the 1951–53 deductions derive from losses of three preceding years; that for 1954,

---

[7] These recent moves toward greater loss offsets are in contrast to an earlier history of very small carryovers. In the 1920's (1921–29), net operating losses could be carried forward two years, but not back. Beginning with 1930, the carryforward was reduced to one year, but even this modest allowance was shortlived. For 1932–38 no carryover provisions existed. Beginning with 1939, a carryforward of two years was once more available. In 1942 a carryback of two years was added. Changes in the carryover allowance made thereafter are shown in the note to Table 35.

[8] Nonbusiness casualty losses tabulated for 1960 on tax returns with AGI less than $1,000 were only $2.6 million. The carryover from this source, although it could arise from returns with positive as well as negative AGI, does not appear to have been significant compared with business losses.

four preceding years; and those for 1960–61, five preceding years. When viewed in relation to a weighted average of the preceding years' losses, the 1945 carryforward deduction was 41 per cent; those for 1951–54, between 14 and 27 per cent; and those for 1960–61, 20 and 12 per cent, of estimated prior year net operating losses on returns with negative income.

In view of the single-year carryback in the early 1950's, the fraction of net operating losses carried forward (about 19 per cent) appears modest. Taxpayers must either have been unable to make use of the carryforward provision for lack of positive income in the years following the loss year, or the then prevailing carryback must have been ample to absorb most of their net operating losses. The above-average frequency in the negative income group of returns which have both sole proprietor and partnership income, noted above, suggests a high income variability. In other words, prior-year income for this group may have been high enough to allow the offset of a large part of net operating loss through carryback. The average unincorporated enterprise net loss on returns with negative income in the early 1950's was somewhat over $3,000, against which various positive income items had to be offset before the loss could be carried to other years. The average loss available for carryback (net operating loss) may thus have been, very roughly, in the neighborhood of $2,500. Table 36 shows a distribution of returns with negative income by size of net loss reported. It shows that for half of the sole proprietor returns, the net loss in 1954 was less than $1,500; and for half of the partner returns, it was less than $2,000. Three-fourths of the returns showed net losses below $3,000 and $5,000, respectively. The concentration of net losses in the small net-loss size groups is greater than the concentration of net profits in the corresponding profit groups.

The loss carryforward figures in Table 35 show little relation between the length of the carryforward period and the proportion of preceding years' operating losses offset. The deductions for 1954, although carried forward from four preceding years, are relatively no greater than those for 1951–53, which are carried forward from only three preceding years each. In addition, some of the loss-years entering the 1951–53 deductions had a two-year carryback, whereas the loss-years entering the 1954 deductions had only a one-year carryback.[9] The

---

[9] For a derivation of the carryback and carryforward periods affecting the deductions of a given year, see the notes to Table 35.

TABLE 36

NUMBER OF RETURNS WITH NEGATIVE AGI AND NET LOSS FROM EITHER
SOLE PROPRIETORSHIP OR PARTNERSHIP, BY SIZE OF NET
LOSS, 1954 AND 1960

Size of Loss from Stated Source (dollars)	Number of 1954 Returns with No AGI and		Number of 1960 Returns with No AGI and	
	Sole Proprietorship Loss	Partnership Loss	Sole Proprietorship Loss	Partnership Loss
Under 100	17,579	2,495	19,090	1,711
100 - 200	17,444	2,543[a]	19,247	1,306
200 - 300	20,960	989[a]	15,102	1,843
300 - 400	19,047	3,505	14,229	1,537
400 - 500	16,950	1,017[a]	15,094	1,336
500 - 1,000	61,871	6,059	56,673	7,732
1,000 - 1,500	43,434	5,136	39,813	4,644
1,500 - 2,000	25,492	5,088	28,699	2,938
2,000 - 2,500	22,968	2,092	18,648	2,903
2,500 - 3,000	16,585	2,551	14,432	3,103
3,000 - 4,000	23,158	2,565	20,792	2,476
4,000 - 5,000	18,753	a	13,728	2,405
5,000 - 10,000	24,876	7,208	31,753	5,749
10,000 - 25,000	16,214	3,911	15,226	5,147
25,000 - 50,000	3,307	1,620[a]	4,022	908[a]
50,000 - 100,000	1,142[a]	a	517 ⎫	375
100,000 or more	26[a]	a	318[a] ⎭	
Total	349,806	47,903	327,383	46,113

Source: Statistics of Income.

[a] Sampling variability of more than 100 per cent. For some of these groups the frequencies could not be separately obtained.

93

sixth and seventh years of loss offsets possible under the 1950–53 provisions may have had little relevance for most persons with net operating loss. By the same token, the eighth and ninth year under the loss offset provisions in force since 1958 may have had slight significance for most.

The figures for 1960 and 1961 bear this out, at least in part. The relative frequency of returns with carryforward declined from over 9 per cent for 1954 to less than 4 per cent for 1960–61 (column 8 of Table 35). But the total amount of carryforward did not decline relative to the amount of net losses reported in prior years. A possible explanation for this increase in the average size of carryforward deductions is the inclusion, since 1958, in the net operating loss deduction of losses from the sale of small business corporation stock and small business investment company stock as well as taxpayers' pro rata share in the losses of corporations electing to be taxed as partnerships. These losses may, on average, be larger than those of sole proprietors and partners.

It is thus possible—though with the information now at our disposal, it is no more than a speculation—that a sizable proportion of net operating losses were offset through carryback. Carryforwards appear to be used primarily by taxpayers with relatively large losses, a supposition supported by a comparison of columns 6 and 8 of Table 35. It shows that even the average carryforward is larger than the average net loss reported on returns with negative income in the preceding year. This follows from the observation that the relative share of loss carryforward returns is greater on a dollar basis (col. 6) than on a frequency basis (col. 8).[10] That those with carryforwards have large losses is not as obvious as it might seem at first, when one considers that loss carryforward is as much a matter of income variability as it is a matter of size of loss. Even very small losses would have to be carried forward if there were no income against which to carry them back.

The probable increase in carrybacks has one distinct advantage. The tax refunds associated with loss carryovers are speeded up and tend to take place shortly after the net operating loss is established. The greater

[10] The number of returns with net loss and negative income in the preceding year, used in computing column 8 of Table 35, is somewhat larger than the number of returns with net operating loss. It is the latter figure we actually desire; the former constitutes a mere proxy. Some overstatement of the desired frequencies results because (a) some returns may have both sole proprietor and partnership net loss and are therefore counted as two frequencies instead of only one; (b) not every return with net loss from unincorporated business and negative AGI has also a net operating loss after the required adjustments are made. However, neither of these overstatements are large enough to alter any conclusions based on the percentage shown in column 8 of Table 35.

the reliance on the carryback provision, the more effective as an automatic stabilizer the individual income tax is likely to be. A carryback calls for tax rebates in the loss year, whereas a carryforward postpones rebates, possibly into prosperity years. The extension of the carryback period has thus probably contributed somewhat to the stabilizing effectiveness of the income tax.[11]

The Conceptual Relation Between Loss Carryover Deductions and Net Losses on Returns with Negative Income

As has been indicated, the connection between loss carryovers and the net losses reported on returns with negative adjusted gross income is only an approximate one. For the purpose of computing net operating loss (the amount which may be carried to other years), a taxpayer in essence computes the excess of allowable deductions over gross income. But some adjustments are required by law to restrict the carryover to specified income components. Thus, taxpayers with capital losses can only take them into account to the extent of capital gains.[12] The deduction from gross income of 50 per cent of the excess of net long-term capital gain over net short-term capital loss is also not allowed. These restrictions are intended to prevent the carryover of these deductions, which might otherwise, in effect, take place. For the same reason a taxpayer's personal exemptions cannot be taken into account when computing his net operating loss. Nonbusiness (personal) deductions may be taken to the extent of "nonbusiness income" only, which for this purpose is defined to exclude wages and salaries.[13]

These adjustments, which are intended to restrict carryovers in the main to business loss deductions and to exclude others, point up the fact that without a generalized carryover system, the carryover for sole proprietor and partnership losses is, in a sense, also limited. A proprietor with net loss from unincorporated enterprise is, in effect, required to offset his loss against any positive income he may have before taking any other deductions. Only if, and to the extent that, positive income is left, can he take the other deductions he is entitled to. To do otherwise would

---

[11] For a more detailed discussion of the advantages and disadvantages of carryforwards compared to carrybacks, see Morris Beck, "Carryover of Business Losses," *National Tax Journal,* March 1953, pp. 82–85. The statistical part of Beck's article deals only with corporate carryovers.

[12] But nonbusiness capital losses are deductible only to the extent of nonbusiness capital gains, even though the taxpayer may have an excess of business capital gains (i.e., gains from sale of property used in his business) over business capital losses. See Treasury Department, Internal Revenue Service, *Tax Guide for Small Business,* 1961 edition, pp. 64–66.

[13] *Ibid.,* p. 65.

amount to letting him carry over other deductions, such as capital losses,[14] personal exemptions, and personal deductions, which other taxpayers are not allowed to carry over to other years. For the sake of uniform treatment, the proprietor is thus required, in the process of deducting his business loss, to "waste" some deductions to which he was entitled.[15]

Thus, the finding that unincorporated enterprise losses are mostly offset is contradicted to some extent. However, our main purpose has been to examine the adequacy of operating loss offset provisions per se. If the offsets which we have shown are at times spurious, because they require the taxpayer to sacrifice other deductions he could have claimed, the fault lies not in inadequate operating loss provisions but rather in inadequate (or totally absent) carryover provisions for other deductions.[16]

True, a taxpayer may care little to which particular provision one ascribes the fact that the loss offset was in fact spurious—that to take one deduction he had to sacrifice another. But from the standpoint of causality there may be merit in stating that the losses of certain taxpayers were largely offset, but their personal exemptions were largely lost. To put the matter in this way suggests that to obtain more adequate loss offsets may not require a change in provisions regarding unincorporated enterprises, but a change in provisions regarding all taxpayers.

[14] Net capital losses can, under present law, be offset against income other than capital gains, only to the extent of $1,000 annually in the year when realized and for five succeeding years. No carryback is allowed.

[15] Vickrey, writing at a time when exemptions were still very high by present standards, proposed to continue the exclusion from carryforward of unused exemptions even in his very comprehensive averaging plan. See William Vickrey, "Averaging of Income for Income-Tax Purposes," reprinted in *Readings in the Economics of Taxation* (Musgrave and Shoup, eds.), Homewood, Ill., 1959, pp. 88–89.

[16] For a proposed remedy, see Joseph A. Pechman, "A Practical Averaging Proposal," *National Tax Journal*, September 1954. Pechman would replace the current requirement—that losses be offset against an individual's entire income for a year before they can be carried to the next year in the averaging period—with a provision allowing the averaging of a number of income (and loss) items over a five-year period. In effect, losses would thereby be credited at the highest bracket rates in each year of the five-year period. While this proposal would greatly mitigate the problem of unused exemptions and deductions, it does not entirely remove it, since in many cases some of the income so averaged may have been covered by exemptions.

CHAPTER 5

Tax Liability on Unincorporated Business and Professions

THE personal income tax has, in principle, no separate tax rates for different sources of income. If this principle were strictly adhered to, the tax collected from any individual would be the same as long as his total income was the same, regardless of whether that income originated from property or personal effort. Such a condition, however, has never existed in the history of United States income tax practice. The tax law has at all times drawn distinctions between income types reflected in differences in rates. Capital gains and losses have been separately treated since 1922; dividends have been subject to somewhat lowered personal income tax rates in recognition of the separate tax on corporate net income; interest on government bonds—in recent years only state and local—has been favored with partial or total exemption; wages, salaries, and income from business and professional practice were for many years eligible for a so-called earned-income credit.[1] In addition to these very explicit differences in rates for different functional components, there are differences in the extent to which their realization for tax purposes can be distributed over time, thus indirectly affecting the rate of tax levied on the individual recipient. Deferred compensation plans, stock options, and corporate income retention are cases in point. Finally, differences in income coverage (dealt with in Chapter 2) influence the effective tax rate on the various functional components.

In view of the variety of ways in which persons may arrange the realization of their income from a given activity, the income tax imputable to unincorporated enterprise becomes of interest. This is especially so because many of those engaged in business and profession have considerable choice as to form of income realization. They may conduct their affairs through incorporation, in which case, as a rule, some combination

---

[1] Each of these devices, except the earned-income credit, have been extensively examined in previous National Bureau studies of the income tax. Capital gains and losses are dealt with in Lawrence H. Seltzer, *The Nature and Tax Treatment of Capital Gains and Losses*, New York, NBER, 1951; dividends in Daniel M. Holland, *The Income-Tax Burden on Stockholders*, Princeton for NBER, 1958, and *Dividends Under the Income Tax*, Princeton for NBER, 1962; interest in George E. Lent, *The Ownership of Tax-Exempt Securities, 1913–1953*, Occasional Paper 47, New York, NBER, 1955, in Lawrence H. Seltzer, *Interest as a Source of Personal Income and Tax Revenue*, Occasional Paper 51, New York, NBER, 1955, and in Roland I. Robinson, *Postwar Market for State and Local Government Securities*, Princeton for NBER, 1960.

97

of corporate and personal income tax rates apply;[2] or they may operate as unincorporated enterprises subject to personal income tax rates. In both cases some conversion of ordinary income into long-term capital gains, which are taxable at one-half the rates applicable to ordinary individual income, with an upper limit of 25 per cent, may be possible.[3] Thus, to gain a balanced picture of the tax on enterprise income, we need to know the tax rates experienced by unincorporated enterprise as well as those imposed on corporate income and capital gains.

We shall first discuss the effective rate of tax on unincorporated enterprise income to show the proportion of the total paid in federal income tax. Secondly, we shall examine marginal rates of tax, that is, the rate at which an additional dollar of income, or loss, has been shared by the Treasury through the income tax.

Effective Tax Rate on Business and Professional Income

The assignment of a tax liability to unincorporated enterprises is the first step in the computation of their average effective rate of income tax. If all those with income from unincorporated enterprise had no other source, their average (mean) effective tax rate would be computed merely by dividing their total tax liability by their income. But as we know (see Chapter 3), such persons also have large amounts of other income. Hence, there is a question of the share of tax liability attributable to their enterprise income. Since a person's tax liability is determined on all of his taxable income simultaneously, we have assigned the same fraction of his tax liability to the business and professional component as the latter is of his total taxable income. In other words, each taxpayer's effective rate of tax was assumed to apply equally to all of his taxable income shares, with appropriate adjustments where the law provides for special tax treatment, as in the case of dividends and capital gains.[4]

---

[2] Beginning with 1958, so-called small business corporations—essentially domestic corporations with no more than ten individuals as shareholders—could elect to have their corporate income taxed at the shareholder level. Their income is thus taxed in the same manner as that of partners, without foregoing the benefits of incorporation. For the number, and net income reported, of such corporations, see Tables 28 and 29 and the discussion relating to them.

[3] For examples of such conversion, see Chapter 3.

[4] Our computations actually do not begin with the incomes of proprietors as such, but simply assign to business and professional income in a given AGI class the effective rate of tax found by dividing tax liability by AGI in that class. Tax liability was computed for each income component before tax credits, and from this gross tax liability, tax credits—where they exist—were subtracted. We thus took account of the special treatment of "earned" income, for which a tax credit was available at various times in the past, the credit on dividends which existed until 1936 and again from 1954 to the present, and the alternative tax available for net long-term capital gains.

TAX LIABILITY ON BUSINESS AND PROFESSIONS

TABLE 37

TAX LIABILITY ATTRIBUTABLE TO UNINCORPORATED BUSINESS AND
PROFESSIONAL INCOME, EMPLOYMENT, AND PROPERTY INCOME
UNDER THE PERSONAL INCOME TAX, 1918-60

	Tax Liability (billion dollars)				Percentage Distribution		
	Total[a]	Business and Professional Income	Employment	Property Income	Business and Professional Income	Employment	Property Income
1918	1.13	.31	.31	.51	27.1	27.4	45.5
1919	1.27	.39	.32	.56	30.8	25.3	43.8
1920	1.08	.28	.36	.44	25.7	33.4	40.9
1921	.72	.16	.25	.31	22.4	34.4	43.2
1922	.86	.17	.25	.44	20.3	29.0	50.7
1923	.66	.13	.19	.34	19.8	28.9	51.3
1924	.70	.13	.17	.41	18.3	23.6	58.2
1925	.73	.13	.13	.48	17.6	17.2	65.2
1926	.73	.12	.13	.48	15.9	18.3	65.9
1927	.83	.13	.14	.56	15.6	17.1	67.3
1928	1.16	.18	.16	.83	15.3	13.6	71.1
1929	1.00	.14	.12	.74	14.0	12.3	73.7
1930	.48	.06	.11	.31	11.7	23.5	64.8
1931	.25	.03	.07	.14	12.6	29.2	58.1
1932	.33	.04	.14	.15	11.7	42.4	45.9
1933	.37	.06	.13	.18	16.4	34.9	48.7
1934	.51	.06	.15	.30	12.4	29.5	58.1
1935	.66	.09	.18	.39	13.4	27.8	58.8
1936	1.21	.15	.27	.79	12.7	22.3	65.0
1937	1.14	.13	.29	.71	11.6	25.8	62.6
1938	.77	.10	.24	.43	13.1	31.0	55.9
1939	.93	.13	.29	.51	13.5	31.0	55.5
1940	1.50	.23	.52	.76	14.7	34.7	50.6
1941	3.91	.83	1.90	1.18	21.1	48.6	30.3
1942	8.93	2.10	5.19	1.64	23.5	58.1	18.4
1943	14.59	3.50	8.98	2.10	24.0	61.6	14.4
1944	16.35	3.69	10.41	2.25	22.6	63.7	13.8
1945	17.23	4.15	10.38	2.70	24.1	60.3	15.7
1946	16.28	4.07	9.18	3.03	25.0	56.4	18.6
1947	18.25	3.91	11.28	3.05	21.4	61.8	16.7
1948	15.62	3.16	9.63	2.83	20.2	61.7	18.1
1949	14.68	2.59	9.39	2.70	17.6	64.0	18.4
1950	18.58	3.25	11.49	3.84	17.5	61.8	20.7
1951	24.44	4.10	16.20	4.14	16.8	66.3	16.9
1952	28.04[b] 27.80[b]	4.38[b] 4.40[b]	19.57[b] 19.61[b]	4.08[b] 3.80[b]	15.6[b] 15.8[b]	69.8[b] 70.5[b]	14.6[b] 13.7[b]

(continued)

99

TAX LIABILITY ON BUSINESS AND PROFESSIONS

TABLE 37 (concluded)

	Tax Liability (billion dollars)				Percentage Distribution		
	Total[a]	Business and Professional Income	Employ-ment	Property Income	Business and Professional Income	Employ-ment	Property Income
1953[b]	29.43	4.29	21.55	3.59	14.6	73.2	12.2
1954[b]	26.67	3.90	19.15	3.61	14.6	71.8	13.5
1955[b]	29.61	4.23	21.23	4.15	14.3	71.7	14.0
1956[b]	32.73	4.66	23.64	4.43	14.2	72.2	13.5
1957[b]	34.39	4.74	25.35	4.30	13.8	73.7	12.5
1958[b]	34.34	4.66	25.28	4.40	13.6	73.6	12.8
1959[b]	38.65	5.11	28.34	5.20	13.2	73.3	13.5
1960[b]	39.46	4.80	29.65	5.01	12.2	75.1	12.7

Source: Estimated from tax liability distributions in Statistics of Income.

a
Discrepancies due to rounding.

b
Individual returns only; does not include fiduciary returns.

The results of this computation are presented in Table 37; total tax liability is divided between unincorporated business and profession, employment, and property. For 1960, unincorporated enterprise accounted for 12 per cent of tax liability, property income for 13 per cent, and wages and salaries for 75 per cent. The fact that unincorporated enterprise and property (especially the latter) account for a greater relative share of tax liability than of reported adjusted gross income (see Tables 3 and 4), is explained by the difference in the income-size distributions among the recipients of each type of income. The extent of the difference in distribution between business and professional income and all other income reported on tax returns is reflected in the difference in effective rates of tax between them (Table 38). In the years before World War II, the rate on business and professional income was less than on other income;[5] since 1940 it has been consistently greater. This is explained by the gradual, but drastic, shift in the composition of income

[5] The sharp rise in the effective rate for 1932 and 1933 may be the result of the absence of an earned-income credit in those two years. For the years 1924–31 and 1934–43, a credit against earned income (from wages and salaries, and unincorporated enterprise) up to a certain size was available. Since wages and salaries and unincorporated enterprise income were both subject to the credit, the effect of its removal showed up much less in 1944 than in 1932, for the importance in the tax base of wages and salaries in the later year had risen so much that the difference in taxation between "earned" and property income no longer had the same significance as formerly.

TABLE 38

EFFECTIVE TAX RATE ON UNINCORPORATED BUSINESS AND PROFESSIONAL INCOME
AND ALL OTHER INCOME REPORTED ON TAX RETURNS, 1929-60
(dollars in billions)

	Other Income Reported on Tax Returns (1)	Tax on Other Income Reported on Tax Returns (2)	Effective Rate on Other Income Col. 2 ÷ Col. 1 (per cent) (3)	Effective Rate on Business and Professional Income (per cent) (4)
1929	22.3	.9	3.9	2.9
1930	16.5	.4	2.6	1.8
1931	12.1	.2	1.8	1.5
1932	11.1	.3	2.6	3.1
1933	10.0	.3	3.1	3.5
1934	12.0	.4	3.7	3.0
1935	13.9	.6	4.1	3.7
1936	17.7	1.1	6.0	4.8
1937	19.8	1.0	5.1	3.9
1938	17.5	.7	3.8	3.2
1939	21.5	.8	3.7	3.4
1940	34.2	1.3	3.7	4.3
1941	54.2	3.1	5.7	9.7
1942	72.7	6.8	9.4	16.9
1943	90.1	11.1	12.3	22.2
1944	99.5	12.7	12.7	21.3
1945	101.4	13.1	12.9	21.7
1946	111.4	12.2	11.0	17.4
1947	126.9	14.3	11.3	16.7
1948	139.5	12.5	8.9	12.8
1949	139.3	12.1	8.7	11.9
1950	156.3	15.3	9.8	13.8
1951	178.1	20.3	11.4	16.4
1952	191.2	23.4	12.2	17.6
1953	203.8	25.1	12.3	17.2
1954	204.3	22.8	11.1	15.3
1955	221.8	25.4	11.4	15.4
1956	238.4	28.1	11.8	15.5
1957	251.5	29.7	11.8	16.0
1958	252.2	29.7	11.8	15.6
1959	275.1	33.5	12.2	16.5
1960	286.5	34.7	12.1	16.0

Source: Col. 1: Table 3, col. 8 minus col. 7, except that AGI
is before exclusions from 1954 on.
Col. 2: Total tax liability, Statistics of Income,
minus Table 37, col. 2.
Col. 4: Table 39, col. 6.
Note: Fiduciaries are excluded from 1953 on. "Other income" is
before exclusions from 1954 on.

TABLE 39

ESTIMATED MEAN EFFECTIVE TAX RATE ON UNINCORPORATED BUSINESS AND
PROFESSIONAL INCOME, REPORTED AND ESTIMATED TOTAL, 1929-60

	Tax Liability (1)	Unincorporated Enterprise Income (billion dollars)			Effective Tax Rate (per cent)		
		Taxable Returns (2)	All Returns (3)	Estimated Total (4)	Col. 1 ÷ Col. 2 (5)	Col. 1 ÷ Col. 3 (6)	Col. 1 ÷ Col. 4 (7)
1929	.14	3.7	4.9	13.0	3.7	2.9	1.1
1930	.06	2.4	3.1	9.5	2.3	1.8	0.6
1931	.03	1.4	2.0	6.6	2.2	1.5	0.5
1932	.04	0.9	1.2	4.1	4.2	3.1	0.9
1933	.06	1.1	1.7	5.6	5.4	3.5	1.1
1934	.06	1.4	2.1	7.6	4.6	3.0	0.8
1935	.09	1.7	2.4	8.6	5.3	3.7	1.0
1936	.15	2.4	3.2	10.3	6.4	4.8	1.5
1937	.13	2.6	3.4	10.8	5.2	3.9	1.2
1938	.10	2.2	3.1	9.6	4.5	3.2	1.1
1939	.13	2.7	3.7	10.6	4.6	3.4	1.2
1940	.23	3.8	5.4	11.7	6.1	4.3	2.0
1941	.83	6.7	8.5	16.2	12.4	9.7	5.1
1942	2.10	10.7	12.5	21.2	19.6	16.9	9.9
1943	3.50	15.6	15.8	26.4	22.5	22.2	13.2
1944	3.69	17.2	17.3	27.8	21.4	21.3	13.2
1945	4.15	19.1	19.1	28.9	21.7	21.7	14.3

(continued)

TABLE 39 (concluded)

	Unincorporated Enterprise Income (billion dollars)				Effective Tax Rate (per cent)		
	Tax Liability (1)	Taxable Returns (2)	All Returns (3)	Estimated Total (4)	Col. 1 ÷ Col. 2 (5)	Col. 1 ÷ Col. 3 (6)	Col. 1 ÷ Col. 4 (7)
1946	4.07	21.4	23.4	34.8	19.0	17.4	11.7
1947	3.91	21.5	23.4	35.0	18.2	16.7	11.2
1948	3.16	21.4	24.6	35.2	14.7	12.8	9.0
1949	2.59	18.8	21.8	32.9	13.8	11.9	7.9
1950	3.25	21.0	23.5	34.6	15.5	13.8	9.4
1951	4.10	24.0	25.0	38.0	17.1	16.4	10.8
1952	4.38	24.1	24.8	38.0	18.2	17.6	11.5
1953	4.29	24.3	25.0	38.6	17.6	17.2	11.1
1954	3.90	23.3	25.5	37.3	16.7	15.3	10.5
1955	4.23	25.2	27.5	39.2	16.8	15.4	10.8
1956	4.66	27.9	30.1	41.8	16.7	15.5	11.1
1957	4.74	27.9	29.7	41.4	17.0	16.0	11.4
1958	4.66	28.0	29.9	42.6	16.7	15.6	10.9
1959	5.11	29.7	31.0	44.2	17.2	16.5	11.6
1960	4.80	28.7	30.0	43.7	16.7	16.0	11.0

Source: Col. 1: Table 37, col. 2. Cols. 2 and 3: Statistics of Income. Col. 4: Table 6, col. 2.

Note: Fiduciaries are excluded after 1952.

103

on tax returns, to the extent that property income was replaced by wages and salaries as the mainstay of the tax base.

How can the tax liability estimates be meaningfully related to income from unincorporated enterprise? No one summary measure is entirely sufficient. If we divide total tax liability by estimated total unincorporated enterprise income, based on estimates of the Departments of Commerce and Agriculture, we obtain an average tax rate in the broadest sense. It shows how much of total unincorporated business and professional income is removed from private use by the income tax. But it may be argued that since the income of nontaxable persons is included, the fraction taken from those who pay the taxes is understated. For 1960, the mean effective rate of tax on business and professional income of tax-payers is nearer to 17 per cent than to 11 per cent (Table 39).[6] Of course, in computing an *average* effective rate of tax, there is no more reason to exclude those returns with a zero effective rate than there is to exclude those with a 1 per cent effective rate. An average, by its nature, does not reveal how high a rate of tax is paid by some. As a summary of the tax experience of all unincorporated enterprise income, the percent-ages shown in the last column of Table 39 are the most valid. They show that before World War II, the individual income tax absorbed less than 2 per cent of the total. But since 1942, the average effective rate has been at, or above, 10 per cent in every year except 1948–50. If the tax liability is viewed in relation to income reported on taxable returns alone, the average effective rate varied from 2 to 6 per cent of income in prewar years, reached a high of 22.5 per cent in 1943, and has been between 15 and 18 per cent since 1950.

EFFECTIVE TAX RATE BY SIZE OF INCOME

To focus on the variation in effective rates applicable to taxpayers with unincorporated enterprise income, we turn to a breakdown of tax liability by income groups for four selected years (Table 40). The mean effective tax rate for 1960 was 15.9 per cent, or slightly below the effective rate for the $10,000 to $25,000 group for that year. Only for those reporting adjusted gross incomes over $500,000 was the mean effective rate greater than 50 per cent; but unincorporated enterprise income in this group has been very small. As the lower part of the table shows, only the 10 per cent of proprietors' returns with the highest incomes were subject to a mean

[6] Seventeen per cent should be considered an upper limit for the mean effective rate on taxpayers' unincorporated enterprise income. To the extent that such income is underreported, the actual average effective rate is overstated when tax liability is divided by reported income. For some rough adjustment for underreporting of income see Table 41, below.

TABLE 40

EFFECTIVE TAX RATES ON UNINCORPORATED BUSINESS AND PROFESSIONAL NET INCOME[a]
REPORTED ON TAX RETURNS, BY INCOME GROUPS, SELECTED YEARS, 1939-60
(million dollars)

Adjusted Gross Income (thousand dollars)	1939			1949		
	Net Income (1)	Tax Liability (2)	Effective Tax Rate[b] Col. 2 ÷ Col. 1 (3)	Net Income (4)	Tax Liability (5)	Effective Tax Rate[b] Col. 5 ÷ Col. 4 (6)
Negative AGI	-126.4	c	c	-919.0	n.a.	n.a.
0 - 2	388.9	0.5	.1	2,815.6	46.7	1.7
2 - 3	629.6	1.3	.2	2,846.8	107.2	3.8
3 - 5	931.6	8.0	.9	4,364.9	267.4	6.1
5 - 10	887.7	21.1	2.4	4,718.6	480.1	10.2
10 - 25c	624.3	35.9	5.8	4,607.1	718.8	15.6
25 - 50c	220.0	26.6	12.1	2,034.8	489.5	24.1
50 - 100	100.4	20.6	20.5	901.9	302.8	33.6
100 - 500	34.0	12.0	35.1	380.4	164.6	43.3
500 and over	-1.1	-0.5	51.1	26.0	13.9	53.6
Deciles						
1st				-827.9	n.a.	n.a.
2nd				518.1	3.7	0.7
3rd				863.2	12.1	1.4
4th				1,091.8	24.2	2.2
5th				1,334.8	42.0	3.2
6th				1,601.9	64.4	4.0
7th				1,853.5	92.6	5.0
8th				2,219.7	149.6	6.7
9th	223.7	4.1	1.8d	3,140.0	279.6	8.9
10th	792.3	46.1	5.8d	9,982.3	1,922.9	19.3
Total	3,689.2	125.5	3.4	21,777.2	2,591.1	11.9

(continued)

TABLE 40 (concluded)

Adjusted Gross Income (thousand dollars)	1952			1960		
	Net Income (7)	Tax Liability (8)	Effective Tax Rate[b] Col. 8 ÷ Col. 7 (9)	Net Income (10)	Tax Liability (11)	Effective Tax Rate[b] Col. 11 ÷ Col. 10 (12)
Negative AGI	-975.1	-23.3	2.4	-1,236.6	-22.0	1.8
0 – 2	1,986.1	84.3	4.3	1,450.2	32.2	2.2
2 – 3	2,366.1	165.1	7.0	1,584.1	82.2	5.2
3 – 5	4,362.4	399.6	9.2	4,095.9	319.4	7.8
5 – 10[e]	5,836.6	776.0	13.3	7,766.0	857.0	11.0
10 – 25[e]	4,964.1	928.5	18.7	9,409.6	1,558.6	16.6
25 – 50	4,384.8	1,233.0	28.1	4,784.8	1,183.8	24.7
50 – 100	1,311.0	541.0	41.3	1,772.6	600.5	33.9
100 – 500	508.8	262.1	51.5	411.6	169.0	41.1
500 and over	9.1	5.8	62.9	.4	.2	50.9
Deciles						
1st	-898.1	-23.2	2.6	-1,147.3	-22.0	1.9
2nd	597.7	18.0	3.0	660.1	8.9	1.4
3rd	905.8	43.7	4.8	1,046.1	39.1	3.7
4th	1,187.6	71.5	6.0	1,426.6	77.8	5.5
5th	1,477.2	107.8	7.3	1,862.0	131.1	7.0
6th	1,725.8	144.9	8.4	2,143.4	185.9	8.7
7th	1,983.6	186.5	9.4	2,512.1	241.8	9.6
8th	2,462.1	272.3	11.1	3,010.7	334.5	11.1
9th	3,796.5	525.5	13.8	4,582.6	614.2	13.4
10th	11,515.7	3,025.3	26.3	13,941.5	3,169.0	22.7
Total	24,753.9	4,372.3[f]	17.7	30,037.8	4,780.4[f]	15.9

effective rate close to 25 per cent. But they accounted for nearly one-third of unincorporated enterprise net income reported. For 70 per cent of the returns, the mean effective rate was less than 10 per cent. For the lowest tenth of returns, which almost coincides with the negative AGI group, the federal government participated in losses by way of tax rebate at an estimated average effective rate of 2 per cent.[7]

This rate, it will be noted, is lower than that shown for the $0-$2,000 income group. It reflects the fact that, for the years on which the estimates are based, the major part of the deduction for loss carryforward was reported on returns with negative income (after the deduction). While we obtain thus a picture of smooth progression of effective rates by income groups, including that with negative income, it should be stressed that this need not be so. The effective rate of loss absorption in the negative income group could be higher than that of some groups above it, if the loss carryovers were taken to returns with high enough incomes in the year the loss offset is made. The fact that this was not found could mean either that the returns with negative income for a given year are of those

---

[7] Estimated tax offset for net loss reported on returns with negative income was not included in the basic tax liability series for 1918–60, shown in Table 37, because data on loss carryovers are extremely fragmentary. Tax offset estimates were only ventured for some recent years and even these are very crude. For the method employed, see Appendix I.

Two somewhat arbitrary assumptions were made to obtain the estimates. First, it was assumed that all of the estimated net operating loss for a given year is either carried back or forward. In view of the average size of carryforwards, discussed in Chapter 4, this seemed to be the most reasonable assumption. However, as shown in Appendix I, by far the greater part of reported loss carryforwards are on returns with negative total income. Second, it is assumed that the distribution by income group of the net operating loss carryforward deduction is also applicable to the carryback portion, and that this size distribution holds for the years for which no such data are published.

NOTES TO TABLE 40

Source: Cols. 1, 4, 7, and 10: Statistics of Income. Cols. 2, 5, 8, and 11: Estimated from tax liability distribution in Statistics of Income.

[a] Business and partnership net profits minus net losses.

[b] Percentages based on unrounded figures.

[c] For 1939, returns with negative income had a tax liability of $32 million. No estimate of net operating loss carryover for that year is included.

[d] Figures shown are for sole proprietors only and the lower of the two figures is for the 85th to 90th percentile only.

[e] For 1952, the class limit was $20,000 instead of $25,000.

[f] Total tax liability in this table for 1952 and 1960 differs from that in Table 37 by the amount shown for the negative AGI group. For most years estimates of negative tax for that group were not possible.

persons whose income is modest even over long periods of time, or that the time which had elapsed between the loss year and the carryforward year was not long enough to allow for a recovery to "normal" positive income.[8]

As has been noted above, the effective rates computed with income reported on tax returns are overstated because of some downward bias in reported incomes. Part of this bias can be eliminated by raising the reported incomes, as shown in Table 40, by multiples based on the Audit Control estimates for 1948–49. Unincorporated enterprise net income for 1949, 1952, and 1960 was raised in each of the broad income groups shown by the same relative amount as was brought about by the 1948 Audit Control Program (Table 16). The results of these adjustments are shown in Table 41. After adjustment by the ACP findings, the effective rate of tax on unincorporated enterprise income reported on all returns was 10.6 per cent for 1949 and 14.3 per cent for 1960; before adjustment, it was 11.9 and 15.9 per cent, respectively. To the extent that the ACP estimates did not uncover all reporting errors these effective rates are still too high.

EFFECTIVE TAX RATE BY SOLE PROPRIETOR AND PARTNERSHIP PROFIT AND LOSS

Our data up to this point have been concerned with tax liabilities on business and professional net income without a separation of sole proprietors from partners, and without regard to the net profit and net loss components of income. The separation of returns with net profit from those with net loss is of interest because of the opposite effect that each has on tax liability; that is, because of the important part their tax treatment plays with respect to risk taking and enterprise.

The dividing line between proprietors who act alone and those with partners may not always be significant. For some purposes it makes little difference whether a shoe store is operated by two brothers or only one, or whether two physicians practice in partnership or separately. Yet, as already suggested in Chapter 1, a separate presentation is useful since it distinguishes, albeit roughly, smaller from larger enterprises, and those in which internally supplied labor, for given size firms, is of less importance, from those in which it is of greater importance. In addition, the farm sector has less weight among partnerships than among sole proprietors.

[8] Without information on the time-shape and amplitude of individual income fluctuations, it is not possible to go beyond the general and inconclusive comments regarding loss carryovers offered in the text.

TABLE 41

EFFECTIVE TAX RATES ON UNINCORPORATED ENTERPRISE NET INCOME
REPORTED ON TAX RETURNS ADJUSTED FOR INCOME-REPORTING
ERRORS, BY INCOME GROUPS, SELECTED YEARS, 1949-60

Adjusted Gross Income (thousand dollars)	Enterprise Net Income		Tax Liability Attributable to Enterprise Income	Effective Tax Rate	
	Reported (1)	Adjusted for Error (2)	(3)	Unadjusted (Col. 3 ÷ Col. 1) (4)	Adjusted (Col. 3 ÷ Col. 2) (5)
1949					
Under 7[a]	11,542	13,277	646	5.6	4.9
7 - 25	6,892	7,754	975	14.2	12.6
25 - 100	2,937	3,082	792	27.0	25.7
100 and over	406	415	179	43.9	43.0
Total	21,777	24,528	2,591	11.9	10.6
1952					
Under 7[a]	10,792	12,415	994	9.2	8.0
7 - 25	9,031	10,160	1,640	18.2	16.1
25 - 100	4,413	4,631	1,471	33.3	31.8
100 and over	518	529	268	51.7	50.6
Total	24,754	27,735	4,372	17.7	15.8
1960					
Under 7[a]	9,548	10,984	772	8.1	7.0
7 - 25	13,521	15,212	2,055	15.2	13.5
25 - 100	6,557	6,882	1,784	27.2	25.9
100 and over	411	420	169	41.0	40.2
Total	30,038	33,497	4,780	15.9	14.3

Source: Cols. 1, 3, and 4 are the same as in Table 40 except for broader
income groupings in this table. Col. 2 equals col. 1 multiplied by the
1948 ratio of our estimate of reported AGI for all sole proprietors plus
col. 4, Table 16, to our estimate of reported AGI for sole proprietors.

[a]Includes all nontaxable returns.

In Table 42, mean effective rates are presented for the reported net
profits and losses of sole proprietors and partners for nine recent years.
Partnership net profits and losses were taxed at a higher rate than those
of sole proprietors, reflecting the fact that the former were reported by
persons with higher incomes, on average, than the latter. The mean
effective rate of tax on net profits reported on taxable returns was 15.5 per
cent for sole proprietors and 20.5 per cent for partners. Net losses on
taxable returns were shared by the Treasury at a higher mean effective

TAX LIABILITY ON BUSINESS AND PROFESSIONS

TABLE 42

MEAN EFFECTIVE TAX RATE ON PROFITS AND LOSSES, BY
SOLE PROPRIETOR AND PARTNERSHIP, 1952-60

		Sole Proprietorship		Partnership	
		Net Profits	Net Losses	Net Profits	Net Losses
			TAXABLE RETURNS		
1952		16.5	21.3	22.1	25.5
1953		15.9	19.2	21.4	25.1
1954		15.1	17.5	20.0	23.2
1955		15.2	17.8	20.0	22.6
1956		15.3	18.3	20.3	23.4
1957		15.5	17.7	20.3	24.2
1958		15.1	16.6	20.1	23.6
1959		15.8	16.4	20.4	23.8
1960		15.4	16.7	19.8	21.3
Average		15.5	17.9	20.5	23.6
			ALL RETURNS		
1952		14.7	9.0	21.6	13.4
1953		14.2	8.4	21.0	12.3
1954		12.5	7.7	19.0	11.6
1955		12.8	8.6	19.0	11.5
1956		13.1	8.9	19.4	12.5
1957		13.5	8.5	19.5	12.2
1958		13.1	8.1	19.2	13.8
1959		14.0	7.9	19.6	13.6
1960		13.6	8.3	19.0	11.0
Average		13.5	8.4	19.7	12.4

Source: See Appendix H.

rate than net profits: at 18 per cent for sole proprietors and 24 per cent for partners. This is, of course, not the result of any deliberate bias in the tax law in favor of losses, but rather the result of the income-size distribution among taxable proprietors with losses as compared to those with profits. In the taxpaying group, those with unincorporated enterprise losses appear, on average, to have higher incomes than those with net profits.

However, when we compare mean effective rates for net profits and net losses reported on all returns (taxable and nontaxable), the picture changes somewhat. The mean effective tax rate on net profits is only slightly lowered by the inclusion of nontaxable returns, but the effective

110

rate on losses is lowered considerably. For sole proprietors the mean rate on net profits is now 13.5 per cent; that on net losses 8 per cent. For partners the respective mean rates are 20 and 12 per cent. This is as one would expect: losses are of greater relative importance on nontaxable than on taxable returns.[9] Whereas all losses on taxable returns are in part absorbed by the government at the taxpayer's effective rate, those reported on nontaxable returns are shared only if the return would have been taxable without the loss, or if the taxpayer is able to offset his losses against taxable income through the carryback or carryforward provisions of the tax law. As we have seen in the preceding chapter this is not always the case.

The relation between the rate of tax at which the government shares net profits and that at which it shares net losses on all returns is no surprise. We would expect net profit to be shared at a higher rate than net losses since the former help to raise income and the latter to lower it. Yet on taxable returns the expected relationship between the effective rate on profits and losses does not prevail. Some reasons for this have been suggested in Chapter 3. Evidently we are encountering two somewhat distinct groups of proprietors.

On the one hand, there is a group with high average expected incomes from other sources (property, salary, etc.) who venture some of their capital in unincorporated enterprises. The conversion of some of their profitable enterprises into corporations, and the transformation of some of their net profits into long-term capital gains, may account in large part for the greater concentration of net losses than net profits on high income returns. And this is reflected in the higher average tax rate on net losses than on net profits reported on taxable returns. In addition, consumption expenditures, disguised for tax purposes as business losses (gentlemen's farms, gift shops, etc.) may play a part in causing a high effective rate of loss sharing. Such "hobby-losses" are positively related to income, first, because of the luxury character of the underlying expenditure, and second, because conversion of the hobby into a business

[9] For 1960, the distribution between taxable and nontaxable returns was as follows (in millions of dollars):

	Sole Proprietors	Partners
Net profit	23,959	9,757
taxable returns	21,099	9,367
nontaxable returns	2,860	390
Net loss	2,887	791
taxable returns	1,345	384
nontaxable returns	1,542	407

makes it cheaper the higher the rate of tax at which the "loss" is shared by the government.

The other group of proprietors may be characterized as the large body of self-employed businessmen, artisans, farmers, and professional persons. Except for the professional group, they are typically low- and middle-income persons whose business is their main source of income. Hence their losses may be frequently only in part, or insignificantly, offset against income from other sources (as could have been inferred from Table 34); they may be largely responsible for the net profit and loss distributions on all returns conforming to the expected pattern. Consequently, absorption of part of this group's loss through the tax system is much more problematical than for the first group, since such absorption largely depends on the possibility of carrying a loss back or forward in time.

Our findings thus far may be summarized as follows. For the aggregate of net profits reported in the 1952–60 period, the federal government's participation has been about 13.5 per cent for sole proprietors and 20 per cent for partners; for net losses, it has assumed an 8 per cent share for sole proprietors and a 12 per cent share for partners. These percentages simply tell us what fraction of total reported unincorporated enterprise income was actually paid in taxes. They are of course the result of a variety of interacting factors, such as the income distribution among those reporting business and professional income and the large number of adjustments that a person can make to a complex tax system. As we have seen, effective rates vary considerably by income groups: from 8 per cent for the $3,000–$5,000 group, to 25 per cent for the $25,000–$50,000 group. This range comprises $26 billion of the total of $30 billion business and professional net income reported for 1960 (Table 40).

The data presented above cover a rather heterogeneous group of proprietors. In particular, the inclusion of persons for whom unincorporated enterprise is only a secondary or minor source of income may affect the mean rates presented. Furthermore, the inclusion of farm income must have lowered the mean rates. The importance of both factors is appraised in the following section.

EFFECTIVE RATE FOR SOLE PROPRIETORS WITH VARYING PROPORTIONS OF
INCOME FROM SOLE PROPRIETORSHIP

One difficulty in working with tax return data is that of obtaining a precise separation of individuals for whom proprietorship in an enterprise is the major occupation and source of income and those for whom it is a secondary occupation and source. Ideally, one might wish to follow the practice of classifying persons as "active proprietors of unincorporated enterprises" if they devote the major portion of their time to the business.[10] While this procedure is not feasible with presently available information, we can nevertheless approximate a separation by major and minor source of income on the basis of available cross tabulations of return frequencies by size of enterprise net profit and by size of total income.

Table 43 shows the frequency of returns with net profit from sole proprietorship for 1960 by size of income and by net-profit-to-total-income percentage bands. The frequency of returns with net profit less than 10 per cent, 10 to 25 per cent, 25 to 50 per cent, and more than 50 per cent of income are shown by income groups.

We find that of the 6.8 million returns covered by the table, 11 per cent reported net profits accounting for less than one-tenth of their total incomes. This represents an upper, though somewhat arbitrary, limit on the relative frequency of returns of "moonlighters"—persons who, in addition to their regular employment, perform odd jobs on their own account. It represents an upper limit because returns of persons who are full-time entrepreneurs, but have a secondary source of income (say stocks and bonds), might also show up in this group in a year of adversity.[11] Over the income range $0–$100,000, the frequency of returns with net profits less than one-tenth of income varies from 3 to 18 per cent of the total in the group. Above that level, the relative frequency rises sharply, suggesting that there are indeed few persons above the $100,000 level whose primary source of income is ordinary (as opposed, for example, to capital gains) income from unincorporated enterprise. The frequency of returns with net profits larger than 10 per cent of income could only be obtained for the incomes up to $200,000; this, however, includes most of such returns. For 10 per cent of the returns with net profits, the latter were greater than 10 but less than 25 per cent of adjusted gross income. The frequency of returns with net profit less than one-fourth of income varied from 8 per cent for the $0–$2,000 group to 51 per cent for the $100,000–$200,000 group.

---

[10] See Department of Commerce, *U.S. Income and Output*, Table VI-16.

[11] On the other hand, some persons whose enterprise is a secondary source may show up in the group deriving the major portion of their income from enterprise, in a year in which the primary source has suffered. This is not as likely as the first case because income from unincorporated business fluctuates with greater amplitude than most other functional components. See Irwin Friend and Irving Kravis, "Entrepreneurial Income, Saving and Investment," *American Economic Review*, June 1957, p. 270.

TABLE 43

ESTIMATED PERCENTAGE OF RETURNS ON WHICH REPORTED SOLE PROPRIETORSHIP NET PROFIT IS
LESS THAN, OR EXCEEDS, STATED PERCENTAGE OF INCOME, BY INCOME GROUPS, 1960

AGI Group (thousand dollars)	Frequency of Returns with Sole Proprietor-ship Net Profit (in thousands) (1)	Percentage of Returns with Net Profit			
		Less Than 10 Per Cent of AGI (2)	Between 10 and 25 Per Cent of AGI (3)	Between 25 and 50 Per Cent of AGI (4)	More Than 50 Per Cent of AGI (5)
Negative AGI	16.3				
0 – 2	1,854.4	2.9	5.4	11.1	80.5
2 – 3	908.2	5.5	8.9	12.9	72.7
3 – 5	1,477.8	11.2	11.5	12.8	64.5
5 – 10	1,719.2	21.0	14.4	16.2	48.3
10 – 25	705.1	14.8	10.0	14.9	60.3
25 – 50	125.1	10.7	8.3	15.9	65.0
50 – 100	22.6	18.3	9.6	18.3	53.8
100 – 200	2.3	36.3	14.4	13.2	36.1
200 – 500	.4	63.4	n.a.	n.a.	n.a.
500 and over	.1	87.5	n.a.	n.a.	n.a.
Total[a]	6,815.1	11.1	n.a.	n.a.	n.a.
Partial total (0–200)	6,814.6	11.1	10.0	13.5	65.4

Source: For detailed frequencies and method of estimation, see Appendix F.

[a]Excluding negative AGI.

Of particular interest is the frequency of returns on which sole proprietor net profits constitute more than half of reported total income. Close to three-fourths in the $2,000–$3,000 group, and over one-third in the $100,000–$200,000 group, derived more than half their income from sole proprietorship. Thus it appears that for well over one-half of the returns with net profit from this source, this is the major source of income, and this holds true for every income group shown in the $0–$100,000 span. Nevertheless, the number of returns showing less than half of income from sole proprietorship is large, indicating that many engage in business "on the side," or are in a transitional stage. But this group accounts for only 14 per cent of reported net profits. Those who derive less than 10 per cent of income from that source account for only an estimated 1 per cent of reported net profits (Table 42).

The information presented in Tables 43 and 44 enables us to show the ratio of net profit to total income for a particular slice of sole proprietors. Previously we have shown this ratio for all sole proprietors with net profit (Table 22). In Table 45 it is shown for those sole proprietors with estimated net profit exceeding 50 per cent of reported income, as well as for all sole proprietors reporting net profit. We find that for all proprietors in the income range $0–$200,000, net profits were slightly below two-thirds of their total income. But for the group more than half of whose income was sole proprietor net profit in 1960, the latter accounted for 91 per cent of total income: 96 per cent in the $0–$2,000 group and 88 per cent in the $100,000–$200,000 group. Thus, over the income range discussed, a very large amount of net profits—86 per cent of the total—was reported on returns for which they constituted, on average, 91 per cent of total income. For this significant group, the loss carryover provisions discussed earlier are of great importance; because this group has relatively small amounts of other income, its business losses can with corresponding ease result in negative total income.

Since sole proprietors whose net profits constitute more than half of their income account for nearly nine-tenths of the net profits reported, the average effective rates presented for all returns in Table 42 are not likely to be greatly modified when we omit those proprietors whose enterprise appears to be a secondary source of income. Average effective rates for two percentage bands, based on the estimates shown in Table 44, were computed. When we eliminate returns whose net profits are less than 10 per cent of total income reported for 1958 and 1960, the average effective rate of tax remains the same as for all net profits (Table 46). With the elimination of all net profits which constitute less

TABLE 44

ESTIMATED NET PROFIT REPORTED ON RETURNS WITH SOLE PROPRIETORSHIP NET PROFIT LESS THAN, OR EXCEEDING, STATED PERCENTAGE OF INCOME, BY INCOME GROUPS, 1960

AGI Group (thousand dollars)	Sole Proprietorship Net Profit (million dollars) (1)	Percentage of Sole Proprietorship Net Profit on Returns with Net Profit			
		Less Than 10 Per Cent of AGI (2)	Between 10 and 25 Per Cent of AGI (3)	Between 25 and 50 Per Cent of AGI (4)	More Than 50 Per Cent of AGI (5)
Negative AGI	53.0				
0 – 2	1,625.3	.2	1.5	5.6	92.6
2 – 3	1,635.1	.4	2.1	6.7	90.8
3 – 5	3,777.3	.8	2.7	7.7	88.7
5 – 10	6,383.2	1.9	3.4	14.6	80.0
10 – 25	6,548.6	1.0	2.7	8.5	87.8
25 – 50	2,910.7	.7	2.6	9.3	87.3
50 – 100	877.0	1.3	3.0	14.1	81.5
100 – 200	118.7	3.2	5.6	12.6	78.6
200 – 500	22.2	13.1	n.a.	n.a.	n.a.
500 and over	7.8	35.6	n.a.	n.a.	n.a.
Total[a]	23,905.9	1.1	n.a.	n.a.	n.a.
Partial total (0–200)	23,876.0	1.1	2.8	10.0	86.1

Source: Amounts of net profit shown in Appendix Table F-2.

[a] Excluding negative AGI.

116

TABLE 45

ESTIMATED NET PROFIT AND AGI REPORTED ON RETURNS FOR WHICH NET PROFIT FROM SOLE
PROPRIETORSHIP WAS OVER 50 PER CENT OF AGI, BY INCOME GROUPS, 1960

Adjusted Gross Income (thousand dollars)	Returns with Net Profit Over 50 Per Cent of AGI			All Returns with Net Profit		
	Net Profit (1)	AGI (2)	Col.1 ÷ Col. 2 (3)	Net Profit (4)	AGI (5)	Col. 4 ÷ Col. 5 (6)
0 – 2	1,506	1,576	95.5	1,625	1,987	81.8
2 – 3	1,484	1,643	90.3	1,635	2,264	72.2
3 – 5	3,352	3,735	89.7	3,777	5,839	64.7
5 – 10	5,104	5,842	87.4	6,383	11,983	53.3
10 – 25	5,752	6,134	93.8	6,550	10,135	64.6
25 – 50	2,541	2,714	93.6	2,911	4,173	69.8
50 – 100	715	798	89.6	876	1,486	59.0
100 – 200	93	107	87.6	119	304	39.1
Total	20,546	22,548	91.1	23,876	38,170	62.6

Source: Col. 1: Table F-2.
Col. 2: Frequencies of returns with net profits more than 50 per cent of AGI,
shown by broad AGI classes in Table F-1, multiplied by average AGI
for narrow income classes as explained in Appendix G.
Cols. 4 and 5: Table G-1.

117

TAX LIABILITY ON BUSINESS AND PROFESSIONS

TABLE 46

ESTIMATED EFFECTIVE PROFIT TAX RATE OF RETURNS WITH SOLE
PROPRIETORSHIP PROFIT GREATER THAN 10 PER CENT, AND
GREATER THAN 50 PER CENT, OF AGI, 1958 AND 1960

	Effective Tax Rate on All Returns with Positive Income	Effective Tax Rate on Returns with Net Profit Greater Than	
		10 Per Cent of AGI	50 Per Cent of AGI
Weighted by amounts of net profit			
1958	13.1	13.1	12.9
1960	13.6	13.6	13.5
Weighted by frequencies			
1958	7.2	7.0	6.6
1960	7.7	7.3	6.9

Source: See Appendix F, Tables F-3 and F-4.

than half of income reported, the average effective rate drops from 13.6 to 13.5 per cent for 1960—only a very small change. It is thus evident that our findings concerning average effective rates of tax are only negligibly altered when we restrict ourselves to the returns of persons whose major source of income appears to be sole proprietorship.[12] All the mean effective rates presented thus far were computed by dividing total tax liability by total net profits of a group of proprietors. As a result, the amount of net profit reported on a return automatically serves as its weight. The mean affective rates thus obtained are therefore representative of business and professional *income,* but not necessarily of proprietors. If each of the latter is given equal weight, so that the weighting is by frequencies rather than amount of net profit, the resulting mean effective rates are much lower than before (7.7 per cent for all

[12] The above test, it should be noted, is only based on the net profits of sole proprietors. They were the major, but of course not the only recipients of unincorporated enterprise income. A breakdown for 1960 is as follows (in million dollars):

Sole proprietor
net profits   23,959
net losses   2,887
Partnership
net profits   9,757
net losses   791

118

TABLE 47

ESTIMATED EFFECTIVE TAX RATE ON NET INCOME FROM SOLE
PROPRIETORSHIP, BY FARMS, PROFESSIONS, AND BUSINESS, 1960

	Net Income (net profit less loss) (1)	Computed Tax Liability (2)	Mean Effective Rate Col. 2 ÷ Col. 1 (3)
All sole proprietorship	21,067	3,014	14.3
Farms	2,998	263	8.8
Professions[a]	5,257	1,048	19.9
Business	12,812	1,703	13.3

Source: Col. 1: *Statistics of Income, U.S. Business Tax Returns,*
1960-61, Table 6.
Cols. 2 and 3: Computed by using mean effective rates for all
returns in given income groups as shown in Table F-3
and explained in Appendix H.

[a]Includes medical, legal, educational, and engineering professional
practitioners. All other services are included in the "business" category.

sole proprietors with net profit, instead of 13.6 per cent; see Table 46).
The merits of each weighting scheme are discussed at greater length
below.

EFFECTIVE RATE FOR SOLE PROPRIETORS, BY INDUSTRIAL GROUPINGS

Computations to obtain the effective rates for sole proprietors by three
broad industrial groupings were made on the basis of data published for
the first time for 1960.[13] Sole proprietor net income for various industrial classifications has not heretofore been broken down by size of total
income (AGI) of proprietors. However, the effective rates for industry
groups now available differ conceptually in one respect from the effective rates presented in Table 46: instead of rates for net profits, they are
for net profits less net losses, or what we have termed net income.

The $21.1 billion net income from sole proprietorship is divided in
Table 47 between farm, professional, and business proprietors. The mean
effective rate for all industrial groups was 14.3 per cent for 1960.[14]
That for the business category, which comprises the majority of sole

[13] U.S. Treasury Department, *U.S. Business Tax Returns, Statistics of Income, 1960-61,* Table 6.
[14] Because this is a composite effective rate on net profits and net losses combined, it is
paradoxically higher than the effective rate on sole proprietor net profits (13.6 per cent) and
net losses (8.3 per cent) separately (Table 42). The explanation is found in the concentration
of net losses at low income levels (when the distribution for all tax returns is used). Since net
losses are a negative item they cancel out some net profits, the latter similarly concentrated
at low income levels. The remainder, after net losses have been offset against net profits, is
therefore more concentrated on high-income returns than before and the result is a higher
mean effective rate than that on net profits before net losses were subtracted.

119

proprietors and well over half the net income reported, was 13.3 per cent. But the farm and professional groups departed significantly from the over-all average. For the former, the computed mean effective rate was only 8.8 per cent; for the latter, almost 20 per cent. Evidently, the use of a mean rate for all sole proprietorship income leads to significant overstatement of the tax rate on farmers and understatement of independent professional practitioners.

These mean effective rates present an *ex post* picture for reported aggregates. The *ex ante* tax treatment of a taxpayer's profit and loss is of course a different matter. If a taxpayer has a given income from other sources, say rentals and interest, an entrepreneurial venture confronts him with a given tax rate on the expected profit, and an equal, or smaller,[15] negative tax rate on the expected loss. The existence of a progressive rate schedule produces a "bias" whereby an anticipated gain is likely to be taxed at a higher rate than an anticipated loss. This effect is clearly deducible from the rate schedule itself and requires no statistical evidence. The figures in Table 42 neither confirm nor deny the *ex ante* bias against losses as compared with profits, but summarize the results *ex post*. For example, if high-income proprietors engage in enterprises more risky than those of low-income proprietors, the mean effective rate on total net losses can be as high, or higher, than on total net profits.

Marginal Tax Rate by Sole Proprietor and Partnership Profit and Loss

The effective rate at which the federal government has absorbed total reported profits and losses does not indicate how it absorbs profit or loss at the margin. In a private enterprise economy the question of how government affects additional enterprise or, more precisely, the results of additional entrepreneurial effort, is of particular interest. What fraction of a small change in profit or loss has been absorbed by federal income tax? The mean marginal tax rate on a 1 per cent change in reported net profits and losses has been computed for the years 1952–60 (Table 48).

If all net profits and net losses reported on taxable returns in 1960 were to change by 1 per cent, 31 per cent of the change in net profits,

---

[15] If he has an "assured" taxable income of $34,000 from other sources and is married, a business net profit of $2,000 will be subject to a marginal rate of 50 per cent at 1963 rates; but a net loss of the same amount will be shared at the same marginal rate because of the width of the tax bracket at that taxable income level. If the same taxable income were $30,000 without entrepreneurial effort, the same net profit would still be shared at 50 per cent, but the loss only at 47 per cent.

TABLE 48

MEAN MARGINAL TAX RATE ON PROFITS AND LOSSES, BY
SOLE PROPRIETOR AND PARTNERSHIP, 1952-60

| | AVERAGE MARGINAL TAX RATE ON 1 PER CENT CHANGE IN PROFIT OR LOSS | | | |
| | Sole Proprietorship | | Partnership | |
	Net Profits	Net Losses	Net Profits	Net Losses
	TAXABLE RETURNS			
1952	32.4	40.2	47.7	44.6
1953	31.3	36.9	40.8	45.8
1954	29.3	33.8	38.0	44.5
1955	29.3	34.2	37.6	41.9
1956	29.9	35.1	38.8	44.0
1957	30.4	34.1	39.2	45.4
1958	29.9	32.7	39.3	45.2
1959	31.3	32.6	40.2	46.5
1960	30.9	33.3	39.5	42.3
Average	30.5	34.8	40.1	44.5
	ALL RETURNS			
1952	28.9	17.1	40.8	24.8
1953	28.0	16.3	39.9	22.8
1954	24.2	15.0	36.1	22.4
1955	24.6	16.6	35.8	21.6
1956	25.6	17.3	37.2	23.6
1957	26.4	16.5	37.6	22.9
1958	26.0	16.0	37.6	26.5
1959	27.6	15.6	38.6	26.5
1960	27.2	16.7	37.9	22.0
Average	26.5	16.3	37.9	23.7

Source: See Appendix H.

and 33 per cent of the change in net losses of sole proprietors would be shared by the federal government. For partners the respective percentages were found to be 39 and 42 per cent. These marginal rates apply to taxpayers only. When nontaxable returns are included in the computation, 27 per cent of a small increase in net profits and 17 per cent of a small increase in net loss of sole proprietors is shared by the government; for partners the percentages are 38 and 22 per cent. The opposite pattern of profit and loss sharing by the government of taxable-return data and all-return data is, of course, explained by the same factors as the similar pattern for mean effective rates shown in Table 42 and discussed at length above. The distribution of net losses on taxable returns is slanted toward the high-income groups, whereas when net losses reported on nontaxable returns are included, the distribution shifts sharply downward.

In computing mean marginal tax rates with a 1 per cent change in profit or loss, we in effect assume a constant Lorenz curve; that is, a constant relative size distribution of unincorporated enterprise income. This amounts to saying that when net profits (losses) change, they change on average by the same relative amount regardless of size. Hence, the weights attached to the marginal tax rates found for each income group are given by the amount of unincorporated enterprise income in each group. This method of computing the mean marginal rate of tax is somewhat in contrast to the usual comparisons of marginal rates on an "additional dollar" of income. Had the latter method been used, the marginal rate for each return would have been given the same weight in computing an average. This implies that when aggregate income

TABLE 49

AMOUNTS OF UNINCORPORATED ENTERPRISE NET PROFIT AND NET LOSS AND
MARGINAL TAX RATE, BY INCOME GROUPS, 1957 AND 1960
(dollars in millions)

Adjusted Gross Income (thousand dollars)	1957			1960		
	Net Profits	Net Losses	Weighted Average Marginal Tax Rate for Group[a]	Net Profits	Net Losses	Weighted Average Marginal Tax Rate for Group[a]
Negative AGI	90	1,052	3.8	84	1,321	3.7
0 - 2	2,054	351	4.9	1,805	355	5.9
2 - 3	2,093	181	11.5	1,849	265	11.9
3 - 5	4,822	286	16.7	4,507	411	16.3
5 - 10	7,756	355	21.1	8,306	540	21.1
10 - 25	8,852	195	31.5	9,734	324	31.2
25 - 50	4,330	122	54.1	4,934	150	53.3
50 - 100	1,853	109	66.7	1,894	122	66.6
100 - 500	601	107	80.1	571	159	80.0
500 and over	38	35	86.0	33	34	88.6
Total	32,490	2,791	28.9	33,716	3,679	31.7

Source: See Appendix H.

[a]The marginal rates shown are derived from average marginal rates for all tax returns in a distribution using narrower income class intervals than those shown above. In weighting the marginal rates for the smaller income groups by the amount of business and professional income in those groups, the rates shown for the larger groupings of the table depart somewhat from the rates for all tax returns.

changes, each taxpayer's income changes by the same absolute amount. Actually, the profits and losses of high-income taxpayers tend to change by larger absolute amounts than those of low-income taxpayers. Of course, it might be argued that marginal rates are of interest because of their effect on enterprise motivations and incentives; and that in the computation of a summary measure, such as an average, equal weight should therefore be given to each return regardless of the amount of enterprise income it represents. In effect this would call for giving each marginal rate a weight of one, instead of using multiple weights proportional to the amount of net profit or net loss reported. In Table 48 the latter method was used on the assumption that size of net profit (loss) is a rough proxy of the scope of enterprise. It has the clear advantage of attaching less weight to part-time and "tax-return" entrepreneurs and more to those whose enterprise is the major source of their income.

For the sake of completeness, however, average marginal rates, with each taxpayer given a weight of one, are presented below, alongside the rates weighted by size of profit or loss, for three years:

	Sole Proprietors		Partners	
	Net Profits	Net Losses	Net Profits	Net Losses
Mean marginal rate for $1 change in profit or loss per taxpayer				
1957	14.8	14.7	22.7	20.9
1959	15.5	15.2	23.2	22.0
1960	15.5	14.9	23.4	21.8
Mean marginal rate for 1% change in profits and losses				
1957	26.4	16.5	37.6	22.9
1959	27.6	15.6	38.6	26.5
1960	27.2	16.7	37.9	22.0

The summary measures of marginal rates applicable to net profits and losses of course hide considerable variation. Mean marginal rates by income groups are shown in Table 49. The rate shown for each group is an average of rates weighted by the combined dollar amounts of net profits and net losses.[16] Over one-fifth of reported net profits and 13 per cent of net losses were on returns subject to marginal rates greater than 50 per cent.

[16] Because the marginal rates shown in Table 49 are weighted averages obtained from an original distribution with narrower income class intervals, the rates for net profits and net losses in each income group if separately computed would actually not be the same. This is because the distribution of net profits and net losses within each of the income groups shown in the table is not the same.

Significance of Annual Mean Tax Rates for
Aggregate Net Profits and Losses

The mean effective and marginal rates presented in the preceding sections describe the actual aggregate tax experience for a year. They do not describe the tax rates a person faces at a moment of time; these can of course be obtained simply from the rate schedule, once a person's income is known. But the rates at which the actual net profits and net losses of a particular taxpayer are shared by government over time are a function of the variability of his total income. If that income is very high when his business is successful (relative to his income when his business results in loss), his profits will be shared at a much higher rate than his losses. If, for some peculiar reason, his total income is low when his business is prosperous, and high when he has a business loss, his profits will be shared by the Treasury at a lower rate than his losses. While the latter may actually be the case for some high-income taxpayers—as suggested by mean effective and mean marginal rates for taxable returns shown in Tables 42 and 48—it does not appear to be the case for the aggregate of reported net profits and net losses.

The variability of unincorporated enterprise income—that is, its ups and downs for a given taxpayer—has an effect on tax liability. The best way to determine this effect is to trace the income and tax experience of a group of identical taxpayers over a period of time. In the absence of information enabling us to do this, the annual cross-section data may give us some preliminary and rough idea. If we had only an annual distribution of net profits, and not also one of net losses, little could be learned about how tax rates vary with variations in unincorporated enterprise income; we would have no way of identifying those whose business or professional income appears temporarily low or temporarily high.

When sole proprietors and partners are each divided into two groups: those with net profits and those with net losses, we have a ready-made, though not ideal, division between those whose enterprise in a given year is in the least favorable part of its income experience and all others. Unfortunately, "all others," that is, those with net profits, is not a category symmetrical with the net loss group. It includes not only those who are in the most favorable phase of their business experience but also some who are in their least favorable phase. As explained in the previous chapter, the tax accounting concept of net profit is so inclusive that what appears at times as a net profit on the tax return would be a net loss in the economic sense. Thus, the business income variability of some proprietors is not caught by the net profit–net loss breakdown. Some proprietors may simply experience high net profits in some years and very low net profits in others without crossing the line from net profits to net loss. Their business income variability, therefore, remains hidden. Variability of unincorporated enterprise income on tax returns may also be understated because on high-income returns there appears to be a bias in favor of reporting losses under sole proprietorship or partnership and against reporting profits in that form (see Chapter 3). How this bias affects mean marginal rates cannot be determined on a priori grounds, for the long-term capital gains rate is lower than the mean marginal rate on net profits of sole proprietors, and the corporate rate on the first $25,000 of net income is less than the mean marginal rate for partners (Table 48). The mean effective rates, however, being lower than the maximum rate on long-term capital gains, tend to be understated (Table 42).

If it were not for these difficulties, the mean rates on net profit and net loss would give us an approximation of the difference in mean rates between those whose enterprises are in a phase above their long-term average and those below it.[17] As it is, the net loss category gives us some of the latter, but we have no adequate counterpart in the mean rates on reported net profits. Without adjustments, we would have the following range between mean rates on sole proprietorships with adverse income experience and those with favorable business experience:

	Net Profits	Net Losses	Difference Between Net Profits and Net Losses
Mean Marginal Rates (per cent)			
1959	27.6	15.6	12.0
1960	27.2	16.7	10.5
1952–60 average	26.5	16.3	10.2
Mean Effective Rates (per cent)			
1959	14.0	7.9	6.1
1960	13.6	8.3	5.3
1952–60 average	13.5	8.4	5.1

[17] The concept of average income in this instance refers to a person's actual, experienced average, since for the moment we are interested in the actual change in tax rates that accompanies a change in enterprise income. It is thus related to, though not the same as, Friedman's "permanent" income which "is to be interpreted as reflecting the effect of those factors that the unit regards as determining its capital value or wealth." See Milton Friedman, *A Theory of the Consumption Function,* Princeton University Press for NBER, 1957, p. 21.

Since the mean rates on net profits reflect also the experience of some enterprises which are in the below-average income phase, the difference shown between mean rates on profits and those on losses may understate the actual spread in rates resulting from profit variability.[18] We may gain perspective as to the possible extent of the bias by making the extreme assumption that every person reporting net loss, which suggests that the enterprise is in an unfavorable transitory state, will eventually file a return showing net profit and an income that will place him in the group of proprietors with the highest tax rates. This amounts to selecting from the group of proprietors reporting net profits, that number with the highest total incomes equal to those reporting net loss. For instance, there were 1.8 million sole proprietor returns reporting net loss for 1960. When they recover from this temporary state, we now assume, they rise to the position held by the 1.8 million net profit returns showing the highest incomes for 1960. Under these extreme assumptions the following mean tax rates are obtained:

	On Net Profits of Returns with Highest Income (1)	On Net Losses (2)	Col. 1 Minus Col. 2 (3)
Mean marginal rates			
1959	36.7	15.6	21.1
1960	35.8	16.7	19.1
Mean effective rates			
1959	18.9	7.9	11.0
1960	18.2	8.3	9.9

Thus, in the ranges within which unincorporated enterprise income is observed to vary, mean tax rates appear to rise by somewhat more than one-half, if simple variation from net loss to net profits is considered. If variation from observed net losses to net profits on high-income returns is assumed, mean tax rates are seen to more than double between lowest and highest income experience.

Obviously the data presented here give only the most tentative evidence on the extent of tax rate variation associated with changing business fortunes. More accurate and detailed data are needed for in-

[18] Because these may also be the enterprises whose income variability is small, inclusion of some of their net "profits" and tax in the group experiencing below-average income might narrow the gap in mean rates between the group with favorable and the group with unfavorable income experience. The direction of the bias in our data is thus not clear.

formed discussion of the possible need for income averaging for tax purposes. Even if the data cited in this section give a correct picture of the variation in rates with variation in unincorporated enterprise income, nothing has been said about the time interval over which this occurs. Again, to consider possible proposals for income averaging, we require information of time periods as well as the amplitude of income fluctuations.

APPENDIXES

APPENDIX A

Tabulation of Sole Proprietor and Partnership Income by Size of Income and Type of Industry: Explanation of Difference

THE statistics for unincorporated business and professional income used in this study are in large part based on two Treasury Department tabulations. 1. The annual tabulations, by size of adjusted gross income, and by size of net profit and loss from sole proprietorship and partnership, as reported on individual returns in *Statistics of Income*. 2. The special tabulations by industry classifications of net profit and loss, presented for recent years in *Statistics of Income, U.S. Business Tax Returns*.

Conceptually, the totals for net profit and net loss obtained from the two types of tabulations should be identical. However, for a number of practical reasons the actual figures have differed, though in most years by only small amounts and only once by more than 5 per cent (Table A-1).

The annual tabulations by size of adjusted gross income are based on the information found on the individual tax return (1040) where the taxpayer summarizes the total amounts of income received from various sources, such as employment, sole proprietorship, partnership, dividends, etc. In the income-size tabulations, the source of the statistics is thus the same for both sole proprietor and partnership profit or loss, i.e., the individual return, 1040.

For the tabulations by type of industry, business tax returns rather than individual tax returns furnished the source. For sole proprietors' profit or loss this merely means that the separate business or farm schedule (schedule C or F, respectively) of the individual return was used as the source. Since the net profit (or loss) arrived at in the business schedule is subsequently transferred to the face of the return to form part of adjusted gross income, summations of net profit and loss based on the two sources should agree, barring copying errors. However, discrepancies do arise, as is evident in Table A-1. Differences in sampling and tabulating procedures employed for the two types of tabulations appear to explain most of the discrepancies.

The reasons for the discrepancies in partnership profits and losses go further than mere differences in sampling and tabulating procedures. The source for the industrial tabulations is the information return (1065) filed by the partnership, whereas the individual return serves as the source for the income-size tabulations. Thus, in the one instance the business itself is the reporting unit, and its profit or loss is tabulated,

131

TABLE A-1

UNINCORPORATED ENTERPRISE INCOME REPORTED ON TAX RETURNS, BY INCOME-SIZE AND INDUSTRIAL TABULATIONS, 1939-60
(dollars in millions)

	Sole Proprietors		Partnerships		Total		Ratio of Industrial Tabulations to Income-Size Tabulations		
	Industrial Tabulation (1)	Income-Size Tabulation (2)	Industrial Tabulation (3)	Income-Size Tabulation (4)	Industrial Tabulation (5)	Income-Size Tabulation (6)	Col. 1 ÷ Col. 2 (7)	Col. 3 ÷ Col. 4 (8)	Col. 5 ÷ Col. 6 (9)
1939	2,478	2,480	1,564	1,194	4,042	3,674	1.00	1.31	1.10
1941	6,226	6,226		2,230		8,455	1.00		
1943	10,668	10,713		5,092		15,805	1.00		
1945	12,069	11,943	6,768	7,060	18,837	19,003	1.01	0.96	0.99
1947	15,105	15,342	7,679	7,953	22,783	23,295	0.98	0.97	0.99
1949	14,459	14,231		7,474		21,705	1.02		
1951	16,552	16,466		8,412		24,878	1.01		
1953	17,007	16,664	8,394	8,287	25,402	24,951	1.02	1.01	1.02
1955	17,588	18,430		9,024		27,454	0.95		
1956	a	21,285	a	8,852	a	30,137			
1957	20,220	20,339	9,761[b]	9,359	29,981	29,698	0.99	1.04	1.01
1958	20,778	20,674	9,558[b]	9,232	30,337	29,906	1.01	1.04	1.01
1959	21,517	21,431	9,869	9,563	31,386	30,995	1.00	1.03	1.01
1960	21,067	21,072	9,386	8,966	30,453	30,038	1.00	1.05	1.01

Source: Statistics of Income.

[a] For 1956, industrial tabulations are only available for sole proprietors and partnerships excluding agriculture.

[b] Partly estimated. For method, see notes to Table B-1 for lines 10 to 18.

whereas in the other, the individual partner is the reporting unit and his *share* in the partnership net profit or loss is tabulated. Again, purely conceptually, the individual shares should add up to the total reported by the partnerships on information returns. But here, aside from the expected sampling variations, there are two additional reasons for discrepancies. 1. Although a partnership is required to file an information return, an individual partner's distributive share may not be reported if his income from all sources is below the filing requirement value. This explains why, for 1939, when personal exemptions were still at prewar levels, total partnership net income tabulated from partnership information returns exceeded the total tabulated from individual returns by 31 per cent.

2. Probably even more significant for recent years is the possible difference in accounting periods of individuals and partnerships. For individual partners who report on a calendar-year basis (as most do), the partnership fiscal year must end between July 1 and December 31 in order that our statistics agree. This is because individuals are required to include their share of partnership ordinary income (loss) in the taxable year in which the partnership fiscal year ends; thus, an individual should have included in his 1961 adjusted gross income his share in the ordinary income of a partnership whose fiscal year ended in 1961. But if the partnership fiscal year had ended on May 31, 1961, the net income of the partnership would be included in our 1960 partnership industrial distribution. The 1960 partnership income figures are for accounting periods ending July 1960-June 1961.[1] The figures on individual returns for income from partnership for 1960 include any share in income from partnership whose fiscal year ends in 1960.[2] This causes the individual-return partnership figures to lag slightly behind those from the industrial tabulation.

[1] The decision to designate these tabulations as 1960 figures rests on data showing that most partnerships have accounting periods ending in the second half of the calendar year. Of 949,396 partnership returns filed between July 1959 and June 1960, as many as 786,188 had accounting periods ending before the end of 1959 (see U.S. Treasury Department, *U.S. Business Tax Returns, 1959–60*, p. 88).

[2] Assuming individuals are on a calendar year basis.

APPENDIX B

Derivation of the Estimates for Farm and Nonfarm Unincorporated Enterprise Income

Tax return data for an industrial breakdown of unincorporated enterprise, as presented in summary form in Table 8, are available at two-year intervals back to 1939. In some years the data are available only for sole proprietors, while for other years, notably 1939, 1945, 1947, 1953, and 1957–60, they are available for both sole proprietors and partnerships. The totals in line 1 of Table 8 differ slightly from the comparable totals in Table 6, because the latter are from the annual income-size tabulations for individuals, whereas the figures in Table 8 are from the less frequent tabulations of returns of sole proprietors and partnerships by type of industry. (For a detailed explanation of the difference between the two tabulations, see Appendix A.)

The figures from the industrial tabulations are shown in detail in Table B-1. Wherever possible the totals are broken down by returns with net profit and net loss, and within each of these classifications, by farm and nonfarm enterprises for sole proprietors and partnerships. For sole proprietors the data shown are, with the exception of 1956, as tabulated in *Statistics of Income*. For partnerships a considerable number of adjustments and interpolations were made. The figures for 1939, 1945, 1947, and 1953 are identical with those in the Treasury Department's special partnership tabulations. For 1941, 1943, 1949, and 1955, however, the partnership figures are those from the income-size tabulations for individuals, and the break between farm and nonfarm is as estimated by us. For 1956–60, the figures are again based on tabulated partnership statistics; but to preserve comparability with earlier years, the item "payments to partners," which became a deduction from ordinary partnership net income after 1954, had to be added back. For the four years 1955–58 "payments to partners" were not available by returns with net income and net loss, but for 1959 and 1960 such separate breakdowns were published. Detailed explanations are given in the notes to Table B-1.

Table B-2 shows the derivation of estimated total farm unincorporated business income from statistics published by the Agricultural Marketing Service (AMS) of the Agriculture Department. They are comparable to the reported amounts shown on line 20, Table B-1. Two variants of farm income estimates were developed: the first follows the letter of the tax law and does not treat taxes, interest, and depreciation on farm dwellings as a deductible expense; the second proceeds on the extreme assumption that all farmers deduct these items in computing taxable income.

134

APPENDIX B

TABLE B-1

NET INCOME AND NET LOSS FROM SOLE PROPRIETORSHIP AND PARTNERSHIP,
BY FARM AND NONFARM ENTERPRISES, AS REPORTED ON BUSINESS TAX
RETURNS, SELECTED YEARS 1930-60[a]
(million dollars)

	1939	1941	1943	1945	1947	1949	1951
Sole Proprietors							
1. Net profit	2,711	6,453	11,041	12,817	16,250	15,979	18,377
2. Farm	194	1,737	3,703	3,745	5,655	4,917	5,213
3. Nonfarm	2,516	4,715	7,338	9,072	10,595	11,062	13,165
4. Net loss	233	227	373	747	1,145	1,520	1,825
5. Farm	86	93	208	404	486	645	n.a.
6. Nonfarm	147	134	164	343	658	874	n.a.
7. Net profit minus net loss	2,478	6,226	10,668	12,069	15,105	14,459	16,552
8. Farm	108	1,645	3,495	3,341	5,168	4,272	n.a.
9. Nonfarm	2,370	4,581	7,174	8,729	9,936	10,187	n.a.
Partnership							
10. Ordinary net income[b]	1,649				6,935	8,008	
11. Farm	62				473	738	
12. Nonfarm	1,587				6,462	7,270	
13. Ordinary net loss	85				167	330	
14. Farm	9				29	47	
15. Nonfarm	76				139	283	
16. Net income minus net loss	1,564	2,230[c]	5,092[c]	6,768	7,679	7,474[c]	
17. Farm	53	214[c]	454[c]	444	691	555[c]	
18. Nonfarm	1,511	2,016[c]	4,638[c]	6,323	6,987	6,919[c]	
Unincorporated Enterprise							
19. Net income minus net loss (sum of lines 7 and 16)	4,042	8,456	15,761	18,837	22,784	21,933	n.a.
20. Farm (sum of lines 8 and 17)	161	1,859	3,949	3,785	5,859	4,827	n.a.
21. Nonfarm (sum of lines 9 and 18)	3,881	6,597	11,812	15,052	16,923	17,106	n.a.

Source   for Lines 1-9

1939-55: All figures are as tabulated in the corresponding annual Statistics of
Income for individuals.
1956: U.S. Treasury Department, Business Indicators, 1956-57. For that year no
figures for agriculture, forestry, and fisheries were tabulated. In the table
above only the farm component of agriculture, forestry, and fisheries, is included in farm income. All other components of agriculture, forestry, and
fisheries are in the nonfarm group. The published nonfarm figures were, therefore
raised slightly by using the 1957 ratio of hunting, trapping, forestry, and fishery
to total nonagricultural income. For instance, the published figure for net
profit less net loss was raised from $16,222 million to $16,425 million, or by
1.25 per cent.
1957-60: Statistics of Income, U.S. Business Tax Returns, 1957-58 and 1958-59.

135

APPENDIX B

TABLE B-1 (concluded)

	1953	1955	1956	1957	1958	1959	1960
Sole Proprietors							
1. Net profit	19,217	19,999		22,807	23,339	24,709	24,269
2. Farm	4,587	4,007		4,460	4,937	4,253	4,265
3. Nonfarm	14,630	15,992	17,530	18,347	18,402	20,455	20,004
4. Net loss	2,210	2,410		2,587	2,562	3,192	3,202
5. Farm	1,214	1,365		1,228	1,175	1,607	1,529
6. Nonfarm	996	1,046	1,078	1,359	1,387	1,585	1,673
7. Net profit minus net loss	17,007	17,588		20,220	20,778	21,517	21,067
8. Farm	3,374	2,642		3,233	3,763	2,647	2,737
9. Nonfarm	13,634	14,946	16,425	16,988	17,015	18,870	18,331
Partnership							
10. Ordinary net income [b]	9,329					10,483	10,113
11. Farm	571					681	664
12. Nonfarm	8,759					9,802	9,449
13. Ordinary net loss [b]	935					614	727
14. Farm	135					133	152
15. Nonfarm	800					481	576
16. Net income minus net loss	8,394	9,024[c]		9,761	9,558	9,869	9,386
17. Farm	436	343–528[c]		628	600	548	512
18. Nonfarm	7,958	8,681–8.496[c]	9,384	9,132	8,959	9,321	8,874
Unincorporated Enterprise							
19. Net income minus net loss (sum of lines 7 and 16)	25,401	26,612		29,981	30,337	31,386	30,453
20. Farm (sum of lines 8 and 17)	3,810	2,985–3,170		3,861	4,363	3,195	3,249
21. Nonfarm (sum of lines 9 and 18)	21,592	23,627–23,442	25,809	26,120	25,974	28,191	27,204

Source for Lines 10-18

1939, 1945, 1947, and 1953: As tabulated in special Statistics of Income supplements for partnership information returns for 1939 and 1953, and in Treasury Department press releases S-2253 and S-2645, respectively, for 1945 and 1947. 1941, 1943, 1949, and 1955: Partnership net income less net loss for these years was obtained from the income-size tabulations for individual returns (col. 4, Table A-1). This figure was then divided into farm and nonfarm components by assuming for 1941, 1943, and 1949 a ratio of farm partnership to farm sole proprietors' income of 0.13, approximately the same as in 1945, 1947, and 1953. The ratio was obtained as follows:

Farm Income

	Sole Proprietors (1)	Partnerships (2)	Col. 2 ÷ Col. 1 (3)
	(dollars in millions)		
1945	3,341	444	.13
1947	5,168	691	.13
1953	3,374	436	.13
1957	3,233	628	.19
1958	3,763	600	.16
1959	2,647	548	.21
1960	2,737	512	.19

136

APPENDIX B

NOTES TO TABLE B-1 (continued)

A sharp rise in farm partnership income is evident from 1953 to 1957-60. For 1955 the farm partnership figure was therefore estimated for a range from .13 to .20 of sole proprietors' farm income, i.e., $343 million to $528 million. The amount of nonfarm partnership income shown for these years was then residually determined.

1956: The same adjustment as for sole proprietors (see note for lines 1-9, 1956 above) was made for partnerships to include hunting, trapping, forestry, and fishery in nonfarm partnership net income less net loss. The reported figure was raised from $8,294 million to $8,375 million, or less than 1 per cent. A further adjustment was required to allow for the omission of "payments to partners" from the partnership tabulations after 1954. This was done by raising $8,375 million by 12 per cent (= $9,384 million), the per cent which payments to partners was to net income less net loss for nonagricultural partnerships for 1957 (see note below). Published sources are the same as for sole proprietors shown above.

1957 and 1958: Ordinary net income and ordinary net loss figures are shown for both years in U.S. Business Tax Returns, 1958-59, Table 17, but these figures are net of payments to partners. The published figures for payments to partners appear in Statistics of Income, Selected Financial Data, 1957-58 and 1958-59, Table 2. Only a figure for payments to partners of nonagricultural partnerships is shown for 1957. The figure for payments to partners of agriculture, forestry, and fisheries partnerships was obtained from unpublished worksheets of the IRS.

The totals for 1957 were obtained by these additions (millions of dollars):

	Agriculture, Forestry, & Fisheries (1)	All Other (2)	Total (3)
1. Ordinary income	819	8,694	9,513
2. Ordinary loss	133	622	755
3. Ordinary income less loss	687	8,072	8,759
4. Payments to partners	30	972	1,002
5. Adjusted ordinary income less loss	717	9,044	9,761

Since payments to partners are not given separately by returns with ordinary income and ordinary loss, no separate adjustments were possible. The figures shown above are divided by agriculture, forestry, and fisheries, and all others, whereas the break throughout this study is between farm and nonfarm. To conform with the rest, the estimated amount for forestry, fisheries, and some miscellaneous items had to be transferred into the "all other" category to yield a nonfarm figure. The amount shown on line 5, column 1, of this note, for agriculture, forestry, and fisheries was reduced by multiplying it by the ratio of farm net profit less net loss to agriculture, forestry, and fisheries net profit less net loss. For net profit and net loss--a somewhat less inclusive concept than the ordinary income and loss concept used here--more detailed industry breakdowns are available for 1957 and 1958 (U.S. Business Tax Returns, 1957-58, p. 11).

	1957 Net profit less net loss (million dollars)
1. Agriculture, forestry, and fisheries	594
2. Farms	521
3. Line 2 ÷ line 1	.876
4. Farm ordinary income-less-loss estimate	.717 X .876 = .628

The last figure is that shown on line 17, Table B-1. The difference between it and $717 million (i.e., $89 million) was added to the "all other" figure of $9,044 million (line 5, this note) to yield $9,132 for nonfarm partnership ordinary net income less loss (shown on line 18, Table B-1).

The figures for 1958 were calculated in a similar way. But data on ordinary income, ordinary loss, and payments to partners were all available by farm and nonfarm in Selected Financial Data, 1958-59.

137

APPENDIX B

Table B-3 shows the derivation of estimated nonfarm unincorporated business and professional income from data published by the National Income Division (NID) of the Commerce Department. Slightly different adjustments in these data were required, depending on whether they were compared with the tabulations based on business tax returns or on individual returns. For instance, income from partnership received by fiduciaries is included in the business return statistics but not in those based on individual returns.

The NID estimates for professional practitioners and the AMS estimates for farm operators are independent of tax return information; however, in its estimates of unincorporated business income, the NID relies heavily on tax return information.[1] Thus, some circularity arises when tax return coverage and NID estimates of unincorporated enterprise are compared. The circularity is to some extent alleviated by the NID's upward adjustment of the tax return figures to correct for (1) understatement of reported net income by use of Internal Revenue Service audit data for the year 1949 and (2) undercoverage of entrepreneurs by use of Census information on sales or number of proprietors.[2]

[1] In the past, the income estimates for unincorporated business have for this reason, as well as others, been considered among the weakest links of United States national income estimates. For instance, the National Accounts Review Committee, in its review of NID estimates, considered improvement of the data for nonfarm sole proprietors and partnerships "the most important single step that could be taken to improve the accuracy of the national accounts." U.S. Congress, Joint Economic Committee: *The National Economic Accounts of the United States,* Hearings before the Subcommittee on Economic Statistics, 85th Congress, 1st Session, Washington, 1957, p. 225. In the most recent discussion of its estimates, the NID itself has taken a more sanguine view, stating that "the entrepreneurial income now, for the first time, is founded for an appreciable span of years on a comprehensive and uniform body of statistical data." *U.S. Income and Output,* Washington, Nov. 1958, pp. 89–90. In contrast, the NID's 1951 discussion stated that "no comprehensive body of data covering any appreciable time interval exists for the income of unincorporated enterprise." *National Income,* 1951 Edition, Washington, 1951, p. 70.

[2] See *U.S. Income and Output,* pp. 90–91.

NOTES TO TABLE B-1 (concluded)

1959 and 1960: Ordinary income and loss from Selected Financial Data, 1959–60 and 1960–61. Payments to partners from U.S. Business Tax Returns, 1959–60 and 1960–61.

[a]Schedule C or F of Form 1040 for sole proprietors; partnership information returns for partnerships. Figures are for accounting periods ending between July 1 of year indicated and June 30 of following year.

[b]Ordinary income (loss) as tabulated by the IRS in Statistics of Income differs slightly from net profit (loss). The latter is defined as the difference between total business receipts and the ordinary and necessary business deductions. Ordinary income (loss) includes, in addition, investment income, income (loss) from other partnerships, gain (loss) from the sale of property other than capital assets, and other income received by the partnership.

[c]Total for partnership is from individual returns 1040. Farm and nonfarm breakdown estimated.

To the extent that they rely on audit data, these corrections, though in the right direction, are not entirely satisfactory for our purpose because the IRS audit control program of 1948–49 could not, and was indeed not designed to, uncover all errors in reporting. In addition, because its estimate for nonfarm unincorporated business is derived from tax return data, the NID made two adjustments based on the assumption that (1) earnings of insurance solicitors are reported as business income on tax returns, and (2) that a significant portion of the income of own-account workers in contract construction (such as carpenters and painters) operating from their own homes is not reported in the business schedule[3] of the return. Insurance solicitors' estimated earnings were subtracted, while the item covering "own-account workers in contract construction" was added in obtaining the Commerce estimates. For our purposes it would be appropriate to reverse the adjustment for insurance solicitors, thereby raising the amount shown for total business and professional proprietors' net income (line 1, Table B-3). But since the item is small,[4] and its size for past years is unknown to us, no correction was attempted. The result is a slight overstatement of the coverage ratios shown in Table 8.

The AMS estimates of farm cash receipts and production expenses, which were used for the farm sector, are generally considered of a high caliber. Since farm cash receipts and expenses include those of corporations as well as sole proprietors and partners, it was necessary to subtract the net income of farm corporations to obtain net income of unincorporated farm enterprises. A further subtraction was necessary for those receipts from farm marketings which are included in the AMS totals but

---

[3] *U.S. Income and Output,* pp. 91–92. Selma F. Goldsmith, whose procedures we have followed in most respects, has in the past adjusted the NID business and professional income estimates for comparability with tax return figures by transferring this portion of the income of own-account workers from the entrepreneurial to the wage and salary component, on the assumption that when reported on income tax returns they would appear under wages and salaries. See "Appraisal of Basic Data Available for Constructing Income Size Distributions," part VI of *Studies in Income and Wealth,*13, New York, NBER, 1951, p. 356. We have not followed this procedure in the present study in the belief that, except for 1941–43, the incentive to report receipts in the business schedule of the tax return may have outweighed other considerations. For recent years, the adjustment may well on balance have to be in the opposite direction. If receipts are reported as business income rather than wages or salaries, it is possible, in many cases, to take a larger total of deductions, since by using schedule C, both business expenses and the standard deduction may be taken.

[4] The NID does not publish detailed statistics of its adjustments. However, it is noted that the addition for depletion allowances, and the subtractions for dividends and interest received by partnerships and earnings of insurance solicitors, entailed on balance a lowering of the tax return total by $300–$400 million a year. (*U.S. Income and Output*). Since the amounts for depletion deductions and dividends and interest received by partnerships have been estimated by us (Table B-2), a rough estimate of $300 million for earnings of insurance solicitors could thus be arrived at residually.

TABLE B-2

ESTIMATES OF FARM OPERATORS' NET MONEY INCOME (AGRICULTURE DEPARTMENT), ADJUSTED FOR COMPARABILITY WITH TAX RETURN CONCEPTS, SELECTED YEARS, 1939-60

(million dollars)

	1939	1941	1943	1945	1947	1949	1953
1. Farm cash receipts	8,635	11,655	20,265	22,405	29,934	28,014	31,339
2. Minus: Production expenses of farm operators	6,060	7,603	11,405	12,839	17,011	18,008	21,339
3. Plus: Taxes, interest, and depreciation on farm dwellings	537	572	643	710	1,113	1,031	1,185
4. Plus: Patronage refunds and stock dividends paid by farmers' cooperatives	30	60	149	122	189	226	321
5. Minus: Estimated net income reported as capital gains	27	-61	137	517	444	360	408
6. Minus: Corporate farm net profit	31	87	129	160	226	200	140
Equals: Farm operators' net money income							
7. Variant I	3,084	4,658	9,386	9,721	13,555	10,703	11,055
8. Variant II (omits line 3)	2,547	4,086	8,743	9,011	12,442	9,672	9,773
Plus: Farm operators' net money income of Hawaii and Alaska							
9. Variant I	12	16	35	37	52	39	41
10. Variant II	10	14	32	34	47	36	36
11. Minus: Depletion deductions	1	1	3	3	5	6	8
12. Minus: Net operating loss deductions				25	22	43	
Equals: Farm net income (income tax concept)							
13. Variant I	3,095	4,673	9,418	9,730	13,580	10,693	11,088
14. Variant II	2,556	4,099	8,772	9,017	12,462	9,659	9,801

(continued)

140

TABLE B-2 (concluded)

	1955	1956	1957	1958	1959	1960
1. Farm cash receipts	29,785	31,117	30,840	34,494	34,194	34,705
2. Minus: Production expenses of farm operators	21,833	22,526	23,246	25,171	26,137	26,177
3. Plus: Taxes, interest, and depreciation on farm dwellings	1,271	1,325	1,363	1,389	1,451	1,461
4. Plus: Patronage refunds and stock dividends paid by farmers' cooperatives	311	351	362	380	362	368
5. Minus: Estimated net income reported as capital gains	624	717	648	713	701	595
6. Minus: Corporate farm net profit	232	151	152	193	149	102
Equals: Farm operators' net money income						
7. Variant I	8,698	9,399	8,519	10,186	9,020	9,660
8. Variant II (omits line 3)	7,427	8,074	7,156	8,797	7,569	8,199
Plus: Farm operators' net money income of Hawaii and Alaska						
9. Variant I	34	34	31	34	34	46
10. Variant II	29	29	26	29	28	39
11. Minus: Depletion deductions	7	7	7	5	24	3
12. Minus: Net operating loss deductions						
Equals: Farm net income (income tax concept)						
13. Variant I	8,725	9,426	8,543	10,215	9,030	9,703
14. Variant II	7,449	8,096	7,175	8,821	7,573	8,235

Line

1. Department of Agriculture, Farm Income Situation, July 1963, p. 44.

2. Ibid., p. 34.

3. Gross rental value of farm dwellings (ibid., p. 45) minus net rent on owner occupied farm dwellings (unpublished Commerce Department estimate).

4. Department of Commerce, unpublished estimate.

141

NOTES TO TABLE B-2 (continued)

Line

5.   Estimated by multiplying total farm cash receipts (line 1) by
the estimated ratio of net capital gains to "sales and receipts
from operations" of unincorporated farm enterprises. Net capital gains of unincorporated farm enterprises was available for
the first time in 1959 (Statistics of Income, 1959, Supplemental
Report, Sales of Capital Assets Reported on Individual Income
Tax Returns, p. 10). For all other years this ratio was estimated on the assumption that the ratio between the ratio of
capital gains to sales for unincorporated farm enterprises and
the ratio of capital gains to sales for farm corporations
(from Statistics of Income, Corporate Returns) was constant.

6.   Treasury Department, Statistics of Income, Corporation Returns.
Figure is compiled net profit minus net realized capital gains
plus compensation of officers.

9
and
10.   For 1939, 1941, and 1957-60, unincorporated enterprise income
of Alaska and Hawaii was tabulated in Statistics of Income.
To estimate the other years, the ratios of Alaskan and Hawaiian
enterprise income to all other enterprise income for the years
mentioned above were averaged and multiplied by reported enterprise income for the years in question. The resulting estimates were then divided between farm and nonfarm in the same
proportion as unincorporated enterprise income reported on tax
returns was divided for each respective year (using figures in
lines 20 and 21 of Table B-1). Total amounts were then estimated on the assumption that nonfarm and farm net income in
Hawaii and Alaska were underreported to the same extent as the
respective types on the mainland.

            In Table 6, col. 2, a different series was used in determining
estimated total unincorporated enterprise income of Alaska and
Hawaii for 1929-60. Estimates of reported amounts were obtained as shown above, and were then raised, to account for
underreporting, by use of the percentages of underreporting
obtained for the mainland. The method for the 1929-60 series
thus differs from that used in this table, in that the farm
and nonfarm breakdowns were not made; therefore, estimated
total income appearing in Table 6 is slightly different from
that which appears in Table B-3.

11.   Series for estimated total depletion (farm and nonfarm), were
constructed separately for partnership and sole proprietorship.
The estimates for partnership are for the most part based on
the data published in the Treasury's special partnership tabulations. For 1939 (Supplement to Statistics of Income for
1939), 1945 (Press Release S-2235), 1947 (Press Release
S-2645), and 1953 (Statistics of Income, 1953 Partnership
Returns), the partnership component is as tabulated. For 1956
(Business Indicators, 1956-1957) and for 1957 (Selected Financial Data, 1957-1958), the tabulated figures omitted agriculture, forestry, and fisheries and were therefore raised by the
ratio of total depletion to total excluding agriculture,
forestry, and fisheries for the years when the ratio was available. For 1958, 1959, and 1960, partnership depletion is again
as tabulated (Selected Financial Data). For all other years
partnership depletion was estimated by straight-line interpolation of the ratio of partnership depletion to net income for
the benchmark years. These ratios were then multiplied by
tabulated partnership net income for the years in question.
Partnership farm depletion is as tabulated for 1939, 1945,

NOTES TO TABLE B-2 (concluded)

Line

11.   1947 and 1953. Depletion for agriculture, forestry, and
        fisheries was also available for these years as well as for
        1958-60. In the latter years this figure was multiplied by
        the ratio of farm depletion to agriculture, forestry, fish-
        eries depletion for the earlier years. For 1957, gross
        receipts of agriculture, forestry, and fisheries was multi-
        plied by the ratio of farm depletion to gross receipts of
        agriculture, forestry, and fisheries for all years for which
        it was available. For the remaining years, 1941, 1943, 1949,
        1955, and 1956, no complete industrial breakdown for partner-
        ship was available. Farm depletion for these years was esti-
        mated by using the average ratio of farm to total depletion
        for 1939, 1945, 1947, 1953, and 1957-60.

             The depletion estimates for sole proprietors are based
        on data for only six years and are therefore not very satis-
        factory. For 1945, a tentative figure for the total was ob-
        tained by subtracting from the total for sole proprietorship
        and partnership (supplied by Joseph Pechman), the depletion
        of partners. For 1956 and 1957 (sources the same as for
        partnership), depletion figures excluding agriculture,
        forestry, and fisheries were published. Sole proprietorship
        is as tabulated in Selected Financial Data for 1958-60. A
        depletion figure for sole proprietors in agriculture,
        forestry, and fisheries was estimated for 1956 and 1957 by
        multiplying 1957 and an estimate of 1956 gross receipts of
        these proprietors by the average ratio of agriculture,
        forestry, and fisheries depletion to gross receipts for
        1958-60. This estimate was added to the tabulated 1956 and
        1957 depletion figures to obtain an estimated total for sole
        proprietors. For all other years, sole proprietorship deple-
        tion was estimated by multiplying net income from sole pro-
        prietorship by estimated ratios of depletion to net income for
        sole proprietors. For 1939-44, the 1945 ratio was used. For
        1946-55 an average of 1945 and the later period was used. De-
        pletion for agriculture, forestry, and fisheries was obtained
        by multiplying agriculture, forestry, and fisheries gross re-
        ceipts (as tabulated in Statistics of Income) by the average
        ratio of agriculture, forestry, and fisheries depletion to
        gross receipts reported by sole proprietorship in agriculture,
        forestry, and fisheries for 1958-60. The latter figure was
        available for all years except 1956 for which an average of
        1955 and 1957 estimated depletion was used. Farm depletion
        is as tabulated in 1959 for sole proprietors. For other
        years, sole proprietor farm depletion was estimated as equal
        to a percentage of depletion for sole proprietors in agricul-
        ture, forestry, and fisheries based on the average ratio ob-
        tained for sole proprietors and partners.

12.   The net operating loss deduction (NOLD) affects only the net
        income of sole proprietors, and only for the years 1944-50.
        Information on NOLD was available for sole proprietors in
        1945 and for sole proprietors and partners for 1951-54 and
        1960-61. Amounts of sole proprietorship NOLD for 1944 and
        1946-50 were estimated by interpolation on the basis of the
        ratio of NOLD to prior year net losses on returns with no
        AGI; for 1944 the 1945 ratio was used and for 1946-50 the ratios
        were interpolated annually between 1945 and the average of the
        1951-54 ratios for sole proprietors and partners. 1945 was the
        only year for which there is a breakdown between farm and non-
        farm NOLD; the 1945 ratio of farm to total NOLD was used to
        separate 1947 and 1949 NOLD by farm and nonfarm sources.

143

TABLE B-3

ESTIMATES OF NONFARM (COMMERCE DEPARTMENT) AND TOTAL
UNINCORPORATED ENTERPRISE INCOME, ADJUSTED FOR
COMPARABILITY WITH TAX RETURN CONCEPTS, 1939-60
(million dollars)

	1939	1941	1943	1945	1947	1949	1953
1. Estimated nonfarm business and professional income	7,459	11,512	16,979	19,117	21,419	22,194	27,613
2. Plus: Dividends and interest received by partnerships	79	87	91	115	138	176	243
3. Plus: Nonfarm business and professional income of Hawaii and Alaska	25	38	62	71	80	81	100
Minus: Income of fiduciaries from either							
4. Sole proprietorship	16	36	75	64	84	55	64
or							
5. Sole proprietorship and partnership							153
6. Minus: Depletion deductions	49	75	102	73	147	163	247
7. Minus: Net operating loss deduction				55	47	92	
Equals: Nonfarm business and professional income—income tax concept							
8. Income size distribution (omits line 4)	7,514	11,562	17,030	19,175	21,443	22,196	27,556
9. Industrial distribution (omits line 5)	7,498	11,526	16,955	19,111	21,359	22,141	27,645
Farm net income—income tax concept							
10. Variant I	3,095	4,673	9,418	9,730	13,580	10,693	11,088
11. Variant II	2,556	4,099	8,772	9,017	12,462	9,659	9,801
Total unincorporated enterprise income—income tax concept							
12. Income size distribution (sum of lines 8 and 10)	10,609	16,235	26,448	28,905	35,023	32,889	38,644
Industrial distribution							
13. Variant I (sum of lines 9 and 10)	10,593	16,199	26,373	28,841	34,939	32,834	38,733
14. Variant II (sum of lines 9 and 11)	10,054	15,625	25,727	28,128	33,821	31,800	37,446

(continued)

TABLE B-3 (concluded)

	1955	1956	1957	1958	1959	1960
1. Estimated nonfarm business and professional income	30,580	32,600	32,977	32,560	35,244	34,221
2. Plus: Dividends and interest received by partnerships	223	257	291	309	350	395
3. Plus: Nonfarm business and professional income of Hawaii and Alaska	117	113	116	106	130	
Minus: Income of fiduciaries from either						
4. Sole proprietorship or	87	107	141	181	189	185
5. Sole proprietorship and partnership	189	205	252	298	310	299
6. Minus: Depletion deductions	296	346	249	338	215	362
7. Minus: Net operating loss deduction						
Equals: Nonfarm business and professional income—income tax concept						
8. Income size distribution (omits line 4)	30,435	32,419	32,883	32,339	35,199	33,955
9. Industrial distribution (omits line 5)	30,537	32,517	32,994	32,456	35,320	34,069
Farm net income—income tax concept						
10. Variant I	8,725	9,426	8,543	10,215	9,030	9,703
11. Variant II	7,449	8,096	7,175	8,821	7,573	8,235
Total unincorporated enterprise income—income tax concept						
12. Income size distribution (sum of lines 8 and 10)	39,160	41,845	41,426	42,554	44,229	43,658
Industrial distribution						
13. Variant I (sum of lines 9 and 10)	39,262	41,943	41,537	42,671	44,350	43,772
14. Variant II (sum of lines 9 and 11)	37,986	40,613	40,169	41,277	42,893	42,304

APPENDIX B

NOTES TO TABLE B-3

Line

1. Department of Commerce, Survey of Current Business, July 1959 and
July 1962, Table I-8, line 14.
2. Dividends from Daniel M. Holland, Dividends Under the Income Tax,
Princeton for NBER, 1962, Table 26, line 12. After 1953, dividends
received were excluded from partnership ordinary income or loss.
For 1939, 1945, 1947, and 1953, interest figures are as tabulated in
Statistics of Income. For all other years, an interest series was
constructed by (a) averaging, for the four years for which we have
data, the ratio of interest received by partnerships to total
interest received by all private businesses, and (b) multiplying
the latter by the average ratio obtained in (a). Interest received
by all private businesses was obtained from Department of Commerce,
Income and Output, 1958, and Survey of Current Business, July 1962,
Table VII-16.
3. See notes to Table B-2, lines 9 and 10.
4. It was arbitrarily assumed that for all years underreporting of sole
proprietorship income of fiduciaries amounted to 10 per cent of the
amount that was reported. Reported or estimated amounts were then
raised by that amount. Prior to 1953, reported amounts were as
tabulated in Statistics of Income. Since 1952, fiduciary return
figures have been published biennially, and gross rather than net
profits have been tabulated. To obtain net profits, it was necessary
to subtract depreciation and "other deductions," which were available
only for sole proprietorship, partnership, and rental income combined.
In estimating the share of sole proprietorship, it was assumed that
depreciation and the increase in "other deductions" were accounted for
by the three income types in proportion to their relative increase
from net to gross for each year in question. First, the increases in
fiduciary income from sole proprietorship for the periods 1952-54,
1954-56, and 1956-58 were divided by the increase in all three income
components combined. This ratio was then applied to depreciation and
to the increase over 1952 in "other deductions" to obtain the share
attributable to sole proprietors for 1954, 1956, and 1958. For 1953,
1955, and 1957 the ratio of sole proprietorship income on fiduciary
returns to sole proprietorship on individual returns was interpolated
from the corresponding ratios of the adjacent years; for 1959 and 1960,
the 1958 ratio was extrapolated. These ratios were then multiplied by
the amounts tabulated from individual returns to obtain estimated
fiduciary income from sole proprietorship.
5. Partnership income of fiduciaries was obtained by the same method outlined above for sole proprietors.
6. See notes to Table B-2, line 11.
7. See notes to Table B-2, line 12.
8. Beginning with 1953, sole proprietorship and partnership income of
fiduciaries (line 5) had to be subtracted from Commerce Department
estimates to make them comparable with tax returns. Before that year,
Statistics of Income figures also included fiduciary income. No
figures are therefore given on line 5 for years before 1953.
9. Estimates differ from line 8 in that fiduciaries' partnership income
is included in the tax return industrial distribution for all years,
whereas their sole proprietorship income is not included for any of
the years shown. This is because the partnership industry breakdown
is tabulated from partnership information returns; the sole proprietor
industry breakdown is tabulated from the returns of individuals only.
10 and 11. See Table B-2, lines 13 and 14.

146

are likely to be treated as capital gains (or losses) on tax returns. Such gains and losses appear to stem primarily from sales of livestock held for draft, breeding, or dairy purposes.[5] Two additions were made to obtain farmers' net income. The AMS total of production expenses includes taxes, interest, and depreciation on farm operators' dwellings. As already noted, these items are not deductible in computing adjusted gross income and our estimate of their value was therefore added back. (In the variant 2 calculation, these items were deducted on the assumption that farmers in practice do not distinguish the amount attributable to business use from that attributable to personal use.) Second, the AMS estimate of farm receipts does not include patronage refunds and dividends from farm cooperatives. These must be reported as taxable farm income and were therefore added in Table B-2 to complete our estimate of farm income to be reported.

The estimates discussed above are not completely consistent in concept with, nor are they comparable in coverage to, the reported figures in Table B-1. Income from Hawaii and Alaska, although included in tax return income, is not included in Commerce Department estimates until 1960. Therefore, an estimate of total unincorporated enterprise income for Hawaii and Alaska was added to the NID and AMS totals. In addition, interest and dividend income of partnerships, taxable as partnership income but treated as property income by the NID, was added to estimated total unincorporated enterprise income; the estimated allowance for depletion of mineral resources was deducted from this income to conform with net profit and loss on tax returns; the same adjustment was required for the so-called net operating loss (loss carryforward) deduction for years when it was tabulated among business deductions in *Statistics of Income*.

From 1953 on, unincorporated enterprise income reported on fiduciary returns has not been included in our tax return figures. In Table B-3, line 12, the estimated total sole proprietorship and partnership net income of fiduciaries has been deducted from the estimated total; in lines 13 and 14 it was necessary to deduct only the sole proprietorship income of fiduciaries, as the partnership income is presumably included in the amounts reported on partnership information returns. It was assumed that all unincorporated enterprise income of fiduciaries was from nonfarm sources and that it was underreported by 10 per cent of the reported amount.

---

[5] This adjustment was first made by Frederick D. Stocker and John C. Ellickson in "How Fully Do Farmers Report Their Income?" *National Tax Journal*, June 1959, p. 120.

After these adjustments are made, it becomes possible to compare, by farm and nonfarm enterprises, the amounts reported on business returns with the estimated amounts potentially available for reporting on these returns; this information is summarized in Table 8. We can also compare amounts of unincorporated enterprise income reported on individual returns with the estimated totals; this information is in Table 6.

Derivation of Estimates of Total Wages and Salaries and AGI

TABLE C-1

ADJUSTMENT OF WAGE AND SALARY DISBURSEMENTS (COMMERCE DEPARTMENT
ESTIMATES) FOR COMPARABILITY WITH AMOUNTS REPORTED ON TAX
RETURNS, SELECTED YEARS, 1939-60
(million dollars)

		1939	1949	1955	1960
1.	Wage and salary disbursements	45,941	134,356	210,902	271,308
2.	Minus: Component in kind	538	1,666	1,940	1,972
3.	Minus: Nontaxable military pay		434	2,435	2,464
4.	Minus: Sick-pay exclusion			444	675
5.	Plus: Taxable other labor income	124	354	598	893
6.	Plus: Total wages and salaries of Hawaii and Alaska	175	625	936	
7.	Equals: Total wages and salaries to be reported	45,702	133,235	207,617	267,090

Source

Line
1. Department of Commerce, U.S. Income and Output, 1958; Survey of Current
   Business, July, 1963, Table I-8.
2. Ibid., Table VII-17, sum of lines 2, 3, 4, and 7.
3. For 1941-53, estimates were supplied by Joseph Pechman. For 1954-60,
   estimates were derived by multiplying military wages and salaries
   (Commerce Department) by the average ratio of nontaxable to total military wages and salaries for 1953 (ratio supplied by Selma Goldsmith)
   and 1962 (data supplied by Defense Department).
4. Statistics of Income.
5. 1929-55 estimates supplied by Joseph Pechman. Taxable other labor income includes pay of military reservists, directors fees, jury and
   witness fees, marriage fees, and compensation of prison inmates. The
   last three items were less than 5 per cent of the total for all years
   they were available; because of their relative insignificance, they
   were estimated by simple straight-line extrapolation. Pay of military
   reservists was available in the Budget of the United States for most
   fiscal years involved. Calendar year figures were obtained by simple
   interpolation. Directors fees were estimated by multiplying compensation of corporation officers (Statistics of Income, Corporation
   Returns) by the 1950-55 ratio of directors fees to compensation of corporation officers.
6. Statistics of Income. For Hawaii, wages and salaries have been tabulated annually by the IRS. For Alaska, tabulated figures were available
   for 1939 and 1955, but not for 1949. For 1949, the published figure
   for Hawaii was therefore raised by the average percentage which Alaska
   was of Hawaii in the period 1939-42 and 1955-60. These combined
   amounts for Hawaii and Alaska were then multiplied by ratio of estimated total wages and salaries to reported wages and salaries for the
   mainland for each of these years in order to obtain estimated total
   wages and salaries for Hawaii and Alaska.

TABLE C-2

ADJUSTMENT OF PERSONAL INCOME ESTIMATE (COMMERCE DEPARTMENT)
TO OBTAIN ESTIMATE OF TOTAL ADJUSTED GROSS INCOME, 1960
(million dollars)

1. Personal income, Commerce Department estimate	401,275
2. Personal income items not included in AGI estimate	
a. Transfer payments	29,518
b. Other labor income	10,103
c. Income in kind	10,008
d. Nonfarm inventory valuation adjustment (noncorporate)	-19
e. Farm inventory	329
f. Imputed interest	11,131
g. Accrued interest	397
h. Tax-exempt interest	824
i. Undistributed fiduciary income other than capital gains	1,776
j. Property income of nonprofit organizations	884
k. Nontaxable military pay	2,464
ℓ. Imputed rental value of tenant occupied houses	521
m. Total, lines 2-a through 2-ℓ	67,936
3. AGI items added to personal income estimate	
a. Personal contributions for social insurance	9,225
b. Net gains from exchanges of property reported on tax	
returns	5,217
c. Other income	2,565
d. AGI of residents of Alaska and Hawaii	-
e. Annuities and pensions	1,796
f. Deductions for depletion	-540
g. Net operating loss deduction reported on tax returns	-166
h. Dividend exclusions	-384
i. Sick pay exclusions	-675
j. Total, lines 3-a through 3-i	17,038
4. Total AGI (sum of lines 1 and 3-j minus line 2-m)	350,377

Source: Unless otherwise indicated, source tables given are from
Department of Commerce, Survey of Current Business, July 1963.

Line
1, 2-a.   Table II-1.
2-b.   Table II-1, line 8 minus line 5 of Table C-1 in this appendix.
2-c.   Table VII-17, sum of lines 1 and 8, minus line 6.
2-d.   Table I-8.
2-e.   Table I-1.
2-f.   Table VII-16, line 4 minus line 6.
2-g.   Treasury Bulletin, July 1963, pp. 57-58. The total amount of
        accrued discount on redemptions during the year was subtracted
        from the amount of "accrued discount" on outstanding debt during
        the calendar year. Accrued interest on series A-D bonds was
        obtained by subtracting the figures for series E-K from the
        figures for "all series combined." The amount of accrued inter-
        est received by individuals was obtained by assuming that 80 per
        cent of series A-D, 66 1/3 per cent of series F, G, J, and K, and
        all of series E bonds, were owned by individuals.
2-h.   The total dollar amounts of state and local government securities
        are available in the 1960 Annual Report of the Secretary of the
        Treasury for the fiscal years 1952-60, and in the 1958 Annual
        Report of the Secretary of the Treasury for the fiscal years
        1941-52. Calendar year amounts were estimated by simple interpo-
        lation. Interest paid by state and local governments is from

APPENDIX C

NOTES TO TABLE C-2 (concluded)

Line
2-h.   Table III-2. Interest paid to individuals is their pro rata share
        based on the dollar amount held by individuals, as calculated by
        George Lent, The Ownership of Tax-Exempt Securities, 1913-1953,
        New York, National Bureau of Economic Research, Occasional Paper
        47, pp. 132-133, for the years 1929-52, and as tabulated in the
        1961 Annual Report of the Secretary of the Treasury for the years
        1952-60.
2-i.   Statistics of Income, 1952, 1954, 1956, and 1958. The amounts for
        1953, 1955, and 1957 are simple averages of the succeeding and pre-
        ceding years. As no data are available for 1960, 1959 and 1960 are
        extrapolated on the assumption that the rate of growth between 1956
        and 1958 holds for the later years. No adjustment was necessary
        for years before 1952, as fiduciary income is included in indi-
        vidual income for this period.
2-j.   Estimated by Joseph Pechman by extrapolating the average amount of
        interest, dividends, and rental income received by nonprofit insti-
        tutions in 1944-47. This average was Selma F. Goldsmith's estimate
        by an index of personal interest, dividends, and rents, as esti-
        mated in Table II-2.
2-k.   See notes to Table C-1, line 3, this appendix.
2-ℓ.   Table II-4, rental value of farm houses, multiplied by 0.26 (ratio
        supplied by Selma F. Goldsmith).
3-a.   Table III-6.
3-b.   Statistics of Income, Part 1.
3-c,3-d,
3-e.   All three estimates are based on Statistics of Income reports. In
        these instances, an adjustment for unreported amounts, obtained by
        multiplying the reported amounts by the ratio of total estimated AGI
        to the reported AGI for all other items, was appropriate.
3-f.   See notes to our appendix Table B-2, lines 5 and 10. Depletion on
        rents and royalties was available only for 1960. Other years were
        extrapolated on the basis of the 1960 ratio of rents and royalties
        depletion to net profits.
3-g.   See notes to our appendix Table B-2, lines 6 and 11.
3-h,
3-i.   Statistics of Income, Part 1.

TABLE C-3

ESTIMATED ADJUSTED GROSS INCOME ON TAX RETURNS, 1918-43
(million dollars)

	Net Income (1)	Personal Deductions (2)	AGI (3)
1918	15,925	1,156	17,081
1919	19,859	1,583	21,442
1920	23,736	1,835	25,571
1921	19,577	2,105	21,682
1922	21,336	2,241	23,577
1923	24,840	2,704	27,544
1924	25,656	2,812	28,468
1925	21,895	2,461	24,356
1926	21,959	2,647	24,606
1927	22,545	2,823	25,368
1928	24,727	3,247	27,974
1929	23,776	3,424	27,200
1930	16,579	2,997	19,576
1931	11,668	2,462	14,131
1932	10,175	2,174	12,349
1933	9,867	1,855	11,722
1934	12,384	1,727	14,111
1935	14,528	1,773	16,302
1936	18,953	2,001	20,954
1937	20,930	2,239	23,169
1938	18,548	2,129	20,672
1939	22,903	2,326	25,234
1940	36,277	3,332	39,609
1941	58,576	4,164	62,740
1942	78,691	6,421	85,112
1943	99,359	6,563	105,922

Source

Column
1. Statistics of Income. For 1918-27, only returns with net
   income were available. Net income on fiduciary returns is
   included throughout.
2. C. Harry Kahn, Personal Deductions in the Federal Income
   Tax, Princeton University Press for NBER, 1960, Table D-2,
   column 5, except that standard deductions are excluded
   from total personal deductions.
3. Col. 1 plus col. 2.

APPENDIX D

Estimates Based on 1948 ACP Data

TABLES 14, 15 and 16 are for the most part based on data from the 1948 Audit Control Program (ACP). Summary data were originally published by the Bureau of Internal Revenue in *The Audit Control Program*, May 1951, as well as by Marius Farioletti, "Some Results from the First Years" Audit Control Program of the Bureau of Internal Revenue, *National Tax Journal*, March 1952, Tables 8, 9 and 10. More detailed figures were only released in mimeographed form.

Table 14

The number of sole proprietors' returns filed and the total number with error are published, by broad income groups, in *The Audit Control Program*. But the breakdown of returns by error resulting in tax decrease, as well as the frequency of returns with error in the business schedule itself, was obtained from the unpublished mimeographed tabulations.

Table 15

The tax liability figures reported for all sole proprietors (column 1) and the estimated total tax change disclosable by audit (columns 3 and 4 combined) are shown in Farioletti. The tax liability voluntarily reported for all sole proprietors with error (column 2), as well as the breakdown of tax change between increase and decrease (columns 3 and 4), and the tax change for returns with error in the business schedule (column 7), were obtained from the mimeographed tabulations.

Table 16

The adjusted gross income estimates shown in columns 3 to 6 are ours. The estimated amount reported (col. 3) was obtained in the same manner as the estimates shown in Tables 20 to 23. For each of 48 income groups given in *Statistics of Income* for 1948, the frequency of sole proprietor returns was multiplied by the average AGI for all returns in the groups, which yielded an estimate of AGI reported by sole proprietors. As noted in the tables, roughly 45 per cent of the returns in the $7,000–$25,000 group of the ACP distribution had AGI of less than $7,000 but gross receipts greater than $25,000. To make the AGI distribution derived from *Statistics of Income* conform to the ACP distribution, it was assumed that these returns had an average AGI of $6,000 and their frequency was multiplied by this amount. The resulting product was subtracted from the AGI of the under $7,000 group and added to the AGI of the $7,000–$25,000 group. The "additional AGI disclosed by audit," shown in column 4 of Table 16, was estimated by blowing up the ACP figures for "net tax increase disclosable by audit" (col. 2) by the reciprocal of the estimated average marginal rate of tax for each of the income groups shown. The marginal rates used are those applicable to average taxable income for each of the groups, taking account of the different rates applying to joint and separate returns. Average taxable income was obtained by subtracting exemptions and deductions from AGI as tabulated in *Statistics of Income*. Because the average marginal rates used as a blow-up factor are for very wide income ranges, the computed AGI equivalent of the net tax increase disclosable by audit is likely to be a very crude estimate.

APPENDIX E

Patterns of Income on Returns Which Have
Unincorporated Enterprise Income as Well as Income
from Wages, Interest, Dividends, or Rents
and Royalties, 1955 and 1959

APPENDIX TABLES E-1 and E-2 show the basic distributions which under-
lie part of Table 33 and all of Table 34 of the text. As a presentation of
"patterns of income" the tables are incomplete, since frequencies for
capital gains and losses and some miscellaneous income types were not
included in the IRS tabulations from which our tables were derived.
Tables E-1 and E-2 permit the interested readers to compute relative
frequencies for any additional income source combinations not included
in Table 34. The average number of sources per return for any particular source combination may also be readily obtained. For instance,
column 15 of Table E-1 shows the frequency with which unincorporated
enterprise income, interest, dividends, and wages and salaries occur on
the same returns.

This differs from the percentage given for returns with unincorporated
enterprise income that show income from specified other sources (columns
6 and 7, Table 34) because the latter does not tell us whether a return
has more than one additional source or not. Conceivably every one of the
returns "with income from specified other sources" could have merely
one additional source. The last columns in the two tables below show
that this is, of course, not so, and that the number of sources per return
rises very steeply as a function of income.

To obtain a fuller picture, *relative* frequencies for the two years shown
may be combined. Interest and dividends, not included in the basic 1959
tabulations, may thus be shown together with rents and royalties. Relative frequencies for the same income groups in the two years are sufficiently similar to justify this procedure. As we have seen in Tables 33 and
34, where identical combinations are available in both years, the frequencies are very similar. For instance, the percentage of returns with
both sole proprietorship and partnership profit or loss rises from 4.7 to
25.4 for 1959 and from 5.3 to 26.0 for 1959.

TABLE E-1

NUMBER OF RETURNS WITH UNINCORPORATED ENTERPRISE PROFIT OR LOSS AND INCOME FROM
WAGES AND SALARIES, DIVIDENDS, OR INTEREST, 1955

Adjusted Gross Income (thousand dollars)	Total with Sole Proprietor and/or Partnership Income (1)	Returns with Sole Proprietor and/or Partnership Income and							
		No Dividends, Interest, or Wages (2)	Only Interest (3)	Only Dividends (4)	Only Wages (5)	Wages and Dividends (6)	Wages and Interest (7)	Dividends and Interest (8)	Wages, Dividends, and Interest (9)
Negative AGI	399,248	267,839	23,327	8,932	74,564	2,651	9,309	11,291	1,335
0 – 2	2,872,156	1,814,469	190,834	41,867	715,868	9,370	46,143	42,836	10,769
2 – 3	1,456,990	679,990	104,682	21,027	549,640	10,478	52,083	30,729	8,361
3 – 5	2,158,793	768,220	132,002	38,217	1,000,146	25,804	115,856	47,149	31,399
5 – 10[a]	1,912,595	480,486	138,651	45,869	848,967	51,256	180,253	93,019	74,094
10 – 25	791,179	194,194	94,353	45,478	140,132	45,162	71,823	102,721	97,316
25 – 50	177,210	25,212	18,006	12,906	11,710	13,991	11,974	40,652	42,759
50 – 100	43,640	2,870	2,460	2,971	1,791	3,789	1,926	10,876	16,957
100 – 500	11,878	231	396	547	221	958	312	2,724	6,489
500 or more	546	3	7	19	1	35	3	129	349
Total	9,824,235	4,233,514	704,718	217,833	3,343,040	163,494	489,682	382,126	289,828

(continued)

156

TABLE E-1 (concluded)

Adjusted Gross Income (thousand dollars)	All Sole Proprietor and/or Partnership Returns with				Frequency of Specified Sources	
	Interest[a] (10)	Dividends[b] (11)	Dividends and/or Interest[c] (12)	Wages[d] (13)	Total[e] (14)	Per Return (Col. 14 ÷ Col. 1) (15)
Negative AGI	45,262	24,209	56,845	87,859	556,578	1.39
0 – 2	290,582	104,842	341,819	782,150	4,049,730	1.41
2 – 3	195,855	70,595	227,360	620,562	2,344,002	1.61
3 – 5[f]	326,406	142,569	390,427	1,173,205	3,800,973	1.76
5 – 10[f]	486,017	264,238	583,142	1,154,570	3,817,420	2.00
10 – 25	366,213	290,677	456,853	354,433	1,802,502	2.28
25 – 50	113,391	110,308	140,288	80,434	481,343	2.72
50 – 100	32,219	34,593	38,979	24,463	134,915	3.09
100 – 500	9,921	10,718	11,426	7,980	40,497	3.41
500 or more	488		542	388	1,954	3.58
Total	1,866,354	1,053,281	2,247,681	4,286,044	17,029,914	1.73

Source: Statistics of Income, 1955, Table 6.

[a] Sum of cols. 3, 7, 8, and 9.
[b] Sum of cols. 4, 6, 8, and 9.
[c] Sum of cols. 4, 6, and 10.
[d] Sum of cols. 5, 6, 7, and 9.
[e] Col. 14 was obtained by adding to col. 2 the sum of cols. 3, 4, and 5 multiplied by two; the sum of cols. 6, 7, and 8 multiplied by three; and col. 9 multiplied by four.
[f] Includes all nontaxable returns with AGI over $5,000.

TABLE E-2

NUMBER OF RETURNS WITH UNINCORPORATED ENTERPRISE PROFIT OR LOSS AND INCOME FROM WAGES AND SALARIES AND/OR RENTS AND ROYALTIES, 1959

Adjusted Gross Income (thousand dollars)	Total with Sole Proprietor and/or Partnership Income (1)	Returns with Sole Proprietor and/or Partnership Income and:				All Sole Proprietor and/or Partnership Returns with		Frequency of Specified Source	
		No Rents, Royalties, or Wages (2)	Wages (3)	Rents and Royalties (4)	Wages and Rents and Royalties (5)	Wages (3) ÷ (5) (6)	Rents and Royalties (4) ÷ (5) (7)	Total[a] (8)	Per Return (8) ÷ (1) (9)
Negative AGI	388,632	248,547	74,207	49,861	16,017	90,224	65,878	544,734	1.40
0 – 2 ⎫ 2 – 3 ⎭	3,702,265	2,151,046	1,026,392	393,983	130,844	1,157,236	524,827	5,384,328	1.45
3 – 5	2,098,432	762,221	974,494	204,235	157,482	1,131,976	361,717	3,592,125	1.71
5 – 10	2,554,567	684,103	1,327,853	252,477	290,134	1,617,987	542,611	4,715,165	1.85
10 – 25	1,107,765	374,275	413,830	173,210	146,450	560,280	319,660	1,987,705	1.79
25 – 50	235,051	84,270	66,111	46,416	38,254	104,365	84,670	424,086	1.80
50 – 100	70,122	20,872	20,971	13,795	14,484	35,455	28,279	133,856	1.91
100 – 500	15,467	3,394	4,922	2,785	4,366	9,288	7,151	31,906	2.06
500 or more	614	73	185	105	251	436	356	1,406	2.29
Total	10,172,915	4,328,801	3,908,965	1,136,867	798,282	4,707,247	1,935,149	16,815,311	1.65

Source: Statistics of Income, 1959, Table 8.

[a] Col. 8 was obtained by adding to col. 2 the sum of cols. 3 and 4 multiplied by two and col. 5 multiplied by three.

The number of specified sources per return with unincorporated enterprise income varies, thus, as follows for 1955–59:

Negative AGI	1.56
0–2 ⎱ 2–3 ⎰	1.63
3–5	1.93
5–10	2.21
10–25	2.57
25–50	3.08
50–100	3.49
100–500	3.87
500 and over	4.16
Total	1.92

Whereas the returns filed by persons with negative income show an average of 1.6 of the specified sources, the returns with income over $50,000 show an average of more than four sources.

APPENDIX F
Derivation of Tables 43 Through 46

Table 43

The frequencies for this table are shown in Table F-1. The basic under-lying data are found in Table 8, *Statistics of Income, Individual Returns, 1960,* where frequencies for returns with net profit from sole proprietorship are tabulated by net profit classes and AGI classes. The breakdown given is for twenty AGI groups and seventeen net profit classes.

To determine the frequency of returns in each AGI group with net profits more than 10 per cent, more than 25 per cent, and more than 50 per cent of the AGI shown on such returns, it was first necessary to determine the respective points in each AGI group that mark off the desired percentage band of frequencies. For instance, for the AGI group $3,000–$4,000, all returns with more than $400 net profit clearly fell into the more-than-10 per cent group. All returns with less than $300 were clearly in the less than 10 per cent group. Returns with net profits $300–$400 could be on either side of the dividing line. It was assumed

TABLE F-1

ESTIMATED NUMBER OF RETURNS WITH REPORTED NET PROFIT FROM SOLE PROPRIETORSHIP
LESS THAN, OR EXCEEDING, STATED PERCENTAGE OF INCOME, BY INCOME GROUPS, 1960

AGI Classes (thousand dollars)	Less Than 10 Per Cent of AGI (1)	Between 10 and 25 Per Cent of AGI (2)	Between 25 and 50 Per Cent of AGI (3)	More Than 50 Per Cent of AGI (4)	Total (5)
Negative AGI					16,303
0 - 2	54,170	100,988	205,915	1,493,307	1,854,380
2 - 3	50,163	80,579	117,366	660,053	908,161
3 - 5	165,832	170,115	189,374	952,451	1,477,772
5 - 10	361,699	247,939	278,955	830,570	1,719,163
10 - 25	104,359	70,161	105,380	425,229	705,129
25 - 50	13,404	10,434	19,901	81,335	125,074
50 - 100	4,140	2,177	4,137	12,162	22,616
100 - 200	853	338	309	847	2,347
200 - 500	255	n.a.	n.a.	n.a.	402
500 and over	70	n.a.	n.a.	n.a.	80
Total	754,945	n.a.	n.a.	n.a.	6,831,427
Partial total (0-200)	754,620	682,731	921,337	4,455,954	6,814,642

Source: Computed from Table 8, Statistics of Income, 1960.

160

CHART F-1
Formulas for Estimating Frequencies for a Fraction of a Class Interval

Fraction of Class Estimated Less Than One Half

Preceding Class Greater   Preceding Class Smaller

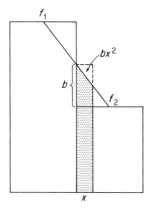 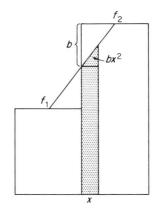

$$\boxed{} = xf_2 + bx(1-x)$$ $$\boxed{} = xf_2 - bx(1-x)$$

Fraction of Class Estimated More Than One Half

Succeeding Class Smaller   Succeeding Class Greater

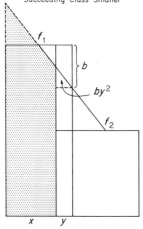 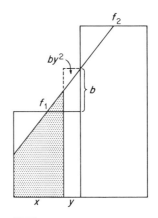

$$\boxed{} = f_1 - \left[yf_1 - by(1-y)\right]$$ $$\boxed{} = f_1 - \left[yf_1 + by(1-y)\right]$$

that the returns in this net profit class are evenly divided in falling to either side of the 10 per cent dividing line. This assumption is most warranted whenever the density distributions with respect to both groupings are very much alike; for instance if the returns tended to be evenly distributed between each of the two sets of class limits. If most of the returns in the group were close to the $4,000 AGI and the $300 net profit level our assumption would be unwarranted. In most instances the assumption that the 10 per cent limit was randomly distributed within the interpolating class had only a small effect on the final result.

In the above example, the class limits within which interpolation was required, $300–$400 net profit, corresponded to the limits of one of the seventeen net profit classes used in the Treasury Department tabulation of frequencies. The frequencies in the class were therefore known. In many instances this was of course not so. When estimating the frequency of returns with net profit greater than 25 per cent of AGI reported on the return, the limit for the $3,000–$4,000 AGI group is in the $750–$1,000 net profit range. This range does not coincide with a given net profit class, but falls into the $500–$1,000 net profit class of the basic

TABLE F-2

ESTIMATED NET PROFIT ON RETURNS WITH NET PROFIT FROM SOLE PROPRIETORSHIP LESS THAN, OR EXCEEDING, STATED PERCENTAGE OF AGI, BY INCOME GROUPS, 1960
(million dollars)

AGI Classes (thousand dollars)	Net Profit				
	Less Than 10 Per Cent of AGI	Between 10 and 25 Per Cent of AGI	Between 25 and 50 Per Cent of AGI	More Than 50 Per Cent of AGI	Total
Negative AGI					53.0
0 - 2	3.5	24.9	91.3	1,505.7	1,625.3
2 - 3	6.6	34.7	109.9	1,483.9	1,635.1
3 - 5	31.7	103.3	290.7	3,351.6	3,777.3
5 - 10	124.4	220.2	934.9	5,103.7	6,383.2
10 - 25	62.2	178.5	556.2	5,751.6	6,548.6
25 - 50	21.7	75.7	272.1	2,541.3	2,910.7
50 - 100	11.6	26.6	123.7	715.1	877.0
100 - 200	3.8	6.7	15.0	93.3	118.7
200 - 500	2.9	n.a.	n.a.	n.a.	22.2
500 and over	2.8	n.a.	n.a.	n.a.	7.8
Total[a]	271.1	n.a.	n.a.	n.a.	23,958.9
Partial total (0-200)	265.4	670.5	2,393.8	20,546.2	23,876.0

Source: Computed from Table 8, Statistics of Income, 1960.

[a]Excluding negative AGI.

162

Treasury tabulation. Hence the frequencies falling into the $750–$1,000 net profit range had to be estimated before one half could be included in the group with net profit over 25 per cent of AGI.

The frequencies for any fractional part of a class interval were estimated, whenever possible, with a formula which took account of changing frequency density within the class. Linear functions were assumed. That is, adjacent class intervals were connected by a straight line, drawn from midpoint to midpoint of two adjacent classes of equal width. Four formulas were employed to cover the four cases illustrated in Chart F-1.

Table 44

Dollar amounts, on which Table 44 is based, are presented in Table F-2. The same basic frequency distribution, used to construct Table 43, was used here also. Frequencies for each net profit class were multiplied by (a) the class midpoint for net profit classes up to $5,000, since classes up to that level were sufficiently small to justify this procedure; (b) a computed mean profit for classes above the $5,000 level. To compute mean profits from the frequency tabulation, a formula based on the Pareto curve was used.[1]

The sum of the computed net profits for each AGI group was in almost all cases very close to the actually tabulated total for the group. For the $3,000–$4,000 AGI group, for example, the actual total was 98.6 per cent of the computed value. The computed net profit in each net profit class for the $3,000–$4,000 AGI group was therefore lowered by 1.4 per cent.

Following the divisions of Table 43, the estimated net profits were tabulated by size of AGI and groups more than 10, more than 25, and more than 50 per cent of AGI reported on returns with net profit.

---

[1] For a given class interval (well beyond the mode of the distribution) with class limits x_1 and x_2, and cumulative frequencies above these limits of F_1 and F_2, respectively, the mean is given by

$$\bar{X} = ab/f, \text{ where } f = F_1 - F_2$$
$$a = F_1 X_1 - F_2 X_2, \text{ and}$$
$$b = \frac{\log (F_1/F_2)}{\log (F_1 X_1/F_2 X_2)}$$

For the open-end interval, with only X_1 and the frequencies above X_1 given, the mean was approximated by computing b for the closed interval immediately preceding the final interval, and using the formula,

$$\bar{X} = x_1 b$$

The formulas are as presented by Maurice Liebenberg and Hyman Kaitz in "An Income Size Distribution from Income Tax and Survey Data, 1944," *Studies in Income and Wealth*, 13, New York, NBER, 1951, p. 444.

TABLE F-3

ESTIMATED MEAN EFFECTIVE TAX RATE ON NET PROFITS FOR RETURNS WITH SOLE PROPRIETORSHIP NET PROFIT
GREATER THAN 10 PER CENT AND GREATER THAN 50 PER CENT OF AGI, 1960
(dollars in millions)

AGI Classes (thousand dollars)	All Returns with Sole Proprietorship Profit			Returns with Net Profit More Than 10 Per Cent of AGI			Returns with Net Profit More Than 50 Per Cent of AGI		
	Net Profit (1)	Tax Liability (2)	Col. 2 ÷ Col. 1 (3)	Net Profit (4)	Tax Liability (5)	Col. 5 ÷ Col. 4 (6)	Net Profit (7)	Tax Liability (8)	Col. 8 ÷ Col. 7 (9)
0 – 2	1,625.3	30.6	1.9	1,621.8	30.5	1.9	1,505.7	28.2	1.9
2 – 3	1,635.1	80.4	4.9	1,628.5	80.0	4.9	1,483.9	72.9	4.9
3 – 5	3,777.3	291.4	7.7	3,745.6	288.9	7.7	3,351.6	258.3	7.7
5 – 10	6,383.2	698.3	10.9	6,258.8	684.7	10.9	5,103.7	558.3	10.9
10 – 25	6,548.6	1,075.4	16.4	6,486.4	1,065.4	16.5	5,751.6	945.7	16.4
25 – 50	2,910.7	720.1	24.7	2,889.1	714.8	24.7	2,541.3	628.7	24.7
50 – 100	877.0	296.9	33.8	865.4	293.0	33.8	715.1	242.1	33.8
100 – 200	118.7	47.8	40.3	114.9	46.3	40.3	93.3	37.6	40.3
200 – 500	22.2	9.6	43.5	19.3	8.4	43.5	n.a.	n.a.	n.a.
500 and over	7.8	3.6	46.0	5.0	2.3	45.8	n.a.	n.a.	n.a.
Total	23,905.9	3,254.1	13.6	23,634.8	3,214.2	13.6	20,576.2	2,771.8	13.5
Partial total (0–200)	23,876.0	3,240.9	13.6	23,610.6	3,203.5	13.6	n.a.	n.a.	n.a.

Source

Col. 1: Statistics of Income.
Col. 2: Statistics of Income, for method see Appendix H.
Cols. 4 and 7: Table F-2.
Cols. 5 and 8: Col. 3 multiplied by cols. 4 and 7 respectively. Computation performed on narrower income classes.

TABLE F-4

ESTIMATED MEAN EFFECTIVE TAX RATE WEIGHTED BY FREQUENCIES ON ALL RETURNS WITH SOLE PROPRIETORSHIP NET PROFIT AND ON RETURNS WITH SOLE PROPRIETORSHIP NET PROFIT GREATER THAN 10 PER CENT AND GREATER THAN 50 PER CENT OF AGI, BY INCOME GROUPS, 1960

AGI Classes (thousand dollars)	All Returns with Sole Proprietorship Profit			Returns with Net Profit Greater Than 10 Per Cent of AGI			Returns with Net Profit Greater Than 50 Per Cent of AGI		
	Frequency (1)	Frequency Multiplied by Effective Tax Rate (2)	Mean Effective Tax Rate Weighted by Frequencies (3)	Frequency (4)	Frequency Multiplied by Effective Tax Rate (5)	Mean Effective Tax Rate Weighted by Frequencies (6)	Frequency (7)	Frequency Multiplied by Effective Tax Rate (8)	Mean Effective Tax Rate Weighted by Frequencies (9)
0 – 2	1,854,380	25,673	1.4	1,800,210	24,769	1.4	1,493,307	20,111	1.3
2 – 3	908,161	43,766	4.8	857,998	41,322	4.8	660,053	31,767	4.8
3 – 5	1,477,772	114,070	7.7	1,311,940	100,954	7.7	952,451	73,104	7.7
5 – 10	1,719,163	187,593	10.9	1,357,464	148,125	10.9	830,570	90,631	10.9
10 – 25	705,129	111,616	15.8	600,770	95,474	15.9	425,229	68,023	16.0
25 – 50	125,074	30,944	24.7	111,670	27,628	24.7	81,335	20,123	24.7
50 – 100	22,616	7,653	33.8	18,476	6,251	33.8	12,162	4,112	33.8
100 – 200	2,347	942	40.1	1,494	596	39.9	847	335	39.6
200 – 500	402	182	45.3	147	66	44.9	n.a.	n.a.	n.a.
500 and over	80	36	45.0	10	4	40.0	n.a.	n.a.	n.a.
Total	6,815,124	522,475	7.7	6,060,179	445,189	7.3	4,455,954	308,206	6.9
Partial total (0 – 200)	6,814,642	522,257	7.7	6,060,022	445,119	7.3	n.a.	n.a.	n.a.

Source

Col. 1: Statistics of Income.
Col. 2: The calculation of effective tax rates is described in Appendix H. Effective tax rates were multiplied by the frequency of taxable returns by narrow AGI classes.
Col. 3: Col. 2 divided by col. 1, the total frequency of returns with sole proprietorship profit, taxable and nontaxable.
Cols. 4,7: Table F-1.
Cols. 5,8: Col. 3 multiplied by cols. 4 and 7 respectively, except that narrower AGI classes were used. A method similar to that used in calculating col. 2 could not be used, as the basic cross classification in Statistics of Income was not available by taxable and nontaxable returns. It was then assumed that within an AGI class the distribution of taxable and nontaxable returns was random with respect to net profit.

Amounts and Frequencies of Reported Net Profits and Net Losses; Estimated Tax Liability Attributable to, and Estimated AGI on Returns with, Net Profit and Net Loss, by Sole Proprietors and Partners, Selected Years, 1939–60

THE net profits, net losses and frequencies for each AGI group are as tabulated in the Treasury Department's annual *Statistics of Income*, except for the consolidation of narrower income classes into the broader groupings shown. Adjusted gross income on returns with net profit or loss from sole proprietorship or partnership was estimated by making the simple, expedient assumption that average AGI for returns with sole proprietorship or partnership income is the same as the average AGI for all returns in the group. For that purpose, narrower income classes than those shown in the tables below were employed, thus minimizing the error which would result from bias in this method. There are no *a priori* reasons to suspect that, within the twenty-five classes used, average AGI for proprietors of unincorporated enterprises differs in a systematic fashion from that reported for all returns.

Tax liability attributable to unincorporated enterprise net income was estimated by multiplying reported net profits and net losses by the mean effective tax rate for each income class. The effective tax rate for each of the twenty-five income classes was obtained by dividing gross tax liability (i.e., tax liability before tax credits) by adjusted gross income reported for each class. Since adjusted gross income for any income class is the algebraic sum of positive and negative income components, the tax liability for unincorporated enterprise net income was obtained by multiplying the mean effective tax rate for any class by both net profits and net losses for the class. The tax liabilities shown are thus the net amounts.

TABLE G-1

AMOUNTS AND FREQUENCIES OF REPORTED NET PROFITS AND NET LOSSES; ESTIMATED TAX LIABILITY ATTRIBUTED TO, AND ESTIMATED AGI ON, RETURNS WITH NET PROFIT AND NET LOSS, BY SOLE PROPRIETORS AND PARTNERS, SELECTED YEARS, 1939-60

AGI Classes (thousand dollars)	Returns with Net Profit			Returns with Net Loss			Tax on Entrepreneurial Net Income Less That Absorbed by Net Losses (million dollars)
	Number of Returns (in thousands)	Amount of Net Profit (million dollars)	AGI	Number of Returns (in thousands)	Amount of Net Loss (million dollars)	AGI (million dollars)	
SOLE PROPRIETORSHIP, 1939							
Negative AGI	7.0	13.7	-60.1	46.5	122.1	-5.2	n.a.
0 – 2	773.7[a]	362.2		67.1[a]	25.5		.4
2 – 3		538.0	1,857.6		11.5	161.2	.9
3 – 5		723.0			13.9		6.0
5 – 10	105.6	589.9	797.9	9.4	14.2	73.0	13.8
10 – 25	29.8	335.6	489.1	5.1	13.8	89.0	18.5
25 – 50	4.0	93.5	153.7	1.7	8.7	64.4	10.4
50 – 100	.8	34.1	65.3	.7	5.1	51.7	6.1
100 – 500	.1	11.0	25.0	.3	4.9	60.7	2.3
500 and over	.0[a]	1.2	3.2	.0[a]	2.8	41.7	-.9
Total	921.1[a]	2,702.3	3,331.7	130.9[a]	222.4	536.4	57.5
PARTNERSHIP, 1939							
Negative AGI	3.7	10.4	n.a.	4.9	28.4	n.a.	n.a.
0 – 2	n.a.	55.7	n.a.	n.a.	5.3	n.a.	.1
2 – 3	n.a.	104.7	n.a.	n.a.	2.8	n.a.	.4
3 – 5	n.a.	224.1	n.a.	n.a.	4.0	n.a.	2.2
5 – 10	62.9	313.8	485.5	4.6	4.5	35.8	7.7
10 – 25	29.4	303.9	501.0	2.7	4.4	47.3	17.8
25 – 50	6.4	135.7	246.8	.9	2.6	34.8	16.3
50 – 100	1.9	71.5	143.3	.3	1.4	25.7	14.6
100 – 500	.4	29.7	78.4	.1	2.4	27.2	9.7
500 and over	.0[b]	1.3	13.9[b]	.0[b]	.4	11.3[b]	.3
Total	104.7[b]	1,250.7	1,468.8	13.5[b]	56.2	182.2	69.0

(continued)

TABLE G-1 (continued)

AGI Classes (thousand dollars)	Returns with Net Profit			Returns with Net Loss			Tax on Entrepreneurial Net Income Less That Absorbed by Net Losses (million dollars)
	Number of Returns (in thousands)	Amount of Net Profit (million dollars)	AGI	Number of Returns (in thousands)	Amount of Net Loss (million dollars)	AGI	
				SOLE PROPRIETORSHIP, 1945			
Negative AGI	6.7	11.5	-10.8	147.3	290.1	-237.1	n.a.
0 - 2	2,666.5	2,503.0	2,960.0	208.6	117.5	225.7	145.6
2 - 3	1,029.0	1,854.9	2,533.4	96.9	46.2	238.7	175.1
3 - 5	893.3	2,428.6	3,380.6	66.2	41.1	246.2	285.8
5 - 10	456.5	2,456.7	3,092.1	27.2	38.2	185.5	427.9
10 - 25	186.9	2,158.7	2,747.3	15.9	46.4	245.7	572.2
25 - 50	32.2	731.8	981.1	6.0	26.4	177.8	284.9
50 - 100	3.7	296.0	425.1	1.4	17.0	153.4	143.8
100 - 500	1.4	131.3	215.6	1.0	14.5	168.7	72.4
500 and over	.0	11.0	31.5	.1	2.9	84.5	6.2
Total	5,276.3	12,583.5	16,356.2	570.6	640.2	1,489.2	2,113.9
				PARTNERSHIP, 1945			
Negative AGI	3.9	12.9	-6.3	15.4	62.4	-24.7	n.a.
0 - 2	369.7	366.4	448.7	29.2	20.3	32.6	22.7
2 - 3	248.7	431.1	619.5	21.0	8.4	51.7	41.1
3 - 5	300.8	786.0	1,161.9	18.1	9.1	68.0	94.2
5 - 10	257.5	1,316.0	1,798.3	12.4	13.7	85.7	235.6
10 - 25	175.0	1,984.6	2,680.8	8.5	16.6	131.5	548.5
25 - 50	53.6	1,198.6	1,626.1	2.7	8.9	81.5	483.4
50 - 100	8.9	716.2	983.5	.6	5.7	63.4	366.1
100 - 500	3.7	364.8	571.3	.4	3.4	69.2	218.7
500 and over	.1	32.2	68.8	.0	.4	25.4	20.9
Total	1,421.9	7,208.7	9,952.7	108.2	148.9	584.3	2,031.2

(continued)

168

AGI Classes (thousand dollars)	Returns with Net Profit			Returns with Net Loss			Tax on Entrepreneurial Net Income Less That Absorbed by Net Losses (million dollars)
	Number of Returns (in thousands)	Amount of Net Profit (million dollars)	AGI	Number of Returns (in thousands)	Amount of Net Loss (million dollars)	AGI	
SOLE PROPRIETORSHIP, 1949							
Negative AGI	13.1	16.5	-20.4	308.9	763.7	-481.9	n.a.
0 – 2	2,481.0	2,512.0	2,878.9	231.4	179.1	236.7	34.2
2 – 3	1,201.1	2,361.1	2,968.4	121.0	78.7	302.5	83.1
3 – 5	1,193.1	3,340.9	4,575.6	147.4	129.7	567.9	191.9
5 – 10	637.0	3,208.1	4,298.8	56.2	70.0	365.3	318.7
10 – 25	241.4	2,730.4	3,535.9	19.7	69.0	296.7	413.3
25 – 50	41.4	994.5	1,377.1	6.9	44.3	236.2	229.8
50 – 100	8.0	336.9	526.2	3.0	30.1	209.5	104.1
100 – 500	1.6	114.9	251.4	1.6	28.2	277.0	39.1
500 and over	.0	14.3	52.8	.1	6.1	144.4	4.7
Total	5,817.8	15,629.5	20,444.8	896.2	1,398.9	2,154.2	1,418.9
PARTNERSHIP, 1949							
Negative AGI	9.5	17.6	-14.9	56.2	189.4	-87.6	n.a.
0 – 2	543.7	540.5	651.8	61.0	61.7	65.3	12.5
2 – 3	329.9	590.6	818.6	40.9	29.4	102.5	24.2
3 – 5	460.2	1,200.1	1,793.7	57.0	52.0	219.5	75.5
5 – 10	359.9	1,605.9	2,476.8	39.1	36.3	260.8	161.4
10 – 25	195.6	1,959.5	2,955.8	17.0	30.9	258.5	305.5
25 – 50	52.1	1,088.9	1,775.6	4.8	16.8	163.0	259.7
50 – 100	15.9	596.9	1,057.4	1.7	10.7	117.5	198.7
100 – 500	4.1	298.9	640.8	.8	8.7	139.3	125.5
500 and over	.1	18.3	88.2	.1	2.3	74.9	9.2
Total	1,971.0	7,912.2	12,243.9	278.3	438.1	1,313.5	1,172.2

(continued)

169

TABLE G-1 (continued)

AGI Classes (thousand dollars)	Returns with Net Profit			Returns with Net Loss			Tax on Entrepreneurial Net Income Less That Absorbed by Net Losses (million dollars)
	Number of Returns (in thousands)	Amount of Net Profit (million dollars)	AGI	Number of Returns (in thousands)	Amount of Net Loss (million dollars)	AGI	
SOLE PROPRIETORSHIP, 1952							
Negative AGI	13.0	14.3	-27.2	295.9	873.9	-558.3	-18.8
0 – 2	1,981.0	2,001.3	2,323.2	250.4	247.0	271.0	70.5
2 – 3	1,089.9	2,132.9	2,717.3	141.5	123.4	356.5	135.1
3 – 5	1,341.7	3,602.6	5,213.2	220.8	203.7	917.3	306.5
5 – 10	920.6	4,087.5	6,215.4	118.8	122.6	779.3	526.5
10 – 20	310.8	3,160.0	4,179.4	28.0	77.6	379.8	575.2
20 – 50	117.9	2,443.8	3,423.7	17.1	99.5	528.0	654.0
50 – 100	14.3	563.4	947.9	5.5	58.2	364.7	208.5
100 – 500	2.6	176.0	395.9	2.6	61.0	445.6	58.7
500 and over	.1	13.2	59.5	.2	16.5	208.5	-2.1
Total	5,791.8	18,195.0	25,448.3	1,080.9	1,883.4	3,692.4	2,514.1
PARTNERSHIP, 1952							
Negative AGI	7.4	34.7	-15.1	38.4	150.2	-72.5	-4.5
0 – 2	270.0	270.6	326.4	35.7	38.8	36.5	13.8
2 – 3	199.2	375.6	499.8	21.5	19.0	53.7	30.0
3 – 5	363.4	1,005.5	1,438.1	43.7	42.0	172.9	93.1
5 – 10	437.6	1,897.7	3,006.0	39.1	26.0	345.6	249.5
10 – 20	210.1	1,913.6	2,865.2	16.4	31.9	223.8	353.3
20 – 50	110.2	2,074.6	3,287.6	9.1	34.1	274.0	579.0
50 – 100	21.7	824.1	1,439.5	2.7	18.3	178.8	332.5
100 – 500	5.5	418.6	848.3	1.4	24.8	248.2	203.4
500 and over	.1	18.9	126.5	.1	6.5	95.6	7.9
Total	1,625.3	8,833.8	13,822.3	208.2	391.5	1,556.6	1,858.1

(continued)

TABLE G-1 (continued)

AGI Classes (thousand dollars)	Returns with Net Profit			Returns with Net Loss			Tax on Entrepreneurial Net Income Less That Absorbed by Net Losses (million dollars)
	Number of Returns (in thousands)	Amount of Net Profit (million dollars)	AGI	Number of Returns (in thousands)	Amount of Net Loss (million dollars)	AGI	
SOLE PROPRIETORSHIP, 1953							
Negative AGI	20.1	30.7	-54.7	317.3	940.6	-868.3	-23.6
0 - 2	2,063.9	2,006.6	2,386.8	286.5	278.8	303.5	70.2
2 - 3	1,087.3	2,108.2	2,711.8	153.3	132.2	382.2	134.9
3 - 5	1,456.7	3,905.3	5,671.4	297.0	213.1	1,167.1	340.3
5 - 10	1,035.4	4,432.8	6,992.9	172.7	150.6	1,132.8	557.0
10 - 20	335.0	3,319.0	4,483.9	33.1	91.1	444.5	596.3
20 - 50	109.5	2,256.1	3,129.7	15.2	93.7	453.3	592.7
50 - 100	11.4	472.7	759.0	4.1	53.8	273.1	171.0
100 - 500	1.9	138.7	293.1	2.0	50.2	340.1	45.0
500 and over	.0	7.6	43.5	.2	10.0	167.3	-1.6
Total	6,121.5	18,677.7	26,417.6	1,281.4	2,014.1	3,795.4	2,482.4
PARTNERSHIP, 1953							
Negative AGI	10.3	18.5	-28.1	55.2	248.9	-150.9	-7.1
0 - 2	303.4	328.8	366.8	39.2	35.9	37.9	15.9
2 - 3	193.3	381.3	479.4	26.0	22.7	64.1	30.0
3 - 5	368.8	1,032.2	1,460.7	45.2	43.7	176.6	98.1
5 - 10	426.9	1,907.9	2,970.7	43.3	34.6	291.6	247.8
10 - 20	208.4	1,900.6	2,839.2	17.4	32.0	237.3	347.5
20 - 50	113.6	2,091.3	3,340.1	10.7	37.4	325.5	571.7
50 - 100	19.9	754.1	1,318.3	3.1	22.0	205.2	298.4
100 - 500	4.9	371.4	750.1	1.4	28.1	245.1	174.8
500 and over	.1	16.7	103.8	.1	10.4	133.7	4.1
Total	1,649.6	8,802.9	13,600.9	241.5	515.7	1,566.0	1,781.2

(continued)

TABLE G-1 (continued)

AGI Classes (thousand dollars)	Returns with Net Profit			Returns with Net Loss			Tax on Entrepreneurial Net Income Less That Absorbed by Net Losses (million dollars)
	Number of Returns (in thousands)	Amount of Net Profit (million dollars)	AGI	Number of Returns (in thousands)	Amount of Net Loss (million dollars)	AGI	
SOLE PROPRIETORSHIP, 1954							
Negative AGI	16.6	16.0	-38.3	349.8	1,015.3	-806.0	-19.3
0 – 2	2,191.7	2,094.3	2,460.4	319.8	298.7	341.7	31.1
2 – 3	1,078.1	2,051.1	2,678.0	192.9	186.1	480.9	83.7
3 – 5	1,426.0	3,690.2	5,547.0	328.8	249.2	1,293.4	253.0
5 – 10	1,095.1	4,587.6	7,450.3	201.4	192.5	1,331.1	506.1
10 – 20	367.5	3,540.9	4,915.6	43.4	110.2	591.9	564.0
20 – 50	128.8	2,551.3	3,692.3	20.0	109.4	591.6	596.0
50 – 100	14.4	546.6	949.3	5.7	69.2	379.5	174.8
100 – 500	2.6	147.9	391.1	2.6	61.5	450.2	38.9
500 and over	.1	8.7	83.4	.2	16.7	230.7	-4.5
Total	6,320.8	19,234.6	28,129.1	1,464.7	2,308.8	4,884.9	2,223.9
PARTNERSHIP, 1954							
Negative AGI	10.8	30.2	-24.9	47.9	218.5	-110.4	-5.5
0 – 2	243.1	246.3	279.1	30.9	25.0	31.0	5.5
2 – 3	171.7	334.5	432.1	21.1	15.9	53.5	17.8
3 – 5	360.5	1,023.8	1,425.7	45.7	49.7	179.0	78.8
5 – 10	423.7	1,919.0	2,966.2	46.4	35.6	314.0	221.5
10 – 25	224.7	1,984.4	3,053.6	19.7	37.0	265.6	321.9
25 – 50	124.6	2,191.5	3,665.0	12.2	34.3	368.5	535.0
50 – 100	23.3	845.9	1,539.4	3.3	21.9	217.7	299.5
100 – 500	5.6	400.7	861.6	1.7	30.3	289.4	170.9
500 and over	.1	27.8	122.4	.2	10.0	170.2	10.1
Total	1,588.0	9,004.0	14,320.1	228.9	478.2	1,778.5	1,655.5

(continued)

TABLE G-1 (continued)

AGI Classes (thousand dollars)	Returns with Net Profit			Returns with Net Loss			Tax on Entrepreneurial Net Income Less That Absorbed by Net Losses (million dollars)
	Number of Returns (in thousands)	Amount of Net Profit (million dollars)	AGI	Number of Returns (in thousands)	Amount of Net Loss (million dollars)	AGI	
SOLE PROPRIETORSHIP, 1955							
Negative AGI	12.5	31.0	−26.1	351.2	870.0	−730.9	−18.3
0 − 2	2,299.4	2,159.4	2,574.1	319.6	263.1	328.8	33.9
2 − 3	1,110.6	2,054.1	2,757.1	169.3	143.4	426.1	88.7
3 − 5	1,486.4	3,803.6	5,807.8	346.2	261.3	1,366.1	270.0
5 − 10	1,240.3	4,821.0	8,410.7	247.6	248.5	1,632.7	524.6
10 − 25	481.8	5,024.1	7,040.9	52.5	138.0	759.6	847.8
25 − 50	87.2	1,963.9	2,899.4	13.7	87.3	458.8	489.2
50 − 100	15.7	594.8	1,041.7	5.3	59.4	352.6	190.8
100 − 500	2.5	136.1	383.2	3.0	77.0	501.3	25.3
500 and over	.1	9.2	61.5	.2	19.2	280.2	−5.4
Total	6,736.4	20,597.2	30,950.3	1,508.7	2,167.2	5,375.5	2,446.7
PARTNERSHIP, 1955							
Negative AGI	7.9	22.6	−16.4	48.6	199.2	−101.0	−4.9
0 − 2	256.0	245.7	289.7	42.2	48.3	39.1	6.3
2 − 3	185.3	352.1	464.3	26.4	24.3	66.5	17.3
3 − 5	350.7	991.6	1,386.0	47.8	31.9	192.2	77.7
5 − 10	461.8	2,020.8	3,245.6	53.4	70.0	365.5	229.5
10 − 25	302.8	2,841.5	4,545.2	31.7	57.2	473.5	488.7
25 − 50	91.0	1,746.1	3,067.9	10.3	32.2	351.0	451.1
50 − 100	25.1	864.4	1,666.8	4.3	26.6	287.5	298.6
100 − 500	6.8	430.4	1,054.0	2.1	29.0	375.2	179.2
500 and over	.2	38.0	206.6	.2	10.7	209.2	15.1
Total	1,687.6	9,553.4	15,909.8	267.1	529.5	2,258.6	1,758.5

(continued)

TABLE G-1 (continued)

AGI Classes (thousand dollars)	Returns with Net Profit			Returns with Net Loss			Tax on Entrepreneurial Net Income Less That Absorbed By Net Losses (million dollars)
	Number of Returns (in thousands)	Amount of Net Profit (million dollars)	AGI	Number of Returns (in thousands)	Amount of Net Loss (million dollars)	AGI	
SOLE PROPRIETORSHIP, 1956							
Negative AGI	16.4	32.0	-35.3	327.2	885.6	-706.5	-17.5
0 – 2	2,256.2	2,141.5	2,542.5	301.4	308.5	309.0	38.1
2 – 3	1,193.1	2,230.7	2,965.1	208.4	186.5	521.7	101.6
3 – 5	1,691.0	4,390.1	6,655.9	351.5	265.3	1,391.6	319.8
5 – 10	1,527.7	5,860.7	10,410.6	303.2	294.1	2,015.3	632.0
10 – 25	571.5	5,735.3	8,257.0	73.3	162.6	1,048.5	956.2
25 – 50	103.7	2,383.2	3,485.5	16.2	80.5	544.3	603.3
50 – 100	18.7	729.1	1,240.3	6.6	65.9	439.2	238.5
100 – 500	2.8	149.9	426.2	3.3	107.7	556.2	17.9
500 and over	.1	9.4	63.7	.3	20.5	294.3	-6.1
Total	7,381.3	23,661.9	36,011.4	1,591.4	2,377.2	6,413.6	2,884.0
PARTNERSHIP, 1956							
Negative AGI	11.1	24.4	-24.0	37.8	207.4	-81.7	-5.1
0 – 2	196.2	203.8	232.7	28.8	42.5	29.5	5.4
2 – 3	140.1	262.2	353.0	19.6	24.1	49.8	13.8
3 – 5	301.7	836.8	1,196.1	40.3	33.4	166.6	63.9
5 – 10	456.7	1,934.2	3,216.0	64.3	58.1	446.4	217.6
10 – 25	318.3	2,998.8	4,768.6	34.7	62.8	523.9	511.2
25 – 50	92.4	1,778.0	3,104.2	11.7	40.1	392.1	455.4
50 – 100	27.6	927.3	1,825.3	5.1	26.5	340.1	323.9
100 – 500	6.7	403.6	1,022.0	2.2	33.4	377.9	164.5
500 and over	.2	23.7	174.0	.2	12.4	214.5	6.2
Total	1,550.8	9,393.0	15,867.9	244.7	540.7	2,459.3	1,756.8

(continued)

TABLE G-1 (continued)

AGI Classes (thousand dollars)	Returns with Net Profit			Returns with Net Loss			Tax on Entrepreneurial Net Income Less That Absorbed by Net Losses (million dollars)
	Number of Returns (in thousands)	Amount of Net Profit (million dollars)	AGI	Number of Returns (in thousands)	Amount of Net Loss (million dollars)	AGI	
SOLE PROPRIETORSHIP, 1957							
Negative AGI	17.6	63.8	-40.2	313.2	834.8	-714.0	-16.0
0 – 2	2,043.6	1,840.6	2,233.6	279.2	289.3	284.2	31.8
2 – 3	997.5	1,812.3	2,484.0	174.0	163.4	434.8	83.6
3 – 5	1,534.4	3,983.3	6,050.6	335.8	240.2	1,329.5	292.6
5 – 10	1,483.9	5,719.7	10,192.5	284.2	262.6	1,906.2	614.4
10 – 25	572.8	5,732.5	8,264.3	64.0	148.4	906.2	950.7
25 – 50	102.0	2,384.6	3,402.7	15.3	86.6	511.5	592.6
50 – 100	20.9	820.8	1,374.2	6.5	76.6	426.5	265.0
100 – 500	2.6	160.9	392.0	2.7	64.6	468.1	42.4
500 and over	.1	7.5	64.0	.2	20.1	202.9	-7.1
Total	6,775.3	22,525.9	34,417.8	1,475.0	2,186.6	5,755.6	2,850.0
PARTNERSHIP, 1957							
Negative AGI	10.7	26.7	-24.4	44.8	217.1	-102.1	-4.9
0 – 2	202.3	213.5	232.7	30.9	61.9	32.5	4.8
2 – 3	147.5	280.4	367.1	16.9	17.6	42.7	14.2
3 – 5	304.2	838.7	1,220.5	50.9	45.5	206.6	64.5
5 – 10	467.9	2,028.8	3,317.2	62.7	69.7	446.4	228.7
10 – 25	338.1	3,124.4	5,067.4	38.2	61.8	579.1	528.0
25 – 50	98.8	1,945.6	3,297.5	13.4	37.2	446.8	492.5
50 – 100	30.3	1,033.2	1,986.3	5.8	33.4	381.5	355.7
100 – 500	6.6	441.8	1,013.4	2.2	45.0	381.2	177.7
500 and over	.2	30.6	186.3	.2	15.4	177.7	8.8
Total	1,606.5	9,963.7	16,664.0	266.0	604.8	2,592.5	1,870.0

(continued)

TABLE G-1 (continued)

AGI Classes (thousand dollars)	Returns with Net Profit			Returns with Net Loss			Tax on Entrepreneurial Net Income Less Net Losses That Absorbed by Net Losses (million dollars)
	Number of Returns (in thousands)	Amount of Net Profit (million dollars)	AGI	Number of Returns (in thousands)	Amount of Net Loss (million dollars)	AGI	
SOLE PROPRIETORSHIP, 1958							
Negative AGI	13.2	21.7	-34.7	278.5	830.7	-733.7	-15.2
0 – 2	2,001.7	1,830.8	2,194.1	285.0	278.0	280.5	31.7
2 – 3	998.6	1,815.5	2,481.9	174.7	158.4	439.1	81.6
3 – 5	1,609.3	4,203.6	6,251.0	330.4	272.5	1,299.6	301.1
5 – 10	1,530.3	5,906.7	10,526.4	330.9	271.8	2,223.8	630.2
10 – 25	602.1	5,862.1	8,701.7	77.9	178.2	1,096.9	962.6
25 – 50	106.4	2,470.7	3,544.9	14.4	87.8	478.2	607.7
50 – 100	16.7	639.4	1,103.9	5.4	58.9	355.4	202.4
100 – 500	2.4	130.2	369.0	2.6	62.8	488.0	28.9
500 and over	.1	9.1	60.3	.2	17.3	214.1	-3.9
Total	6,880.8	22,890.0	35,198.5	1,499.9	2,216.4	6,102.1	2,827.3
PARTNERSHIP, 1958							
Negative AGI	7.7	17.4	-20.2	37.5	205.9	-98.9	-5.0
0 – 2	215.9	222.7	240.9	32.2	36.2	30.3	5.4
2 – 3	142.1	261.7	354.4	18.0	18.0	45.2	13.1
3 – 5	301.4	825.4	1,180.1	42.6	39.8	167.4	60.8
5 – 10	463.5	1,982.1	3,253.0	67.2	55.7	485.1	216.6
10 – 25	343.7	3,073.4	5,154.1	47.5	78.3	722.5	512.3
25 – 50	100.2	1,900.4	3,337.3	13.0	48.7	434.4	472.1
50 – 100	30.5	1,077.7	2,011.8	5.4	33.1	355.2	362.9
100 – 500	6.3	422.3	964.2	2.4	44.6	418.1	165.1
500 and over	.2	27.2	186.8	.2	18.2	236.9	4.8
Total	1,611.5	9,810.2	16,662.4	266.3	578.4	2,796.2	1,808.1

(continued)

TABLE G-1 (continued)

AGI Classes (thousand dollars)	Returns with Net Profit			Returns with Net Loss			Tax on Entrepreneurial Net Income Less That Absorbed by Net Losses (million dollars)
	Number of Returns (in thousands)	Amount of Net Profit (million dollars)	AGI (million dollars)	Number of Returns (in thousands)	Amount of Net Loss (million dollars)	AGI (million dollars)	
SOLE PROPRIETORSHIP, 1959							
Negative AGI	16.4	76.4	-57.8	338.6	1,187.9	-1,189.7	-21.0
0 - 2	1,958.5	1,720.1	2,104.2	315.2	322.4	319.5	29.5
2 - 3	932.0	1,670.9	2,318.6	173.6	182.4	435.6	74.2
3 - 5	1,464.9	3,777.6	5,779.6	358.1	337.2	1,427.1	269.9
5 - 10	1,679.2	6,300.4	11,625.1	399.8	373.8	2,716.4	657.2
10 - 25	684.9	6,557.4	9,852.4	99.7	209.5	1,402.7	1,061.1
25 - 50	127.8	2,969.5	4,281.5	17.8	96.7	595.5	726.0
50 - 100	27.3	1,060.7	1,795.2	8.7	89.5	570.3	334.0
100 - 500	3.5	181.5	512.4	3.4	71.0	570.4	45.0
500 and over	.1	8.2	56.1	.2	21.2	274.2	-6.4
Total	6,894.6	24,322.7	38,267.3	1,715.1	2,891.5	7,122.0	3,169.6
PARTNERSHIP, 1959							
Negative AGI	7.8	23.7	-27.4	44.2	198.1	-155.2	-4.2
0 - 2	202.6	204.8	230.9	30.0	66.6	30.0	4.9
2 - 3	132.9	253.6	330.6	20.9	19.0	51.9	12.4
3 - 5	290.9	799.7	1,167.4	41.0	46.7	164.6	62.8
5 - 10	491.3	2,005.2	3,479.4	83.7	70.0	584.1	215.5
10 - 25	368.6	3,190.0	5,530.1	52.6	83.6	782.5	526.3
25 - 50	105.0	1,906.3	3,518.1	18.7	58.6	626.6	467.0
50 - 100	38.2	1,269.1	2,512.1	7.6	44.2	499.7	421.3
100 - 500	8.3	528.0	1,292.2	3.1	53.9	540.8	198.7
500 and over	.2	40.1	227.3	.2	16.2	273.4	11.5
Total	1,645.7	10,220.4	18,260.8	302.0	656.9	3,398.5	1,916.0

(continued)

177

TABLE G-1 (concluded)

AGI Classes (thousand dollars)	Returns with Net Profit			Returns with Net Loss			Tax on Entrepreneurial Net Income Less That Absorbed by Net Losses (million dollars)
	Number of Returns (in thousands)	Amount of Net Profit (million dollars)	AGI	Number of Returns (in thousands)	Amount of Net Loss (million dollars)	AGI	
				SOLE PROPRIETORSHIP, 1960			
Negative AGI	16.3	53.0	-40.9	327.4	1,058.9	-820.7	-16.3
0 - 2	1,854.4	1,625.3	1,986.6	309.9	311.1	308.3	28.1
2 - 3	908.2	1,635.1	2,264.4	179.8	198.3	449.9	71.6
3 - 5	1,477.8	3,777.3	5,838.8	370.7	356.3	1,482.2	264.0
5 - 10	1,719.2	6,383.2	11,982.6	441.7	434.0	3,006.1	653.0
10 - 25	705.2	6,549.8	10,134.6	109.0	220.7	1,519.3	1,042.2
25 - 50	125.1	2,910.7	4,173.1	18.4	89.2	613.3	698.1
50 - 100	22.6	876.5	1,485.9	7.3	82.3	477.9	269.0
100 - 500	2.7	140.3	417.7	3.1	114.6	540.7	10.2
500 and over	.1	7.7	78.0	.2	21.8	258.6	-6.6
Total	6,831.4	23,958.9	38,320.8	1,767.5	2,887.2	7,835.6	3,013.2
				PARTNERSHIP, 1960			
Negative AGI	10.2	31.1	-25.7	46.1	261.7	-115.6	-5.7
0 - 2	185.6	179.6	209.8	33.7	43.6	33.0	4.1
2 - 3	120.6	213.5	301.3	18.7	66.3	46.2	10.6
3 - 5	264.5	729.6	1,060.8	45.1	54.7	184.7	55.4
5 - 10	480.4	1,922.6	3,438.2	87.5	105.7	626.9	204.0
10 - 25	377.6	3,184.1	5,690.9	66.2	103.6	981.2	516.4
25 - 50	111.1	2,023.6	3,705.7	21.8	60.4	725.8	485.7
50 - 100	32.2	1,017.7	2,115.6	7.6	39.2	501.2	331.5
100 - 500	6.9	430.2	1,091.0	2.7	44.3	486.7	158.8
500 and over	.2	25.6	198.5	.2	11.9	257.8	6.4
Total	1,589.2	9,757.5	17,786.2	329.7	791.4	3,727.9	1,767.2

Source: Statistics of Income.

^aFigure based on number of businesses, not total number of returns. ^b0-5 AGI class not available and not in totals.

APPENDIX H

Computation of Mean Effective and Marginal Tax Rates (Derivation of Tables 42 and 48)

Mean Effective Rates

THE mean effective tax rates on net profits and net losses—as summarized in Table 42 of the text—are simply weighted averages of effective tax rates computed by income groups. For the years 1952–60, gross tax liabilities (i.e., tax liabilities before tax credits) were divided by adjusted gross income for twenty-five AGI groups. The gross effective rate thus obtained for a given income group is the effective rate assigned to net profits and net losses reported in that income group. In summing effective rates for the whole distribution, the rates for each income group were weighted by the net profits reported in that group to obtain a mean effective rate on net profits, and by the net losses reported in the group to obtain a mean rate on net losses.

By this method, the fact that effective rates are at all times the joint product of a number of income components is taken into account. It would have been inconsistent with the concept of an average effective rate to have treated net losses in an incremental manner. This accounts for our resistance to the temptation to impute a higher effective rate to net losses than to net profits reported in the same income group. The argument in favor of such a procedure would be that net losses have the effect of lowering tax and effective rate below what it would otherwise have been. Indeed, our method assigns zero effective rate to net losses reported on nontaxable returns although such returns might have been taxable in the absence of net loss.

But it is obvious that had negative income items been treated in this incremental fashion the same would have had to be done for positive income items. For had we assigned to negative income the rates at which positive income would have been taxed in the absence of negative components, the same rates would now have to be assigned to the positive components. The effective rates assigned to the various components of income would now be higher than those actually paid. A simple example will illustrate the problem. A taxpayer whose adjusted gross income is $10,000 and whose tax is $1,000 is said to have an effective rate of .10.

His income consists of

Wages	$9,000
Dividends	3,000
Business	− 2,000
AGI	10,000

We can say that his dividends are taxed at 10 per cent, but only if we consider his business income also taxed at 10 per cent. If this were not done, a 10 per cent effective rate would overstate his tax load since it results in $1,200 of tax.

To use a higher effective tax rate on net losses, on the grounds that the latter account for a lower tax liability than would have had to be paid, would lead to obvious difficulties. All negative income components would have to be assigned a higher effective rate than positive income components of identical incomes.

The mean effective rates computed, as described above, are weighted by amounts of net profits (net loss). For some purposes it may be desired to give the effective rate of each return with net profit (net loss) equal weight, i.e., to weight the averages obtained for a given income group by frequencies. Below, mean rates computed by both methods are presented for 1960 for all returns (taxable and nontaxable):

	Sole Proprietorship		Partnership	
	Net Profit	Net Loss	Net Profit	Net Loss
Effective rates weighted by:				
dollar amounts	13.6	8.3	19.0	11.0
frequencies	7.6	7.5	17.7	11.1

Mean Marginal Rates

Mean marginal rates on net profits and net losses are calculated to measure the change in tax liability associated with a small change in net profit or net loss. The procedure used was to compute the change between income groups in tax liability per return and in taxable income per return. The change in tax liability was then divided by the change in taxable income, which gave us a marginal tax rate. The marginal rate thus computed was always assigned to the lower of the two income groups involved in computing the ratio. This procedure, of course, left the highest income group in the distribution—returns with more than $1 million AGI—without a computed rate. The highest marginal rate in the schedule was therefore assigned to the (quantitatively unimportant) open-end group. It should be noted that the procedure employed in computing the marginal rates automatically takes into account variations, by income groups, in family size and marital status as well as variations in personal deductions.

The marginal rates computed for each of twenty-four income groups were then once more weighted to obtain a mean marginal rate. The weights used were the amounts of net profit (net loss) reported in the income group for which the marginal rate was computed. The mean marginal rate thus obtained gives most weight to the income groups with the greatest concentration of net profits (net losses). The reasons for this procedure have been fully explained in the text. A second method for which results were presented in the text, weighting by frequencies, requires no further explanation.

Note on Estimate of Net Operating Loss Deduction

PRACTICALLY no data have been published on net operating losses for given years and resulting net operating loss deductions for prior and succeeding years. For the sake of completeness, rough estimates of net operating loss were made, and tax equivalents for net operating loss deductions were included, in Tables 40, 42, and 48.

To estimate net operating loss for a given year, the amount of net losses reported on returns with negative AGI was used as a starting point. Because persons filing such returns had also income from other sources, the net losses reported on these returns did not immediately become net operating losses subject to carryback and carryforward.

To explain the rough estimates of net operating loss, which were possible with the available data, the computations made are shown for 1952 and 1959 in Table I-1. Of the 433,135 returns with negative AGI for 1959, 388,632, or 90 per cent, were returns with profit or loss (mainly loss) from unincorporated enterprise. Most of the other income reported in the negative AGI group alongside sole proprietor and partnership losses must then have been reported on the same returns as these losses. The ratio of the number of returns with unincorporated enterprise net loss to all returns in the group was used to compute the amounts of other income that must be offset against the reported net losses in the group to obtain an estimate of net operating loss.

For 1959, a net operating loss of $858 million on returns of sole proprietors and $172 million on returns of partners was estimated. Since some returns have both sole proprietor and partnership net loss, these two figures are not additive. Separate estimates were required, however, since the effective and marginal rate estimates in Tables 42 and 48 are for sole proprietors and partners separately.

The most tenuous element in the estimates is the amount of negative tax liability ascribed to net operating losses. It was assumed that all of the net operating loss is either carried back or carried forward. The only hint on the distribution, by income groups, of the carryover to other years is the published net operating loss carryforward deductions for 1951–54 and 1960–61. The distributions for these years for taxable and nontaxable returns were combined and averaged. The percentage distribution of the average carryforward for five years is shown in Table I-2. It was used as the basis for distributing the estimated net operating loss for 1960 by income groups. Only the four-year average of 1951–54 carryforwards was used to obtain annual net operating loss distributions

TABLE 1-1

COMPUTATION OF NET OPERATING LOSS ESTIMATE FOR 1952 AND 1959
(million dollars)

	Net Operating Loss on 1952 Returns with				Net Operating Loss on 1959 Returns with			
	Total in Negative AGI Group (1)	Sole Proprietor Net Loss (2)	Partnership Net Loss (3)	Sole Proprietorship and/or Partnership Net Loss (4)	Total in Negative AGI Group (5)	Sole Proprietor Net Loss (6)	Partnership Net Loss (7)	Sole Proprietorship and/or Partnership Net Loss (8)
A. Net operating loss components								
1. Partnership net loss	150	59	150	150	198	77	198	198
2. Sole proprietor net loss	874	874	44	874	1,188	1,188	60	1,188
3. Other negative components:								
Net loss from sale of property other than capital assets	51				93			
Net loss from estates and trusts	n.a.				3			
Itemized personal deductions	27				n.a.			
Rents and royalties net loss	25				70			
Total, line 3	102	72	9	77	166	130	17	140
4. Total (lines 1 through 3)[a]	1,126	1,004	204	1,101	1,552	1,395	275	1,526
B. Net operating loss offset components								
5. Positive income components other than unincorporated enterprise net profits	430	302	39	325	661	517	67	556
6. Partnership net profits	35	27		27	24	21		21
7. Sole proprietorship net profits	14		4	4	76		36	36
8. Total (lines 5 through 7)	481	330	44	356	763	539	103	612
C. Estimated net operating loss (line 4 minus line 8)[a]		676	160	746		858	172	914

for 1952–59. To each such distribution, the effective and marginal rates of that year were then applied for the computations underlying Tables 42 and 48, respectively. It was in this manner that the estimated negative tax liability of $23 million for 1952 and $22 million for 1960, shown in Table 40, were arrived at.

NOTES TO TABLE I-1

Line	
1 and 2.	Proportion of partnership (sole proprietor) net loss assigned to returns with sole proprietor (partnership) net loss was determined by utilizing the information on frequency of returns with both sole proprietor and partnership income for 1955 and 1959 (see Appendix E). For the negative AGI group, 5 per cent had profit or loss from both sources. This meant that a large proportion of partnership net loss (39 per cent for both years) would be reported on returns with sole proprietor net loss, but a much smaller proportion of sole proprietor net loss would be on returns with partnership net loss (5.1 per cent in both years) simply because there were far more sole proprietor than partnership returns in the group.
3.	The share of other negative components reported on returns with net loss from sole proprietorship, or partnership, respectively, was estimated by multiplying the negative components shown by the ratio of the frequency of returns with sole proprietor loss to all returns in the group (.70 for 1952 and .78 for 1959) and the ratio of the frequency of returns with partnership loss to all returns (.09 for 1952 and .10 for 1959), respectively. The share for sole proprietors and/or partners with loss was estimated by summing the frequencies of returns with sole proprietorship and partnership loss, correcting for double counting, and dividing by all returns in the group (.76 for 1952 and .84 for 1959).
5.	Positive income components were wages and salaries, dividends, interest, annuities and pensions, rents and royalties net profit, net capital gains before deduction for net long-term gain, income from estates and trusts, and miscellaneous income. The apportionment was made by the same ratios as described for "other negative components in line 3." Miscellaneous income, which includes the net operating loss carryforward after 1954 and was negative for 1959, was therefore estimated for 1957–59 on the basis of prior year averages.
6 and 7.	To estimate partnership net profit reported on returns with sole proprietor net loss, the former was multiplied by the ratio of the frequency of returns with sole proprietor net loss to all returns, excluding those with partnership net loss. An analogous procedure was used to estimate sole proprietor net profit on returns with partnership net loss. The ratios for 1952 and 1959, respectively, were .77 and .87 for line 7 and .30 and .47 for line 8.

a Figures may not add to totals because of rounding.

TABLE I-2

DISTRIBUTION OF NET OPERATING LOSS CARRYFORWARD DEDUCTION, BY INCOME GROUPS, SELECTED YEARS, 1951-61
(thousand dollars)

AGI Classes (thousand dollars)	1951	1952	1953	1954	1960	1961	Percentage Distribution Based on Five-Year Average, 1951-54 and 1960
Negative AGI	68,668	90,865	161,411	86,136	123,399	68,103	70.48
Nontaxable returns	4,811	18,135	10,889	28,533	19,774	16,897	10.91
Taxable returns							
.6 - 2	6,782	5,913	9,130	2,431			
2 - 3	3,207	7,247	2,253	2,304			
3 - 4	2,748	926	869	5,274	8,012	1,427	8.13
4 - 5	2,105	886	1,609	2,424			
5 - 10	9,863	2,990	8,409	10,653	2,134	1,521	4.63
10 - 15	2,153	2,711	3,093	3,351	200	1,456	1.79
15 - 20	1,224	1,505	902	1,477	1,953	870	.70
20 - 30[a]	1,888	1,126	1,383	445	4,720	185	.59
30[a] - 50	1,114	1,048	1,176	716	4,153	373	1.48
50 - 100	581	1,108	786	1,044	738	768	1.02
100 - 200	27	115	224	120	398	36	.16
200 - 500	7	14	145	5	153	85	.08
500 - 1,000			23	1		90	.02
1,000 and over				51			.01
Total	105,179	134,589	202,302	144,965	165,634	91,897	100.00

Source: Statistics of Income, 1951-1954.

[a]For 1960 and 1961, class limits were $25,000 instead of $30,000.

185

INDEX